ATTRIBUTION THEORY:
Applications to Achievement, Mental Health, and Interpersonal Conflict

APPLIED SOCIAL PSYCHOLOGY

A series of volumes edited by
Michael J. Saks and **Leonard Saxe**

Kidd and Saks / Advances in
Applied Social Psychology, Volume 1

Kidd and Saks / Advances in
Applied Social Psychology, Volume 2

Saks and Saxe / Advances in
Applied Social Psychology, Volume 3

Carroll / Applied Social Psychology
and Organizational Settings

Graham and Folkes / Attribution Theory: Applications to
Achievement, Mental Health, and Interpersonal Conflict

ATTRIBUTION THEORY:

Applications to Achievement, Mental Health, and Interpersonal Conflict

Edited by

SANDRA GRAHAM
University of California, Los Angeles

VALERIE S. FOLKES
University of Southern California

LEA LAWRENCE ERLBAUM ASSOCIATES, PUBLISHERS
1990   Hillsdale, New Jersey   Hove and London

HM
291
.A883
1990

Lawrence Erlbaum Associates, Inc., Publishers
365 Broadway
Hillsdale, New Jersey 07642

Library of Congress Cataloging in Publication Data

Attribution theory : applications to achievement, mental health, and
  interpersonal conflict / edited by Sandra Graham, Valerie S. Folkes.
       p.   cm.—(Applied social psychology)
    Includes bibliographical references.
    ISBN 0–8058–0531–1
    1. Attribution (Social psychology)   I. Graham, Sandra, 1947–   .
II. Folkes, Valerie S.   III. Series.
HM291.A883   1990
302'.12—dc20   90–3145
                                                                    CIP

Printed in the United States of America
10 9 8 7 6 5 4 3 2

Contents

Preface   **ix**

1. Searching for the Roots of Applied Attribution Theory   **1**
   Bernard Weiner

   Kurt Lewin: The Practical Theorist   *1*
   The Social Psychological Approach to Attributions:
      The Influence of Heider and Weiner   *5*
   Attributional Theory and Applied Psychology   *10*
   A Summary Statement   *12*
   References   *12*

PART I: APPLICATIONS TO ACHIEVEMENT

**2. Communicating Low Ability in the Classroom: Bad Things
   Good Teachers Sometimes Do**   **17**
   Sandra Graham

   Pity and Anger as Attributional Cues   *19*
   Praise and Blame   *23*
   Help Versus Neglect   *27*
   Implications and Applications   *32*
   Summary   *34*
   References   *35*

3. **The Causal Attribution Process in Sport and Physical Activity**   37
Edward McAuley and Terry E. Duncan

Attribution Theory and Sport: An Update   *38*
Causal Attributions, Affect and Self-Perceptions   *39*
Future Directions and Applications   *46*
Summary   *49*
References   *50*

4. **Explanatory Style in the Classroom and on the Playing Field**   53
Christopher Peterson

The Theory of Learned Helplessness and Explanatory Style   *53*
The Measurement of Explanatory Style   *56*
Why Explanatory Style is not Simply
    a Risk Factor for Depression   *59*
Explanatory Style and Academic Performance   *59*
Explanatory Style and Athletic Performance   *66*
A Critical Evaluation   *69*
Conclusion: Some Pitfalls in Applying Attribution Theory   *71*
Summary   *73*
References   *73*

PART II: APPLICATIONS TO MENTAL HEALTH

5. **Applying Attribution Theory to the Study of Stress and Coping**   79
James H. Amirkhan

"Thinking": The Influence of Perceived Control   *81*
"Doing": The Influence of Coping   *85*
Control and Coping: Causal Chronologies   *89*
Applying Attribution Theory   *92*
Summary   *97*
References   *98*

6. **Attributions, Person Perception, and Clinical Issues**   103
Steven Regeser López and Bonnie H. Wolkenstein

Clinical Judgment   *104*
Families' Attributions of a Relative's
    Serious Mental Disorder   *112*
Conclusion   *118*
References   *118*

7. **Attributional Therapies**   **123**
    Friedrich Försterling

    Introduction   *123*
    Consequences of Causal Attributions   *124*
    Attribution and Attributional Theories and Their Relation to Models
        of Psychotherapy   *130*
    Causal Antecedents   *130*
    Beliefs and Attributions   *132*
    An Attributional Analysis of Beck's Cognitive Therapy   *134*
    Summary   *136*
    References   *136*

**PART III: APPLICATION TO CONFLICT IN INTERPERSONAL AND
         INTERGROUP RELATIONSHIPS**

8. **Conflict in the Marketplace: Explaining Why
    Products Fail**   **143**
    Valerie S. Folkes

    Attributional Conflict in Exchange Relationships   *144*
    The Roots of Attributional Conflict   *144*
    Consequences of Attributions for Product Failure   *150*
    Conflict Over Contributions of Causes   *155*
    Reducing Buyer-Seller Conflict   *156*
    Summary   *158*
    References   *159*

9. **Conflict in Close Relationships: The Role of Intrapersonal
    Phenomena**   **161**
    *Frank D. Fincham, Thomas N. Bradbury, and
    John H. Grych*

    Research on Conflict in Close Relationships   *162*
    Prerequisites for a Model of Conflict   *164*
    A Model of Conflict in Close Relationships   *175*
    Caveats   *180*
    Conclusion   *181*
    References   *182*

10. **Attributions and Organizational Conflict**   **185**
    Robert A. Baron

    The Relevance of Attributions to Organizational Conflict:
        Empirical and Theoretical Foundations   *186*

Attributions and Organizational Conflict: Initial Evidence   *188*
Attributions and Organizational Conflict: Apparent Sincerity
    and the 'My Hands Are Tied' Strategy   *191*
Related Research: Excuses and Causal Accounts   *198*
Attributions and Organizational Conflict:
    Practical Implications   *201*
Summary   *202*
References   *203*

11. An Attributional Approach to Intergroup and International Conflict   **205**

Hector Betancourt

From Individual to Intergroup and International Phenomena   *206*
An Attributional View of Intergroup Behavior and Conflict   *208*
An Attributional View of International Conflict   *213*
Summary   *217*
References   *218*

Author Index   *221*
Subject Index   *229*

Preface

Five of us who contributed to this volume—Jim Amirkhan, Hector Betancourt, Valerie Folkes, Sandra Graham, and Steve López—share two characteristics in common. We were all students of Bernie Weiner within the last decade and, through a series of propitious events, we all managed to acquire academic positions at universities in the greater Los Angeles area. About 3 years ago, at Bernie's suggestion, we initiated a series of regular meetings at UCLA for the purpose of discussing and critiquing one another's research ideas. Since we had all continued to do attribution research after earning our doctorates, we fondly (and modestly) began to refer to ourselves as the "Attribution Elders."

It soon became evident in these monthly gatherings that our respective research focuses represented a number of the domains outside of social psychology to which attribution theory had been applied. Sandra Graham was concentrating on achievement concerns; Steve López and Jim Amirkhan had continued their respective research programs on clinical issues; Valerie Folkes was investigating consumer behavior and marketing, and Hector Betancourt had followed his long-standing interest in international conflict. With active research programs in these diverse areas, we realized that together we formed the nucleus for a book on attributional applications. Graham and Folkes assumed the role of editors and together with the other Elders, we worked out a general organizational framework for the book that would both capture our own research foci and be appealing to other attribution researchers whom we identified as potential contributors. Thus the idea for this volume had a natural evolution and was, from its inception, a collaborative effort.

The book begins with a chapter by Bernie Weiner that provides an historical overview of the growth of attribution theory, tracing the basic conception back to its intellectual origin in the writings of Kurt Lewin and up to present-day extensions in applied domains. The introductory chapter sets the stage for the three broad domains of application addressed in the remainder of the book. The first section addresses applications to achievement strivings with chapters by Sandra Graham on the communication of low-ability cues in the classroom; by Edward McAuley and Terry Duncan on attributional processes in the sports domain, and by Christopher Peterson on the role of attributional style in both academic and athletic achievement. The second section addresses application to issues of mental health. Included here are chapters by Jim Amirkhan on attributional analyses of stress and coping, by Steve López and Bonnie Wolkenstein on causal perceptions of clinicians and family members concerning patient mental status, and by Friedrich Försterling on attributional interpretations of psychotherapy. Finally, the third section of the book broadly addresses the topic of conflict from an attributional perspective, with chapters by Valerie Folkes on buyer-seller disagreement; by Frank Fincham, Thomas Bradbury, and John Grych on marital discord; by Robert Baron on dissension in the workplace, and by Hector Betancourt on conflict among nations. Reflecting the orientation and expertises of the various authors, the chapters are more research-based than practice-oriented. Thus the audience for this book is more the applied psychologist with a research focus than the practitioner, although we hope that the practical implications evident in each author's contribution will also make this volume appealing to the latter group.

Skeptics may wonder whether there is a need for another edited book on attribution research, inasmuch as a series of such volumes with an emphasis on applications preceded us in the 1980s (see, for example, Antaki & Brewin, 1982; Harvey & Weary, 1985; Jaspars, Fincham, & Hewstone, 1983). We view the present volume as complementary to, rather than redundant with, the prior books. The continued vitality of attribution research in applied settings has instigated a wealth of new findings and research directions over the past few years, many of which are represented in this book. Furthermore, some of the topics presented here, such as attributional analyses of international conflict and buyer–seller discord, have not been addressed in any of the prior volumes.

We also view our book as distinctly different from its predecessors. As the reader may well be aware, there is no single attribution theory, but rather a range of attributional conceptions, each with its own particular approach to causal thinking and its own particular set of pertinent empirical findings. Prior volumes reflect this diversity in attributional approaches. Our book is more focused, inasmuch as most of the chapters here fit within the attributional theory formulated by Bernard Weiner (see Weiner, 1985, 1986). This means that there is an emphasis on attributional consequences rather than antecedents, on dimensions or properties of causes rather than specific attributions per se, and on affective as well as cognitive determinants of behavior. We believe that this adherence to a particular attributional approach gives our volume a unity not achieved by its predecessors.

We had been forewarned by some cynical colleagues experienced in editing books about the difficulties of the process but, frankly, we found none of this to be true. As the editors, we therefore want to acknowledge those who made our job easier. First and foremost, we thank all of our contributing authors for both their scholarship and conscientious adherence to deadlines. Appreciation also is extended to Julie Carney at UCLA for her secretarial help and assistance with the index. In Larry Erlbaum and his editorial staff we found a friendly and receptive publisher for which we also are grateful. Finally, we would like to acknowledge our intellectual debt to our mentor and friend, Bernie Weiner.

Sandra Graham
Valerie Folkes

REFERENCES

Antaki, C., & Brewin, C. (Eds.). (1982). *Attributions and psychological change*. New York: Academic.

Harvey, J. H., & Weary, G. (Eds.). (1985). *Attribution: Basic issues and applications*. New York: Academic.

Jaspars, J., Fincham, F. D., & Hewstone, M. (Eds.). (1983). *Attribution theory and research: Conceptual, developmental, and social dimensions*. New York: Academic.

Weiner, B. (1985). An attributional theory of achievement motivation and emotion. *Psychological Review, 92*, 548–573.

Weiner, B. (1986). *An attributional theory of motivation and emotion*. New York: Springer–Verlag.

To Justin, Jason, and Brandon

1

Searching for the Roots of Applied Attribution Theory

Bernard Weiner
University of California, Los Angeles

One of the unexpected consequences of the growth of attribution theory has been a corresponding increment in attributional applications to everyday problems and concerns. This introduction looks into the past to find an answer to the question: "Why has attribution theory been so amenable to practical use?" The products of my search also provide a historical context for the present book.

The theories that are highlighted in this chapter were proposed by Lewin, Heider, Rotter, and Weiner, with secondary discussion of Atkinson and Kelley. The editors have asked me to focus upon my work and how this was influenced by others. I do this with great modesty: My approach happens to provide the guiding theoretical system for *this* book, which includes a number of my former students as chapter contributors. However, it is known by this writer as well as by the readers that there are many attributional analyses, these are often incommensurate, and each has its own historical antecedents and confirmatory set of data.

I begin this chapter by documenting the overriding influence of Kurt Lewin on attribution theory and attribution theorists. Lewin is the starting point because of his known focus on theory utilization (action research) and because his role in attribution theory has been insufficiently acknowledged. In addition, he was an important influence on two theorists who greatly influenced my work.

KURT LEWIN: THE PRACTICAL THEORIST

In his biography of Lewin, Alfred Marrow (1969) pointed out the simultaneous thrust of theory and application that directed Lewin's vast energies. Lewin's

1

dictum, "there is nothing so practical as a good theory," is one of the few (the only?) aphorisms that has originated in experimental psychology. It is therefore not unreasonable to presume that students and coworkers of Lewin would be guided by his unified theory-application aims. Thus, to the extent that Lewin's influence on attributional thinking can be documented, we should be alerted to look for both theoretical development and theory utilization among the proponents of attribution theory.

Lewin's (1935, 1938) approach was so catholic that different aspects of his thinking were incorporated by different psychologists. In seeking the roots of attribution theory, Lewin's ideas require classification into two categories. First, he championed Expectancy-value theory, and illustrated the power of that conception in his explication of level of aspiration. These features of his work strongly affected Julian Rotter (1954) and John Atkinson (1957, 1964). Both these theorists embraced Expectancy-value theory and used level of aspiration, that is, the choice among tasks differing in difficulty, as one of their main research paradigms. Secondly, Lewin (as well as other Gestaltists of the period) clarified some of the determinants of object and person perception and expanded the knowledge of psychologists by pointing out the dynamics of part–whole relationships and force fields. These components of Lewin's thinking are reflected in Heider's (1958) elucidation of balanced states and attributions (as well as Festinger's theory of cognitive dissonance and some aspects of Kelley's writings). Both balance and attribution in part concern cognitive dynamics arising from the formation of units or wholes. For example, a prediction of balance theory is that if a good act is performed by a bad person, then a state of imbalance exists. This initiates a force toward cognitive change or balance so that the act is perceived as less positive or the person is perceived as more positive. Similarly, attribution theorists have documented that there is a tendency to attribute a good act to a person perceived as good (such as the self). That is, given a positive outcome, the perceived attributional source is in part determined by motivational forces, as documented by phenomena such as the so-called "hedonic bias" (the tendency to attribute success rather than failure to oneself). Hence, both balance and attribution are in part derived from identical Gestalt principles related to cognitive dynamics.

The contributions of Rotter, Atkinson, and Heider soon will be elaborated. For now, I merely wanted to note the immediate influence of Lewin on these three theorists (see Table 1.1).

In Table 1.1, Lewin and Heider are distinguished in terms of hierarchical levels, although they were contemporaries and Heider had an effect on others not necessarily familiar with the writings of Lewin. However, Lewin already had an impact on psychology in the 1930s and 1940s, whereas Heider did not dramatically influence psychological thinking until the 1960s. In addition, Table 1.1 is an oversimplification in that Heider also influenced Lewin, and all the theorists included in Table 1.1 as descendants of Lewin also were guided by major psychologists other than Lewin. What perhaps is most curious about the table is the

TABLE 1.1
Historical Influences in the Study of Attribution

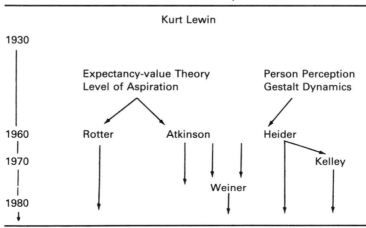

relative independence of Rotter, Atkinson, and Heider. In spite of their partly shared origins and partly shared interests, they did not cite one another.

Table 1.1 includes two other names "lower" in the time-frame hierarchy who are primarily associated with attribution theory: Harold Kelley and this writer. Kelley is a descendant of Heider inasmuch as the well-known "Kelley cube" is an in-depth examination of the covariation principle of causal inference, which was championed by Heider and philosophers before him. And I owe a great deal to Heider, particularly to his distinction between can and try as determinants of achievement performance. However, I also was guided by Expectancy-value theory as interpreted by Atkinson. These influences also will be examined in somewhat more detail later in the chapter.

I now want to turn to the attributional contributions of the psychologists in Table 1.1 who were directly or indirectly affected by Kurt Lewin. The discussion is organized into three sections. First, the contributions of Julian Rotter and the personality approach to causal ascriptions is presented. Next, and in much greater detail, the focus is on the social psychological approach to causal ascriptions, particularly as evidenced in the thinking of Fritz Heider and this writer. This section includes a reinterpretation of achievement theory as developed by Atkinson. Finally, I address why attribution theory has made such an impact on applied psychology.

The Personality Approach to Attributions: The Influence of Rotter

Rotter is identified with social learning and, as a clinician, wanted to develop a conceptual system that could be useful in dealing with clinical problems while remaining true to the logical positivism represented in social learning theory. Thus, he surely had both theoretical and applied concerns. As previously indicated, Rotter also accepted Expectancy-value theory, contending that the strength of motivation to perform an action is determined by the reinforcement value of a goal and the expectancy of attaining that goal. Clinical difficulties were anticipated when expectancy of success was nonveridical and when there was a low expectancy for a highly valued goal. Hence, one of Rotter's central quests was to identify the determinants of expectancy of success.

In a series of experimental studies, Rotter and his colleagues (e.g., James & Rotter, 1958) documented that performance at skill tasks results in differential changes in expectancy of success when compared with performance at chance tasks. This laboratory experimental research led Rotter to speculate that some individuals might perceive the world as if it were composed of skill tasks, whereas others would perceive life outcomes as chance-determined. That is, there are individual differences in causal perceptions and these, in turn, result in disparate subjective likelihoods of success and failure across a variety of situations.

The locus of control, or I–E scale (I for internal, E for external) was constructed to measure individual differences in personal construction of the world as skill (internal) or chance (external) related (Rotter, 1966). However, to the best of my knowledge, the scale never has been successfully reported to relate to differences in expectancy of success or expectancy change. Rather, the I–E scale took on a life of its own, and it was indeed an active life. Locus of control was related to hundreds of different variables, few of any particular relevance to social learning theory or Expectancy-value theory. It also began to evoke comparions with a "good–bad" scale: It was "good" to be an "internal" inasmuch as this was thought to be related to information seeking, openness to experience, positive adaptation, and so on. Correspondingly, it was "bad" to be an "external."

Even during the heyday of the I–E scale (say, from 1965 to 1980) questions were being raised about the breadth of personality traits, or their cross-situational generality. It was known, for example, that internal attributions for success were unrelated to the tendency to ascribe failure internally. In addition, it has long been recognized that the closer any set of scale items is to the situation in which a prediction is being made, the better the predictive validity of the scale. For example, if predicting motivation at high jumping, it is probably best to ask how motivated one is when high jumping, good to ask how motivated one is at sports, and conceivably of little value to determine how much one is motivated to achieve. Hence, specific scales began to be developed, such as the Health Locus of Control scale, which examines whether individuals perceive health-related outcomes as subject to personal or environmental control. In addition, individual difference scales began to be developed that incorporated properties of perceived causality in addition to locus, such as the stability of causes. These scales were particularly used to understand and predict depression (Abramson, Seligman, & Teasdale, 1978).

To summarize, the historical antecedents of the individual difference approach to attributions include Rotter's attention to expectancy estimates, which was in part derived from his investigations involving skill and chance tasks, his acceptance of Lewin's Expectancy-value theory, and research on level of aspiration. Over time, scales became more specific to particular situations and included properties of causality other than locus. In this book, this influence will be evident in the chapters by Amirkhan on stress, and Peterson on achievement strivings.

THE SOCIAL PSYCHOLOGICAL APPROACH TO ATTRIBUTIONS: THE INFLUENCE OF HEIDER AND WEINER

Festinger's theory of cognitive dissonance provided the dominant research paradigm for social psychology in the 1960s. Dissonance theory offered a noncommonsense approach to attitude formation and change based on the "fit" between cognitive elements. Thus, it also was a balance formulation. Inasmuch as attitudes have been the backbone of social psychology, and since there was a very conscious desire in the 1950s to progress beyond what was known as "bubba" (grandmother) psychology, the dominance of dissonance theory can be readily understood. But by the end of the 1960s dissonance theory had run its course. And this also is understandable. The many studies that were conducted left scholars searching for new places to leave their personal mark. In addition, dissonance was linked to drive theory, but this conception already had been discarded by most motivational psychologists. And of greatest importance, dissonance was conceptually sparse, so that there were few new directions toward which the theory could turn (hence resulting in increasingly novel experimental procedures to examine the same phenomena).

Attribution theory as first proposed by Heider and elaborated by Kelley replaced dissonance as the dominant paradigm within social psychology in the 1970s. This was in part because attribution theory fit within the overriding cognitive context of psychology that emerged in the early 1960s. Attribution theory was concerned with epistemology, or how people know. Heider, Kelley, and others presumed that individuals search for mastery and understanding, asking why events occurred and inferring the intents of others. Second, attribution theory is a psychology that does not rely on the nonobvious. People are accepted as attempting to be rational, guided in their inferences by informational inputs and directed in their actions by naïve psychological beliefs.

Heider, like Rotter, was concerned with causal perceptions in achievement-related contexts, but not from the perspective of an individual difference theorist.

Rather, he began by analyzing the perceived determinents of achievement performance. He intuited that behavior is influenced by both "can" and "try;" can, in turn, was conceived as the relation between ability and the difficulty of the task. Both ability and effort hence were considered internal to the actor and components of skill, whereas objective task difficulty was an external determinant of behavior. Hence, Heider also emphasized the locus of causality in his theorizing.

The Weiner Approach

My contribution to attribution was in part to emphasize other dimensions or properties of causality in addition to locus. Starting from the ability–effort distinction made by Heider, it was reasoned that to the extent that these two causes of achievement performance differentially predict or determine some aspect of judgment or action, then an additional distinction between causes other than internal–external is needed.

One of my initial experiments linking attributional thinking to achievement strivings (Weiner & Kukla, 1970) documented that evaluation is particularly influenced by perceived effort expenditure: High effort is rewarded in achievement settings while low effort tends to be punished. This is not true for ability, which has little direct effect on evaluation when not confounded with outcome. Thus, given the differential consequences of ability and effort information on evaluation, a need to differentiate these causes was established.

My colleagues and I (Weiner et al., 1971) labeled the property distinguishing ability from effort as "causal stability." Stability refers to the lability of a cause over time. Ability was considered to be rather fixed (akin to aptitude), whereas effort was conceived as variable, subject to fluctuation over short periods. Inasmuch as effort expenditure is perceived as variable, we speculated it would be linked with reward and punishment, which could then be used to influence expended effort. On the other hand, it appeared to us that rewarding or punishing ability had little instrumental function, since ability was conceived as fixed.

We had an additional insight at that time (Weiner et al., 1971). When Rotter contrasted skill (ability) with luck perceptions, he was actually comparing a respective internal, stable cause with an external, unstable cause. Hence, the disparate expectancy shifts that he documented could be attributed to either the locus or the stability dimension of causality. We later definitively documented that expectancy shifts are determined by causal stability rather than causal locus (see reviews in Weiner, 1985, 1986). For example, failure because of lack of ability produces lower expectancy of success than failure perceived as due to lack of effort, although both are internal determinants of behavior. Furthermore, failure because of low ability and failure due to an objectively difficult task may produce the same expectancy decrements, although ability is an internal determinant and task difficulty an external determinant of behavior.

But if causal stability is linked with expectancy of success (as it surely is), then what is the psychological significance of causal locus? To answer this question, we returned to Expectancy-value theory as construed by Lewin and later by Atkinson and Rotter (1957, 1964) and concluded that causal locus must be associated with the value of goal attainment. In this case, value was equated with affective reactions, or pride in accomplishment, which Atkinson (1957) had proposed to be the incentive associated with successful goal attainment. More specifically, it was contended that the greater the degree to which one ascribes success to internal factors (the self), the greater the pride in accomplishment.

Along with many coworkers, I continued with this line of thinking, seeking to isolate still other causal dimensions and their unique consequences. A third dimension of causality was recognized when poor strategy as a cause of failure was contrasted with lack of effort. Both these causes are internal and variable, yet lack of effort elicits greater punishment for failure than does poor strategy. This logic resulted in the postulation of a third causal dimension, which I labeled "controllability" (Weiner, 1979). Inasmuch as causal controllability was conceived as independent of causal locus, a cause could be classified as internal and controllable (e.g., effort) or internal and uncontrollable (e.g., aptitude). Hence, locus *and* control, not locus *of* control as conceived by Rotter, is the proper nomenclature to characterize causes such as ability, effort, luck, and strategy. It became evident that I also had erred in the past in my understanding of phenomenal causality; ability and effort differ not only in stability, but also in controllability. Hence, the differential reward elicited by these two causes could be attributed to either dimension of causality. I now strongly suspect that perceived controllability rather than stability is the causal mediator of reward and punishment.

It further was realized that there are many possible affective responses to success and failure in addition to pride and shame, which historically were the only affects linked with achievement strivings. For example, failure due to volitional interference from others elicits anger, whereas uncontrollable failure by others because of, for example, a physical handicap, evokes pity. It soon became apparent that each causal dimension is linked with a specific set of affects (see reviews in Weiner, 1985, 1986). A key issue then became to discover these cognition–emotion unions and in so doing develop a miniature theory of emotion.

A Reinterpretation of Atkinson's Theory of Achievement Strivings.   The theory proposed by John Atkinson (1957, 1964) provided the dominant interpretation of achievement strivings during the two decades beginning around 1957 and ending around 1977. Atkinson argued that achievement strivings are in part mediated by individual differences in what he called the "motive for success" and the "motive to avoid failure." These were conceived as relatively enduring dispositions to go toward or away from achievement-related contexts. In addition, motivation was presumed to be determined by the expectancy of success and the incentive value of success, with the latter conceived as the amount of pride one experiences given goal attainment.

These ideas were in the background during the development of an attributional interpretation of achievement strivings. For example, it was reasoned that individuals highly motivated to achieve have a disposition to ascribe success internally. Hence, individual differences in achievement needs (motives) were conceived as causal dispositions, and achievement theory as construed by Atkinson thus was brought into contact with Rotter's thoughts about causal tendencies. Increased reward for success resulting from self-ascription then might result in continued goal strivings, thus accounting for the linkage between achievement motives and achievement behavior documented by Atkinson.

As already noted, Atkinson also included expectancy (probability of success) and incentive as determinants of achievement performance. He further specified that the incentive value of achievement success is higher for difficult than for easy tasks. We then documented that when a task is easy, the incentive value of success (pride) is low because success is externally ascribed (to the ease of the task). On the other hand, when the task is difficult, the incentive value is high because the attribution for success is internal (Weiner & Kukla, 1970). To use the language of Kelley (1967), in the former instance the positive outcome is consistent with social norms and thus is externally attributed (there is covariation of the outcome with the task), whereas in the latter instance the outcome is inconsistent with social norms and thus internally attributed (there is covariation of the outcome with the person). Hence, Kelley's insights about covariation principles also played an important role in the development of an attributional approach to achievement strivings.

Current State of the Theory. The concerns with causal dimensions and achievement performance that have been discussed were further refined and eventuated in an attributional theory of motivation, which is depicted in Fig. 1.1 in its most current version. Fig. 1.1 reveals that a motivational sequence is initiated by an outcome that individuals interpret as positive (goal attainment) or negative (nonattainment of a goal). Inasmuch as some affects are directly linked with outcome, Fig. 1.1 includes a connection between outcome and the reactions of happy (for success) and frustrated or sad (for failure). These associations are designated with a "1" in the figure. A causal search is then undertaken to determine why the outcome occurred (Linkage 2). Some of the conditions that promote this search are indicated in the figure, such as negative, unexpected, and important outcomes. A large number of antecedents influence the causal explanation(s) that is reached. Some of the known antecedents are included in Fig. 1.1, such as the specific information outlined by Kelley (e.g., past personal history, social norms, etc.). The blanket etcetera at the bottom of the antecedents merely conveys that there are many unlisted determinants of the selected attribution.

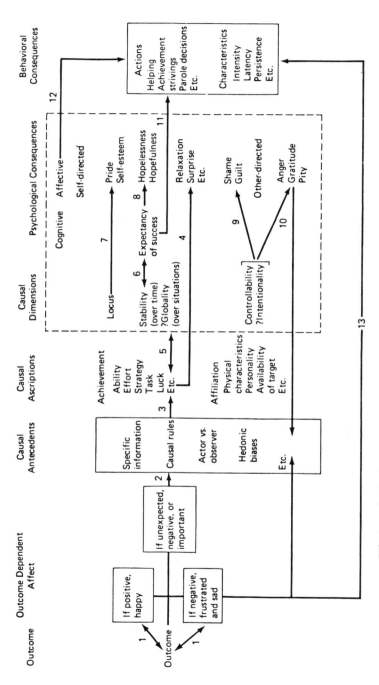

FIG. 1.1. An Attributional Theory of Motivation and Emotion. From Weiner (1986, p. 240).

9

The causal decision is biased toward a relatively small number of causes, such as ability and effort in the achievement domain. Again Fig. 1.1 is not complete, as denoted by the etcetera at the bottom of the causal lists. The cause is then located in dimensional space. This is depicted as Linkage 5. The three main properties of causes are locus, stability, and controllability, with globality and intentionality considered possible causal properties.

Causal dimensions have psychological consequences. being related to both expectancy and affect (in this conception, affect is presumed to be the value of goal attainment). The stability of a cause influences the relative expectancy of future success (Linkage 6). Turning to the affective consequences, the locus of a cause exerts an influence on self-esteem and pride; the stability of a cause, by affecting expectancy, fosters feelings of hopelessness and hopefulness (see Linkage 8); and controllability influences social emotions. More specifically, controllable causes of personal failure promote feelings of guilt, whereas uncontrollable causes generate shame (Linkage 9). These are represented in Fig. 1.1 as self-directed affects, as are the specific attribution-linked emotions of relaxation and surprise. Among the affects directed toward others are anger (given a cause of failure controllable by others), pity (given an uncontrollable cause of failure), and gratitude (given a controllable cause for success; see Linkage 10). Finally, expectancy and affect are presumed to determine action (Linkages 11, 12, and 13).

To add to this complexity, the linkages in Fig. 1.1 are not unidirectional. For example, feelings of happiness and sadness influence outcome perceptions (Linkage 1); expectancy of success influences attributions (Linkage 6); and affects such as pity and anger are important attributional cues when communicated to others (Linkage 10).

ATTRIBUTION THEORY AND APPLIED PSYCHOLOGY

Now, what does all this theoretical complexity and conceptual reinterpretation have to do with applied psychology, and more specifically with the topics addressed in this book, such as interpersonal and intergroup conflict, teacher behavior in the classroom, student persistence, marriage and divorce, and so on? When attributional thinking was confined to the locus dimension of causality, some application was possible, particularly when specific scales were devised as predictors of, for example, reactions to stressful events. But there was relatively little to be done other than assess internal and external tendencies. However, with the additional causal dimensions and a host of affects, greater application became possible. For example, one could examine if distressed partners in marriage perceive causes of negative events as stable, so that perceived expectancy of future success of the marriage is low, or if attributions were being made for negative events to controllable causes, hence increasing anger. If this were the case, then potential avenues for change were indicated. One also could examine if the cause of a need was ascribed to uncontrollable causes, thus evoking pity and help, or to controllable causes, thereby giving rise to anger and neglect. If the latter, then again a direction for application was evident. One could also determine if buyers ascribed bad products to stable causes, so that future purchases of that product were unlikely. And one could investigate disagreements between members of a dyad, both in terms of causal ascriptions and generated affects. Do the buyer and the seller perceive the causes of a defective product differently, so that the seller cannot understand the anger of the buyer? These are the kinds of questions pursued by Baron, Betancourt, Fincham et al., and Folkes in their chapters on conflict in this book.

In a similar manner, those interested in achievement strivings began to examine the wide array of attributions, experienced affects, and communicated feelings that might influence behavior in the classroom or on the sports field. This freeing of attributions from just the locus dimension can be seen in the chapters by Graham, McAuley and Duncan, and Peterson.

Attribution Theory and Clinical Psychology

Clinical psychology also has benefited from the growth of attribution theory. Like social psychology, clinical psychology was ready to undergo change in the 1970s. Academic psychologists had long been suspicious (at best) of the nonempirical stance of psychoanalytic theorists. While alternative approaches in clinical psychology were available in the 1960s, none dominated the imagination of psychologists. At about this time, cognitive therapies began to gain increasing attention. Sparked by the ideas of Beck, Ellis, and G. Kelly, how clients make sense out of their world and how these interpretations direct their feelings and actions became a central theme in change attempts. Even behaviorally oriented therapists began to recognize the importance of thought processes, and there grew an influential school of cognitive behavioral modification.

These trends provided the background for the growth of attributional therapy and the application of attributional language to explain clinical phenomena, especially depression. The initial change programs guided by attribution theory involved children exhibiting maladaptive behavior in achievement contexts, such as quitting in the face of failure and displaying little frustration tolerance. The goal of the change program was to have these children think differently about the cause(s) of their failures. This was anticipated to then produce behavioral change.

Now there is a rapidly expanding use of attribution therapy, with the potential to deal with a range of clinical problems and populations. This is illustrated in the chapters by Försterling, López, and Wolkenstein, and Amirkhan. These chapters document the efficacy of attributional therapy and how diagnostic inferences are directed by attributional information, such as the perceived normative behavior of disparate cultural groups.

A SUMMARY STATEMENT

Now let us return to the question that instigated this chapter: "Why has attribution theory been so amenable to practical use?" To summarize my answer, I have contended that:

1. The important historical predecessors and contributors to this area, particularly Kurt Lewin, were strongly committed to both theory development and theory utilization.
2. Some of the central theorists, including Rotter and Atkinson, were engaged in basic research on issues that readily lent themselves to application, such as the determinants of expectancy of success and achievement strivings.
3. Instruments such as the I–E scale, even given its flaws, were easily modifiable and proved useful in enhancing predictions of coping behaviors in health-endangering situations.
4. The *zeitgeist* of cognitive psychology and the dissatisfaction with dissonance and psychoanalytical theory paved the way for new approaches in social psychology and new paths to clinical phenomena and psychotherapy.
5. Above all, attribution theory provides a rich framework, incorporating many causal concepts, expectancy of success, a variety of affects, and disparate phenomena. Thus, the tools are provided for application. As Lewin stated: "There is nothing so practical as a good theory."

REFERENCES

Abramson, L. Y., Seligman, M. E. P., & Teasdale, J. D. (1978). Learned helplessness in humans: Critique and reformulation. *Journal of Abnormal Psychology, 87*, 49–74.

Atkinson, J. W. (1957). Motivational determinants of risk-taking behavior. *Psychological Review, 64*, 359–372.

Atkinson, J. W. (1964). *An introduction to motivation*. Princeton, NJ: Van Nostrand.

Heider, F. (1958). *The psychology of interpersonal relations*. New York: Wiley.

James, W., & Rotter, J. B. (1958). Partial and 100% reinforcement under chance and skill conditions. *Journal of Experimental Psychology, 55*, 397–403.

Kelley, H. H. (1967). Attribution theory in social psychology. In D. Levine (Ed.), *Nebraska symposium on motivation* (pp. 192–238). Lincoln: University of Nebraska Press.

Lewin, K. (1935). *A dynamic theory of personality*. New York: McGraw–Hill.

Lewin, K. (1938). *The conceptual representation and the measurement of psychological forces*. Durham, NC: Duke University Press.

Marrow, A. J. (1969). *The practical theorist: The life and work of Kurt Lewin*. New York: Basic Books.

Rotter, J. B. (1954). *Social learning and clinical psychology*. Englewood Cliffs, NJ: Prentice–Hall.

Rotter, J. B. (1966). Generalized expectancies for internal versus external control of reinforcement. *Psychological Monographs, 80*(1, Whole No. 609).

Weiner, B. (1979). A theory of motivation for some classroom experiences. *Journal of Educational Psychology, 71,* 3–25.

Weiner, B. (1985). An attributional theory of achievement motivation and emotion. *Psychological Review, 92,* 548–573.

Weiner, B. (1986). *An attributional theory of motivation and emotion.* New York: Springer–Verlag.

Weiner, B., Frieze, I. H., Kukla, A., Reed, L. Rest, S., & Rosenbaum, R. M. (1971). *Perceiving the causes of success and failure.* Morristown, NJ: General Learning Press.

Weiner, B., & Kukla, A. (1970). An attributional analysis of achievement motivation. *Journal of Personality and Social Psychology, 15,* 1–20.

APPLICATIONS TO ACHIEVEMENT

As a theory of causal explanations for success and failure, attribution research found a natural context for study in the achievement domain. Inspired largely by Weiner's empirical and theoretical contributions, a vast literature has accumulated that applies attributional analyses to achievement-related concerns. These concerns have been many and varied, including causal ascriptions of teachers and students in academic contexts and of coaches and players in athletic settings. Furthermore, the type of attributional activity examined has ranged from relatively situationally specific reactions to particular experiences of exam success and failure or team wins and losses, to more generalized causal belief systems that take on a trait-like conception. The three chapters in this section of the book reflect some of this diversity (and richness) in the application of attribution theory to the achievement domain.

It is well documented in attribution research that perceiving oneself as low in ability has far-reaching negative consequences. Drawing on several attribution principles related to perceived ability, Graham (Chapter 2) focuses on classroom achievement and describes a number of seemingly positive teacher behaviors, such as communicated praise for success and unsolicited offers of help, that can subtly and indirectly communicate low ability to students. Unlike the remaining chapters in the book, this chapter takes a distinctly developmental approach to the study of attributions. By examining age-related changes in attributional thinking across the elementary-school years, Graham documents that the potentially negative consequences of indirect low-ability cues are mediated by the cognitive maturity of children. This chapter serves as a reminder that the application-oriented attribution researcher concerned with school performance must take into account the more general growth and changes in the cognitive competencies of children that can influence causal reasoning.

Achievement outcomes occur not only in the classroom, but on the athletic field as well. Hence, attributional analyses of academic success and failure should also be applicable to winning and losing in sports. In Chapter 3, McAuley and Duncan present a cogent review of a number of attributional studies on athletic outcomes (e.g., table tennis and gymnastic competition) that they and their colleagues have conducted over the past several years. Their work underscores the consistency of attributional reasoning, whether outcomes involve sport or academic achievement. That is, causal attributions for wins and losses in sport predict affective reactions and expectations for future performance in much the same way that they predict these consequences of academic success and failure. The domain of sport may ultimately prove to be a particularly important testing ground for attributional principles, inasmuch as winning and losing at athletic competitions often are more unambiguous achievement outcomes than are good and poor scores on academic tasks.

Whereas Graham and McAuley and Duncan take a situational approach to the study of achievement attributions, Peterson (Chapter 4) conceives of attributional reasoning as a stable and generalized personality trait that he and his colleagues have labeled explanatory (attributional) style. Thus attributional dispositions are systematically measured and individuals are classified as relatively optimistic or pessimistic in their explanatory style. In Peterson's work, individual differences in explanatory style are then correlated with a range of achievement outcomes in both academic and athletic contexts. The author reports a consistent set of findings indicating, for example, that a pessimistic explanatory style predicts poor GPA among college undergraduates and even perhaps the losing streaks of professional baseball teams! The power of explanatory style as a predictor of achievement outcomes is not yet known; a number of the more general complexities in the study of personality traits remain as issues to be dealt with. Nonetheless, Peterson's research has gained wide recognition and it has been most influential in moving the individual difference approach toward the forefront of attribution research in achievement contexts.

2 Communicating Low Ability in the Classroom: Bad Things Good Teachers Sometimes Do

Sandra Graham
Graduate School of Education, University of California, Los Angeles

Of all the perceived causes of success and failure, ability and effort appear to be the most dominant. When explaining achievement outcomes, we tend to attach the most importance to what our perceived competencies are and how hard we try. Recognizing the import of these two prevalent self-ascriptions, much of the applied attribution research in achievement-related contexts has been concerned with ability and effort, particularly the role they play in coping with academic failure.

One well-established finding to have emerged from the prior research is that self-perceptions of low ability versus lack of effort have far-reaching and disparate consequences (see Weiner, 1985, 1986). Failure because of perceived low ability reflects on the failing individual and therefore has implications for self-esteem. As a chronic cause of failure, a self-ascription to low ability also tends to lower one's expectations for future success. And because low ability is perceived as uncontrollable, it leads to the belief that there is no response in one's repertoire to alter the course of failure. Hardly a more debilitating attributional pattern is imaginable. Attributing failure to lack of effort, on the other hand, is more adaptive because effort is perceived as both changeable and under one's volitional control. Thus the failing student who believes that he or she did not try hard enough can be bolstered by the expectation that failure need not occur again and by the belief that there is a relationship between one's efforts and subsequent outcomes. Guided by these causal distinctions, a number of application-oriented investigations have attempted to change the failing student's attribution for failure from low ability to lack of effort (see Försterling, 1985; Chapter 7 this volume).

In contrast to this more dominant focus on attributional change and its conse-

17

quences, a smaller body of application-oriented research has focused on the *antecedents* or determinants of maladaptive versus adaptive causal ascriptions. A number of the more obvious antecedents have been identified, such as one's own performance history or the performance of others (see Kelley & Michela, 1980). For example, a history of failure on exams at which most others excel certainly leads the student to question his or her ability.

In classroom contexts, the information provided by others, such as a teacher, is also likely to be an important source of attributional information. Sometimes this information may be quite direct, as when a teacher tells a pupil "You didn't work hard enough on that math exam" or "You belong in the low reading group." At other times, however, attributional information may be subtly, indirectly, and even unknowingly conveyed. This unintended communication of attributional information appears to be particularly likely when the teacher wishes to protect the self-esteem of the failure-prone student. In this chapter, I will make the argument that three prevalent and seemingly positive teacher behaviors can be conceptualized in this manner and can therefore unintentionally function as low-ability cues. The particular behaviors that I include in this category are communicated pity following failure; the offering of praise following success, particularly at easy tasks; and unsolicited offers of help. These feedback types will be contrasted to three equally prevalent but seemingly negative teacher behaviors that might indirectly communicate the more adaptive lack of effort attribution. This latter group includes communicated anger following failure; the assignment of blame following failure, particularly at easy tasks; and the withholding of help. Thus, the indirect sources of attributional information are to be found in a full range of teacher behaviors and in situations of success as well as imminent failure.

The psychological processes underlying this analysis are shown in Fig. 2.1. Briefly, the process begins with the teacher's private attributions for the target student's outcome. Attributional inferences about students then lead to particular teacher reactions toward that pupil, such as pity or anger, praise or blame, or help or neglect. In the next step, the student uses that reaction to infer the teacher's underlying attribution. The inferred attribution of the teacher then influences self-perceptions of ability or effort. Finally, particular self-ascriptions lead to specific consequences related to, for example, expectancy and achievement-related affect.

In the following sections, I present the empirical evidence documenting the linkages proposed in Fig. 2.1. Unlike the other chapters in this volume, most of the research that I describe was conducted in a developmental context. My colleagues and I have examined the attributional cue value of pity versus anger, praise versus blame, and help versus neglect among children from prekindergarten to the late elementary years. There are two main reasons for this developmental focus in our research, one practical and the other more theoretical. Practically speaking, many of the teacher behaviors that may function as attributional cues are more prevalent in elementary-school classrooms (see Sti-

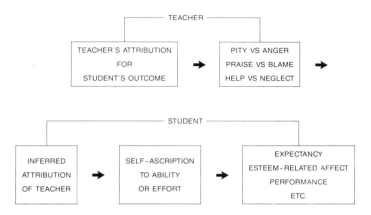

FIG. 2.1.   An Attributional Process Depicting Teacher Behaviors That Function as Indirect Causal Cues.

pek, 1984). It is therefore essential that the application-oriented researcher be sensitive to age differences in children's attributional understanding that may influence the interpretation of ability-implicating classroom cues. At a more theoretical level, the study of developmental growth and change in, for example, children's understanding of the *meaning* of an attribution such as ability or of an emotion such as pity provides the attribution theorist with insights into how these same attributions and affects are perceived in adulthood. We know a good deal more about different conceptions of ability that adults readily utilize, and about the prevalence of our naïve theories of when people "should" feel pity versus anger, based on studies of the acquisition of these concepts in children (Graham & Weiner, 1986; Nicholls & Miller, 1984; also see Graham & Brown, 1988). Thus, there is much of value in the study of developmental processes for the attribution researcher concerned with theory generality and theory refinement.

PITY AND ANGER AS ATTRIBUTIONAL CUES

I begin with pity and anger as causal cues because these were the first set of relations that we examined developmentally. The format adopted here will be followed throughout the chapter. First I describe the relevant attribution principles suggesting relations between a particular teacher behavior and causal ascriptions. Then the pertinent developmental investigations are presented.

Principle One: Some Emotions Are Responses to Causal Attributions

That our thoughts determine how we feel is a fundamental principle of attribution theory (Weiner, 1985, 1986). Thus pity and anger are among a prevalent set of human emotions that share in common the fact that they are preceded and determined by causal thoughts. In the case of pity and anger, these thoughts relate to the perceived controllability of causes. Pity is elicited when another's failure is perceived as caused by uncontrollable causes, such as low ability (think of the teacher's reaction to the retarded child who continuously experiences academic difficulty). In contrast, anger is aroused when another's failure is attributed to controllable factors, such as lack of effort (consider the teacher's feelings toward the bright student who never completes assignments). These linkages are not confined to the achievement domain. For example, we pity the disabled but feel anger toward the able-bodied who are unwilling to work because they are perceived as responsible for their plight. Anger is thus an "ought" emotion that often accompanies the belief that the target of anger is capable of changing his or her behavior. In contrast, pity has been conceptualized as a more positive emotional reaction to those whose negative state is viewed as both chronic and not subject to personal influence.

Now suppose that a teacher does respond with pity or anger toward a failing student. According to the sequence outlined in Fig. 2.1, the student may then use this affective display to infer, first, the teacher's attribution and then his or her own self-ascription for failure. In other words, failing students can gain information about the causes of their achievement outcomes, based on the affective displays of teachers.

Developmental Research

We began our developmental study of pity and anger as attributional cues with a pair of simulational studies. We simply wanted to document that given knowledge of a teacher's emotional reaction of pity or anger, conveyed by verbal labels, individuals could use this information to infer antecedent thoughts in a manner consistent with the theory. In the first investigation (Weiner, Graham, Stern, & Lawson, 1982, Experiment 1) college students and children ages 9 and 11 were given scenarios such as the following:

A student failed a test and the teacher became angry.
Why did the teacher think the student failed?

We manipulated a number of teacher affects including anger and pity. Four attributions—low ability, lack of effort, task difficulty, and bad luck—were presented as possible causes for the student's failure and these were rated on simple Likert scales. Here we will only be concerned with the data for ability and effort which were quite systematic across the age groups. Consistent with our analysis, all subjects reported that the sympathetic teacher believed the student to be low in ability and that the angry teacher believed the student had not tried hard enough. Thus, these linkages between pity-inferred ability and between anger-inferred effort appeared to be rather robust.

Guided by our developmental interest, in a second study we investigated these same linkages with children who ranged in age from 5 to 9 (Weiner et al., 1982), Experiment 2). With these younger age groups, we had reason to expect developmental differences in the understanding of attribution–affect relations. If causal thoughts precede particular emotional experiences such as anger and pity, then developmental changes in children's understanding of specific causal thoughts should influence their understanding of the associated affects and the attribution-affect linkages (see Graham & Weiner, 1986). The attributions of concern here are effort and ability. There is a substantial body of research indicating that children are able to reason accurately about effort at an earlier age than they are able to reason about ability (Nicholls, 1978; Nicholls & Miller, 1984). This appears to be so because children understand the concept of effort as something controllable and unstable before they understand the concept of ability as an uncontrollable and stable causal factor (Nicholls, 1978; Nicholls & Miller, 1984). Before middle childhood, children tend to view ability as fluctuating and to some degree modifiable through practice and effort. Carol Dweck and her colleagues have labeled this an "incremental" conception of ability or intelligence, as opposed to an "entity" view which is more characteristic of older children and adult perceptions (Dweck & Elliott, 1983; Dweck & Leggett, 1988). However, the basic distinction even in the analysis by Dweck concerns underlying attributional properties of ability.

The documented developmental differences in children's understanding of effort and ability led us to predict in our study with younger children that the anger–effort relation would be understood earlier than the pity–ability association. In this study children selected, rather than rated, ability or effort as the causal ascription of the sympathetic-versus-angry teacher. Table 2.1 shows the causal alternative selected as a function of the communicated affect and age of subjects.

Our predictions were confirmed. The anger-inferred effort linkage is stronger than the pity-inferred ability relation in all age groups. Even 5-year-olds understand that anger can be a cue to lack of effort attributions, but pity as a cue to low ability is not understood by children younger than about age 9. This means that younger children may not be as susceptible as their older counterparts to the ability-implicating messages of communicated pity *in academic contexts*. I want to emphasize this last point because we now have a good deal of developmental evidence indicating that very young children understand the relationship between pity and antecedent thoughts about uncontrollability in nonachievement domains, such as helping or affiliation (Graham, Doubleday, & Guarino, 1984; Graham & Weiner, 1989). What appears to be changing and increasing with age is the child's conception of academic ability as something uncontrollable and stable.

TABLE 2.1
Percentage Choice of Effort, Given the Anger Cue, and Ability,
Given the Pity Cue, as a Function of Age[a]

	Age Group		
Linkage	5 (n=30)	7 (n=37)	9 (n=36)
Anger-effort	77	89	100
Pity-ability	50	62	72

[a]From Weiner, Graham, Stern, and Lawson (1982).

Pity and Anger as Cues Guiding Self-perception

The studies that have been described document the *possibility* that pity and anger can function as attributional cues for the target of these affective displays. We have taken the analysis a step further and documented that these communicated affects are indeed used by students to infer why they failed, that is, whether they are deficient in ability or effort (see Graham, 1984). Although this was not a developmental study, I want to digress briefly to describe this research because it is highly pertinent to the general discussion of pity and anger as indirect attributional cues.

In this study (Graham, 1984), sixth-grade participants were induced to fail at a novel puzzle-solving task. Following failure, a female experimenter posing as a teacher communicated either pity, anger, or no affective reaction. The subjects then reported their causal attributions for failure and their expectation for success on the next puzzle. Note that in contrast to the simulational studies presented herein, this was a laboratory situation where participants actually experienced failure and the affects were indeed communicated. This methodology provided us with a way to capture more closely the ecology of the classroom, but without sacrificing the experimental control needed to focus on the phenomenon of interest.

In support of our analysis, the findings revealed that children were most likely to attribute their puzzle-solving failure to low ability when pity was conveyed and most likely to report lack of effort as the cause for failure when anger was conveyed. In addition, they had the lowest expectations for future success in response to the pity cue. These data led me to speculate that failing children, at least from the middle elementary grades on, might progress through communicated affect–self-perception scenarios such as the following:

I haven't solved any of these puzzles so far and the teacher obviously feels sorry for me. She must think I'm not good at this task. I really did get the puzzles wrong because I'm not good at puzzle solving, and I don't expect to do better in the future.

Or alternatively:

> I haven't solved any of these puzzles so far and the teacher obviously is angry with me. She must think I'm not trying. I really did get the puzzles wrong because I didn't try hard enough, but I expect to do better in the future.

Of all the subtle attributional cues in classroom context, the emotional reactions of teachers may be among the most important antecedents of perceived personal competence.

PRAISE AND BLAME

When I was a classroom teacher a number of years ago, I recall reading a published interview with a teacher of low-achieving African–American fifth graders in an inner city school. This woman was considered a master teacher and in the interview she was questioned about a number of her instructional practices, including her general beliefs about feedback and evaluation of her students. The following is a portion of her response to the question about her particular evaluation practices:

> Oh, I complement them. That is the best way to get children to work. Always commendations, always. Never . . . well, I can't say that I *never* say I'm not pleased. Sometimes I get angry and say I am not pleased with this kind of paper and I want it rewritten, but I'll always find one word and I say, "This is beautifully written." . . . This is my best way . . . I always try to stress the positive, accent the positive. (Leacock, 1969, p. 128)

At the time, as I struggled with my own class of unruly middle schoolers, I remember being impressed with these remarks, thinking they represented a very positive and humane approach to evaluating failure-prone minority students. The teacher's reluctance to criticize her pupils seemed to reflect a genuine desire to protect their self-esteem. She recognized the incentive value of praise and readily dispensed it for even small accomplishments. Looking back at these remarks now as an attribution researcher, I feel less reassured by them. The attributional process depicted in Fig. 2.1 suggests that there may be unintended messages communicated by this teacher's generous use of praise and minimal assignment of blame. According to our analysis, the student might use such feedback to conclude that the teacher views him or her as low in ability.

The possibility that praise and blame can function as attributional cues was first documented in a series of studies by Meyer and his colleagues (Meyer et al., 1979). Subjects read a questionnaire containing information about two students who successfully solved a math problem. One student was praised by the teacher and the other was simply told that his answer was correct. The research participants then indicated which of the two students the teacher believed to be higher in ability. The data clearly revealed that subjects inferred less ability in the student who received praise than in the student who received neutral feedback. Meyer et al. (1979, Experiments 3–5) also examined teacher blame following failure as an attributional cue. This time participants read that one of two failing students was blamed or criticized by the teacher and that the other student received no such reprimand. When they inferred the teacher's beliefs about the two students' abilities, subjects reported that the student *not* blamed by the teacher was less competent. In other words, the absence of blame, like the conveying of praise, functioned as an indirect low-ability cue. What attribution principles underlie these somewhat paradoxical effects of praise and blame on perceptions of ability? Two principles appear to be particularly relevant, one related to evaluation and the other related to the relationship between effort and ability.

Principle Two: Attributions Are Determinants of Achievement Evaluation

Evaluative feedbacks such as praise and blame are known to be related to the perceived causes of success and failure, particularly effort expenditure (Weiner & Kukla, 1970). The successful student who tries hard is maximally praised or rewarded, whereas the failing student who puts forth little effort elicits the most blame or punishment. Thus, praise and blame from others can allow us to make inferences about effort as a cause for success and failure.

Principle Three: Ability and Effort are Perceived as Compensatory Causes of Achievement

A second attribution principle relevant to this analysis has to do with the perceived relationship between effort and ability. Among adults, effort and ability are often perceived as compensatory causes of achievement (Kun & Weiner, 1973). In both success and failure, the higher one's effort, the lower one's perceived ability and vice versa. Thus if two students achieve the same outcome, often the one who tried harder is judged as lower in ability. Similarly, the one who is higher in ability is often perceived to have tried less hard than his or her equally successful counterpart. Applied to the cue value of praise and blame, these two attribution principles thus suggest the following: Praise, relative to neutral feedback, leads to the inference of high effort, and the higher one's perceived effort, the lower one's perceived ability. In contrast, blame relative to neutral feedback, leads to the inference of low effort, and the lower one's perceived effort, the higher one's perceived ability.

Developmental Evidence

This analysis presumes a complex reasoning process where individuals progress from evaluative feedback about one cause (effort) to judgments about a second cause (ability). We wondered whether very young children have the cognitive maturity to infer attributions from information about praise and blame in the manner that has been proposed. We did not anticipate that inferring effort would be a problem, since a number of developmental studies indicate that relations between praise and blame and inferences about effort are understood by children as young as age 5 (Harari & Covington, 1981; Weiner & Peter, 1973). These young children reward high effort and punish low effort much like adult subjects do. However, progressing from judgments about effort to inferences about ability using a compensatory rule may require a more advanced level of cognitive functioning, for there is a good deal of developmental research indicating that young children may not perceive this inverse relationship between effort and ability. For example, Kun (1977) documented that up to about age 10, children expect effort and ability to covary positively: The student who tries harder is believed to be smarter, a phenomenon that Kun labeled the "halo schema" (also see Nicholls, 1978). This earlier research led us to speculate that young children's ability inferences in response to praise and blame cues would vary positively with effort rather than negatively. That is, if young children perceive effort as high in response to praise and low in response to blame, then the same pattern would prevail for their ability inferences.

George Barker and I investigated these developmental hypotheses in a study modeled after the Meyer et al. research (Barker & Graham, 1987). Children between the ages of 4 and 12 watched videotaped teaching sessions depicting a pair of students solving a set of objectively easy math problems. We chose videotaped sessions over verbal scenarios to increase the realism of the stimuli. In one videotape, both students successfully solved the easy problems. One student was praised by the teacher with such positive statements as: "Good thinking!" or "Great job!.". The other student received neutral feedback such as "Correct." In the second videotape, both students failed the easy problems, but one student was criticized (e.g., "What's the matter with you? That's not the right answer!"). The other student merely received feedback that his answers were incorrect. The research participants then rated the effort and ability of the two students on 5-point scales.

The results of these ratings are shown in Fig. 2.2. The top two panels show effort and ability ratings by age group and feedback condition for success. For effort (left panel), subjects inferred that the praised student tried harder than his neutral feedback counterpart and this was true for all three age groups. Recall that we expected even young children to be able to infer effort accurately from evaluative feedback. With ability, however, there was the anticipated developmental trend. Whereas 11- and 12-year-olds "correctly" inferred that the praised

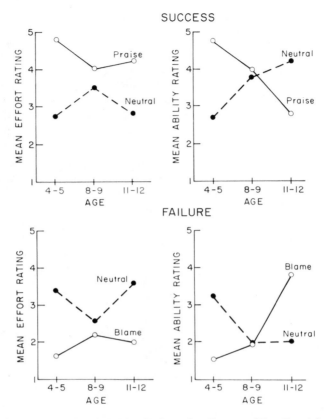

FIG. 2.2. Effort and Ability Ratings for Success (Top Panels) and Failure (Bottom Panels) as a Function of Age Group and Type of Feedback. (From Barker & Graham, 1987)

student was lower in ability, the opposite pattern prevailed for the youngest children who reported that the praised student was smarter. Eight-year-olds, in addition, fell clearly between these two extreme age groups.

There was a very similar pattern to the data for failure where the feedback was blame or neutral (bottom panels). All the children inferred less effort in the blamed student (left panel), but only the oldest children inferred that this student was also smarter (right panel). For very young children, the absence of blame, like the presence of praise, was the high-ability cue. Eight-year-olds were again in the middle, not making a clear distinction between effort and ability as a function of feedback type.

Our predicted developmental hypothesis was therefore supported in this data. Very young children were not susceptible to the ability-implicating messages of praise and blame. We argued that this was because they do not yet perceive a compensatory relationship between effort and ability. In our next analysis, we tested this understanding. We calculated correlations between effort and ability ratings for each age group, and we plotted these two causal ratings together to graphically display the meaning of these correlations (see Fig. 2.3). We predicted positive correlations between young children's ability-effort ratings in contrast to negative correlations implied by use of a compensatory rule. This is exactly what emerged in this analysis. Fig. 2.3 shows the praise data by age group and feedback condition. Among 5-year-olds, when effort was perceived as high, ability was perceived as high ($r = .84$). With 12-year-olds, the opposite was true: When effort was high, ability was perceived as low ($r = -.79$). The 8-year-old group was again between these two extremes, with a correlation that was positive but more moderate ($r = .24$). The data for blame were virtually identical and are not reported here (see Barker & Graham, 1987).

In sum, young children and older children have different interpretations of the ability-implicating messages of praise and blame. We were able to trace this difference to growth and change in a particular aspect of causal thinking. Use of a compensatory schema is no doubt an important cognitive prerequisite to processing information about ability and effort.

HELP VERSUS NEGLECT

We turn now to research on unsolicited help (versus neglect) as the third teacher behavior that can indirectly function as a low-ability cue. As in the case of praise, simple reinforcement principles underscore the desirable consequences of help.

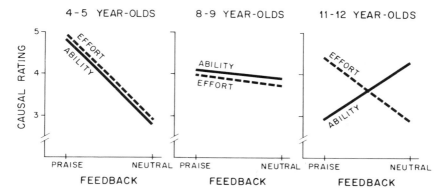

FIG. 2.3. Ability and Effort Ratings Plotted Together for Each Age Group as a Function of Feedback Condition in the Success Scenario. (Data From Barker & Graham, 1987)

Being the recipient of aid usually results in some tangible gain, at least when compared with undesirable alternatives such as failure. Why, then, might the offering of help have unintended effects on perceptions of ability?

Principle Four: Helping Behavior is Often a Response to Particular Attributions

The possibility that help may be a cue to low ability is based on an attributional analysis of helping (Schmidt & Weiner, 1988; Weiner, 1986). According to this analysis, we are more likely to help others when the cause of their need is due to uncontrollable factors such as low ability than when the need is perceived as due to controllable factors such as insufficient effort. A prevalent example of this attributional principle is the public's reaction to government assistance in the form of welfare. People perceive that welfare is appropriate for the physically disabled because their dependency is perceived as uncontrollable, whereas the able-bodied who are unwilling to work are perceived as undeserving of aid (Graham & Clayton, 1989). This linkage between perceived controllability and helping behavior is a basic attributional principle that also has been documented in actual classroom contexts. For example, Brophy and Rohrkemper (1981) reported that teachers expressed greater commitment to help "problem" students when the causes of need were uncontrollable factors such as low ability or shyness. Perceived controllable problems, such as lack of effort or disruptive behavior, resulted in relative neglect.

If a teacher's attributions determine likelihood of help, then again we reasoned that these behaviors might serve as indirect attributional cues (Fig. 2.1). In other words, one can gain information about others' perceptions of their ability based on the offering or withholding of help.

Developmental Research

We examined this possibility in two developmental studies (Graham & Barker, in press). Drawing on the videotape methodology used by Barker and Graham (1987), we filmed a classroom sequence depicting two male students solving a set of math problems in the presence of their teacher. As the students worked, the teacher circulated around their desks, much as she might do in a regular class-room, stopping unobtrusively to gaze at their papers. With one of the problem solvers (the nonhelped student), the teacher casually looked over his shoulder and then moved on without comment. With the other problem solver (the helped student) the teacher also looked over his shoulder and then, without apparent knowledge of the student's immediate performance, leaned down to offer help. Unsolicited help was administered when the teacher said: "Let me give you a hint. Don't forget to carry your tens." The help manipulation was therefore intended to coincide with the early stages of problem solving when the outcome was unknown and it was unclear whether the student could have solved the problems successfully on his own.

After viewing this videotape, participants rated the two students' ability and effort. Four groups of children, ranging in age from 5 to 12, participated in this first experiment. Guided by our previous findings, we expected developmental differences in the use of teacher cues to infer attributions. We anticipated that our youngest children would not be able to reason accurately about ability—in other words, we did not expect ability judgments to differ systematically as a function of help versus relative neglect. Furthermore, we expected that relative neglect would be a cue to low effort (and high ability) but only among the older children who perceive a compensatory relationship between effort and ability.

Table 2.2 shows the ability and effort ratings as a function of age group and helping condition. It is evident here that all of the age groups, including the youngest, perceived the helped student to be lower in ability than the nonhelped student. Thus all the subjects in this investigation understood the cue function of unsolicited help. However, only the oldest children inferred less effort in the student with higher ability—that is, the nonhelped student. This again suggested changing relations between ability and effort, or developmental differences in the understanding of the compensatory schema.

Correlations were than calculated between ability and effort ratings in each age group (Fig. 2.4). Ability and effort linkages were strongly positive among 5- and 6-year-olds ($r = .94$). For these young children, the helped student was perceived to be lower in ability *and* effort. By 9 or 10 a shift toward negativity in this relationship begins to emerge and that negative association is quite evident by age 11 or 12 ($r = -.39$). When two students achieved the same outcome, 12-year-olds reported that the less competent student put forth more effort (the

TABLE 2.2
Ability and Effort Ratings as a Function of Age Group and
Help Condition[a]

Condition	Age Group			
	5–6	7–8	9–10	11–12
	Perceived Student Ability			
Helped	3.1	2.3	3.3	4.3
Not helped	5.7	6.9	6.4	6.0
	Perceived Student Effort			
Helped	3.6	3.6	5.2	6.1
Not Helped	5.7	6.8	6.4	4.3

Note. n=20 in each age group. Rating scales range from 1 to 7. High scores indicate more perceived ability and effort.
[a]From Graham and Barker (in press, Experiment 1).

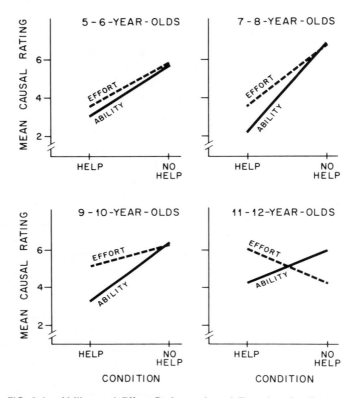

FIG. 2.4. Ability and Effort Ratings plotted Together for Each Age Group as a Function of Help Condition. (From Graham & Barker, In Press)

helped student), whereas the smarter student did not work as hard (the nonhelped student). Note the close parallel in the pattern of developmental data found here to that for praise depicted in Fig. 2.3.

Three findings from this study are particularly noteworthy. First, unsolicited help, like pity and praise, can function as a low-ability cue. Second, this cue function of help appears to be quite salient, for it is apparent even to 5- and 6-year-olds. And thirdly, the understanding of this help–low ability linkage is not dependent on children's use of complex inferential rules such as a compensatory schema. That is, even when children see ability and effort as positively covarying, they still infer lower ability in the target of unsolicited help. This suggested to us that the cognitive prerequisites for inferring ability from helping information may not be as complex as we initially thought.

At what age does the cue function of unsolicited help actually emerge? In a follow-up study (Graham & Barker, in press, Experiment 2) we used the same methodology with still younger participants to address this question. Our youngest children in this study, mostly 4–5-year-old preschoolers, were tested along with a group of 7–8-year-olds and a group of 11–12-year olds. With these groups of children we documented the expected developmental trend. Four-year-olds inferred about the same level of ability in both the helped and the nonhelped student.

Insight into how these very young children think about help was provided by an additional question we asked in this study. After they completed the attributional ratings, we asked children to imagine that they were going to work on a group math task, and to choose one of the two students in the videotape to be a member of their group. Table 2.3 shows the choice data for each age group. Seventy percent of the 8-year-olds and all of the 12-year-olds chose the student not helped by the teacher—in other words, the student they inferred to be smarter. In contrast, two-thirds of the very young children chose the helped student as their preferred groupmate.

As part of the postexperimental debriefing, we informally asked a random sample of children in each age group why they made the choice they did. Predictably, all of the children in the oldest group indicated perceived ability differences as their reason for the unanimous choice of the nonhelped student (e.g., "because he is better in math and is smarter"). But the youngest children made few references to ability or any other attributional factor. Their most frequently reported reason for choosing the helped student was the belief that the teacher liked him more. Most other reasons offered were quite idiosyncratic and unrelated to the help-giving context (e.g., "because he has a yellow shirt"). These data are consistent with the nonattributional developmental literature on children's conceptions of help (see Eisenberg, 1983). It has been reported that kindergartners are less likely than third or sixth graders to mention competence as a characteristic of a good helper (Barnett, Darcie, Holland, & Kobasigawa, 1982). Nor do they recognize that competence level might be a limiting condition

TABLE 2.3
Choice of Workmate as a Function of Age Group
and Help Condition[a]

	Age Group		
Condition	4–5	7–8	11–12
Helped	20	9	0
	(67%)	(30%)	(0%)
Not Helped	10	21	30
	(33%)	(70%)	(100%)

Note. n=30 in each age group. Number in parentheses indicates percentages of children making that choice.
[a]From Graham and Barker (in press, Experiment 2).

for even a very willing potential help giver. It seems quite likely that before elementary school, the young child does not systematically consider ability-related factors in his or her judgments about help in achievement contexts.

IMPLICATIONS AND APPLICATIONS

The arguments and empirical evidence presented here are based on laboratory investigations. My colleagues and I have not, for example, directly examined teachers' affective displays or evaluative practices during the course of their actual instruction. Instead, what has been offered is a conceptual analysis of pity versus anger, praise versus blame, and help versus neglect that I believe has many implications for classroom instruction. In keeping with the applied focus of this volume, I turn now to some of the implications and applications of this research.

The teacher behaviors that can carry ability-implicating messages are pervasive in educational practice. Praise, after all, is at the heart of reinforcement theory in the classroom. Only recently, as studies of teacher praise continue to show weak correlations with student outcomes has the value of praise as a reinforcer been questioned and the contribution of attribution principles to a conceptual analysis of its function been acknowledged (Brophy, 1981). These conceptual analyses have been put to the test in actual classroom contexts with large-scale observational studies such as those of Parsons and her colleagues (Parsons, Kaczala, & Meece, 1982). Parsons et al. recorded extensive observations of feedback patterns between teachers and students in nearly 20 fifth-to-ninth grade math classrooms. These researchers found that frequent blame or criticism for quality of one's work was positively related to high self-concept of math ability and high future expectancies among students. Praise, on the other hand, was unrelated to math self-concept, although boys who were not praised believed that their teachers had high expectations for them. Parsons et al. concluded that:

> To suggest that teachers should avoid criticism or give praise more freely overlooks the power of the context in determining the meaning of any message. A well chosen criticism can convey as much positive information as a praise; abundant or indiscriminant praise can be meaningless; insincere praise which does not covary with the teachers' expectations for the student can have detrimental effects on many students. (p. 336)

With the growing influence of attributional concepts, the multifaceted effects of praise and blame have become more evident. It is now apparent that there are no simple relations between these feedbacks and academic achievement.

A concrete example of an instructional practice that relies heavily on help-giving is cooperative learning. Cooperative learning is an instructional strategy in which individuals in a group help one another to attain a prescribed goal (see Slavin, 1983). The structure of cooperative groups typically is heterogeneous so that low-ability students can benefit from the assistance of their higher achieving peers. Although cooperative learning is known to increase help giving among cooperating group members, it is less clear that such behavior leads to improved academic performance or enhanced self-esteem, particularly for the lower achieving group members (Slavin, 1983). The attributional analysis presented here might help explain why this seemingly positive instructional strategy does not always have the desired effect. Perhaps other instructional strategies that entail help giving, such as special class placement or some forms of remedial tutoring, will also benefit from an attributional analysis as the evidence mounts that these practices lead to neither improved student performance nor enhanced self-perception of ability. Of course, with all of these instructional strategies, one must distinguish between what we might label "instrumental help," such as probing when appropriate, from "gratuitous help," such as supplying answers outright, for it is only this latter form of premature unsolicited help that is thought to be detrimental to ability self-perception.

Concerning affective reactions, in some instances pity may be directly displayed in the classroom through certain gestures, postures, or subtle verbal content. In other instances this emotion, while privately experienced, may be the motivator of particular classroom behaviors. For example, in the teacher expectancy literature, Brophy and Good (1974) suggest that a set of well-documented teacher behaviors toward low-expectancy students, such as teaching less difficult material, setting lower mastery levels, and praise for marginal or even incorrect answers, may be determined, in part, by "excessive sympathy for the student" (p. 311).

Are Minority Children the Particular Targets of Low-ability Cues?

The analyses presented here are based on general attributional principles and are believed to apply to a broad segment of the population. One wonders, however, whether minority children, with their frequent history of chronic school failure, might be the particular targets of classroom low-ability cues. There is some indirect evidence that this might be the case. For example, it is known that teachers have lower expectations for African–American than for white students (Cooper, Baron, & Lowe, 1975; Rubovitz & Maehr, 1973; Taylor, 1979). Thus any of the low-expectancy behaviors cataloged by Brophy and Good (1974) and motivated by sympathy might be particularly directed toward the African—American student. Consider also the Direct Instruction model, a widely embraced instructional program for low-achieving minority children (Rosenshine, 1979). The principal components of this model have been described as "simple questions, a high percentage of correct answers, help when the student does not know the answer, and infrequent criticism" (p. 43.). It is evident that there are close similarities between these instructional strategies and all of the behaviors believed to communicate low-ability attributions.

Developmental Processes

The prior discussion must be qualified to some degree, inasmuch as we did find consistent effects of age on the perception of pity, praise, and unsolicited help as low-ability cues. Among very young children, the student receiving pity, the praised student, the student not blamed, and the student receiving unsolicited help were either seen as higher in ability than their counterparts, or there were no differences as a function of feedback cue. In typical developmental fashion, we tended to focus on growth and change in cognitive capacities of children to explain age-related differences in the cue function of teacher behavior. That is, we concentrated on changes in the structure of children's thinking about the properties of low ability (e.g., its uncontrollability and stability) and in their understanding of a compensatory relationship between ability and effort. Life most developmental researchers, we found that as children got older they processed attributional information in a more "logical" or "adult-like" fashion.

But paralleling this *age*-related cognitive growth are systematic *grade*-related changes in classroom environments that must also play an important role in developmental differences such as those documented here. For example, as children progress through elementary school, there is an increasing focus on ability assessment and comparison with others through such common classroom practices as letter grades, report cards, ability grouping, and movement from a mastery to a competitive feedback orientation (Eccles, Midgley, & Adler; Stipek, 1984; Stipek & Daniels, 1988). All of these practices operate to enhance the conception of ability where being smart means being smarter than others but having to try less hard, and doing well means succeeding on hard tasks at which others encounter difficulty (Nicholls & Miller, 1984). This appears to be the conception of ability that is necessary for the more differentiated inferences about potential low-ability cues shown by the older children in our studies.

The degree to which both ability and ability-implicating classroom cues become salient will be influenced by both cognitive growth across age and by changes in classroom environments across grade. The application-oriented researcher with a developmental focus needs to take into account both of these important determinants of perceived personal competence.

SUMMARY

The research presented in this chapter tells a simple and straightforward story. By the early elementary years, a prevalent set of teacher behaviors including sympathetic affect, generous praise, minimal blame, and unsolicited help share in common the fact that they are positively motivated behaviors that can sometimes function as low-ability cues. I should emphasize here that I am not advocating that such behaviors should never be employed, for I readily acknowledge that the use of praise, sympathetic affect, and offers of help are useful instructional practices that often neutralize some of the immediate impact of failure, such as public embarrassment or frustration. But over time, with increasing age of children, or if indiscriminately adopted, such well-intentioned behaviors can have uncertain and uneasy consequences.

REFERENCES

Barker, G., & Graham, S. (1987). Developmental study of praise and blame as attributional cues. *Journal of Educational Psychology, 79*, 62–66.

Barnett, K., Darcie, G., Holland, C., & Kobasigawa, A. (1982). Children's cognitions about effective helping. *Developmental Psychology, 18*, 267–277.

Brophy, J. (1981). Teacher praise: A functional analysis. *Review of Educational Research, 51*, 5–32.

Brophy, J., & Good, T. (1974). *Teacher–student relationships: Causes and consequences.* New York: Holt, Rinehart, & Winston.

Brophy, J., & Rohrkemper, M. (1981). The influence of problem ownership on teachers' perceptions of and strategies for coping with problem students. *Journal of Educational Psychology, 73*, 295–311.

Cooper, H., Baron, R., & Lowe, C. (1975). The importance of race and social class in the formation of expectancies about academic performance. *Journal of Educational Psychology, 67*, 312–319.

Dweck, C., & Elliott, E. (1983). Achievement motivation. in P. Mussen (Gen. Ed.) & E. M. Hetherington (Vol. Ed.), *Handbook of child psychology: Vol. 4. Social and personality development* (pp. 643–691). New York: Wiley.

Dweck, C.& Leggett E. (1988). A social-cognitive approach to motivation and personality. *Psychological Review, 95*, 256–273.

Eccles, J., Midgley, C., & Adler, T. (1984). Grade-related changes in the school environment: Effects on achievement motivation. In J. Nicholls (Ed.), *Advances in motivation and achievement: Vol. 3. The development of achievement motivation* (pp. 283–331). Greenwich, CT: JAI Press.

Eisenberg, N. (1983). Developmental aspects of recipients' reactions to aid. In J. Fisher, A. Nadler, & B. DePaulo (Eds.), *New directions in helping* (Vol. 1, pp. 189–222). New York: Academic.

Försterling, F. (1985). Attributional retraining: A review. *Psychological Bulletin, 98*, 495–512.

Graham, S. (1984). Communicating sympathy and anger to black and white children: The cognitive (attributional) consequences of affective cues. *Journal of Personality and Social Psychology, 47*, 40–54.

Graham, S., & Barker, G. (in press). The downside of help: An attributional-developmental analysis of helping behavior as a low ability cue. *Journal of Educational Psychology.*

Graham, S., & Brown, J. (1988). Attributional mediators of expectancy, evaluation, and affect: A response time analysis. *Journal of Personality and Social Psychology, 55*, 873–881.

Graham, S., & Clayton, S. (1989). *In the eye of the beholder: The "stigma" of public assistance.* Manuscript in preparation.

Graham, S., Doubleday, C., & Guarino, P. (1984). The development of relations between perceived controllability and the emotions of pity, anger, and guilt. *Child Development, 55,* 561–565.

Graham, S., & Weiner, B. (1986). From attribution theory to developmental psychology: A round-trip ticket? *Social Cognition, 4,* 152–179.

Graham, S., & Weiner, B. (1989). *Attributions, emotions, and action across the lifespan.* Manuscript submitted for publication.

Harari, O., & Covington, M. (1981). Reactions to achievement behavior from a teacher and student perspective: A developmental analysis. *American Educational Research Journal, 18,* 15–28.

Kelley, H., & Michela, J. (1980). Attribution theory and research. In M. Rosenzweig & L. Porter (Eds.), *Annual review of psychology* (Vol. 31, pp. 457–501). Palo Alto, CA: Annual Reviews.

Kun, A. (1977.) Development of the magnitude-covariation and compensation schemata in ability and effort attributions of performance. *Child Development, 48,* 862–873.

Kun, A., & Weiner, B. (1973). Necessary versus sufficient causal schemata for success and failure. *Journal of Research in Personality, 7,* 197–207.

Leacock, E. (1969). *Teaching and learning in inner city schools.* New York: Basic Books.

Meyer, W., Bachmann, M., Biermann, U., Hempelmann, M., Ploger, F., & Spiller, H. (1979). The informational value of evaluative behavior: Influence of praise and blame on perceptions of ability. *Journal of Educational Psychology, 71,* 259–268.

Nicholls, J. (1978). The development of the concepts of effort and ability, perception of own attainment, and the understanding that difficult tasks demand more ability. *Child Development, 49,* 800–814.

Nicholls, J. G., & Miller, A. T. (184). Development and its discontents: The differentiation of the concept of ability. In J. G. Nicholls (Ed.), *The development of achievement motivation* (pp. 185–218). Greenwich, CT: JAI Press.

Parsons, J., Kaczala, C., & Meece, J. (1982). Socialization of achievement attitudes and beliefs. *Child Development, 53,* 322–339.

Rosenshine, B. (1979). Content, time, and direct instruction. In P. Peterson & H. Walberg (Eds.), *Research on teaching* (pp. 28–56). Berkeley, CA: McCutchan.

Rubovitz, P., & Maehr, M. (1973). Pygmalion black and white. *Journal of Personality and Social Psychology, 25,* 210–218.

Schmidt, G., & Weiner, G. (1988). An attribution–affect–action theory of motivated behavior: Replications examining help-giving. *Personality and Social Psychology Bulletin, 14,* 610–621.

Slavin, R. E. (1983). *Cooperative learning.* New York: Longman.

Stipek, D. (1984). The development of achievement motivation. In R. Ames & C. Ames (Eds.), *Research on motivation in education: Vol. 1. Student motivation* (pp. 145–174). New York: Academic.

Stipek, D., & Daniels, D. (1988). Declining perceptions of competence: A consequence of changes in the child or the educational environment. *Journal of Educational Psychology, 80,* 352–356.

Taylor, M. (1979). Race, sex, and the expression of the self-fulfilling prophesy in a laboratory teaching situation. *Journal of Personality and Social Psychology, 37,* 897–912.

Weiner, B. (1985). An attributional theory of achievement motivation and emotion. *Psychological Review, 92,* 548–573.

Weiner, B. (1986). *An attributional theory of motivation and emotion.* New York: Springer–Verlag.

Weiner, B., Graham, S., Stern, P., & Lawson, M. (1982). Using affective cues to infer causal thoughts. *Developmental Psychology, 18,* 278–286.

Weiner, B., & Kukla. A. (1970). An attributional analysis of achievement motivation. *Journal of Personality and Social Psychology, 15,* 1–20.

Weiner, B., & Peter, N. (1973). A cognitive-developmental analysis of achievement and moral judgments. *Developmental Psychology, 9,* 290–309.

3 The Causal Attribution Process in Sport and Physical Activity

Edward McAuley
University of Illinois

Terry E. Duncan
University of Oregon

Research in the social psychology of sport and physical activity has undergone rapid expansion and development in the past decade, providing social and behavioral scientists with a better comprehension of an integral part of American society. Attribution theory has been one of the three most systematically tested social psychological theories in the sport and physical activity domain (Landers, 1983). Indeed, it would appear that sport outcomes provide a very logical testing ground for a theory that attempts to understand the psychological underpinnings of "why" questions.

Although other models such as Kelley's (1973) analysis of variance model and Jones and Davis's (1965) correspondent inference theory exist, empirical investigation of attribution theory with respect to achievement in sport has been predominantly driven by Bernard Weiner's (1972, 1979, 1985) attributional model of achievement motivation and emotion. Weiner's model, and in particular his recent reformulation (Weiner, 1985, 1986), is an elegant and sophisticated attempt to explain the layperson's interpretation of achievement outcomes and to understand how that interpretation may influence future behavior. Weiner has repeatedly made it clear that causal attributions formed as a function of causal search are better understood and become more meaningful when they are classified along a taxonomy of dimensions. Empirical evidence provides consistent support for the existence of three causal dimensions—locus of causality, stability, and controllability—although it is conceivable that other dimensions exist (Weiner, 1985). These three dimensions are proposed by Weiner to impact upon future behavior through the mediation of affective reactions and future expectancies.

In this chapter we examine the application of attribution theory to sport and physical activity. First, we provide a brief overview of the general findings in the sport attribution literature and discuss two of the more problematical issues in this area: the measurement of causal attributions, and the incomplete testing of Weiner's model. We then report and discuss a series of studies that we have conducted over the past 5 years representing an attempt to test more fully the relationships among attribution, affects, and self-perceptions suggested by Weiner's model. Finally, we identify some future directions that sport attribution theorists might explore.

ATTRIBUTION THEORY AND SPORT: AN UPDATE

As previously indicated, the last decade or so has spawned a number of empirical investigations of the attribution process in sport. Rejeski and Brawley (1983) provide a comprehensive and well-written review identifying some general characteristics of this body of literature. It is not the purpose of this chapter to review the sport attribution research in its entirety, but rather to identify some of the shortcomings of that research, explore a number of studies that have attempted to overcome some of those shortcomings, and suggest future directions for attributional study.

The majority of the attributional research prior to 1983 had relied upon Weiner's (1972) early two-dimensional taxonomy and, in spite of cries to the contrary (e.g., Bukowski & Moore, 1980; Roberts & Pascuzzi, 1979), a rather myopic employment of the classic four causal elements of ability, luck, effort, and task difficulty. Unfortunately, these theoretical limitations still plague much of the empirical investigations that have been conducted in the last several years.

In any given event, numerous causal ascriptions can be offered to explain the outcome. Although these ascriptions may be important in and of themselves, it is the taxonomy of causal structure that gives meaning to these many causes. Identifying the underlying causal dimensions of locus of causality, stability, and control enable one to make quantitative comparisons between causes by being able to determine how myriad causal explanations differ or are alike. However, sport attribution researchers have largely failed to consider that the respondent's perception of the link between specific causal attributions and the corresponding causal dimensions may be radically different from that of the investigator. In many contemporary sport attributional studies, investigators, endeavoring to associate different attributional elements with their respective causal dimensions, have often, through the use of raters or judges (e.g., Auvergne, 1983; Martin & Huang, 1984; Riordan, Thomas, & James, 1985) arbitrarily assigned elements to dimensional space. In effect, these researchers are committing what Russell (1982) has referred to as "the fundamental attribution researcher error," by assuming that the investigator can accurately predict how the subject perceives an attribution in terms of causal structure, and thus precluding the role of the respondent as an active agent in the attribution process.

To rectify this problem, Russell (1982) developed the Causal Dimension Scale (CDS), a measure of how individuals perceive causes. The (CDS) represents an important advance in the measurement of causal attributions as it allows the respondent to make an open-ended attribution and then classify that cause with respect to dimensional properties. These dimensions (locus of causality, stability, and control) are assessed by nine semantic differential scales with three of the subscales representing each dimension. High scores on each dimension indicate that the cause is internal, stable, and controllable. McAuley and Gross (1983) designed one of the first studies, utilizing the CDS to assess attributional patterns in the sport domain, examining attributions given for outcome following a table tennis match. They reported adequate reliability for the locus of causality and stability dimensions, but expressed concern over the control dimension, perhaps indicating that the dimension of controllability may be less clear-cut and more difficult to assess in sport than in academic situations. Other researchers (e.g., Mark, Mutrie, Brooks, & Harris, 1984; McAuley, Russell, & Gross, 1983; Vallerand, 1987) have since employed the CDS in sport achievement settings, providing further evidence for its utility in involving the subject as an active agent.

The necessity for accurate measurement and the involvement of the subject as an active agent in the attribution process is of paramount importance if we are to be able to test the assumptions of Weiner's (1985) attributional model. A great deal of the extant sport literature has concentrated on such basic relationships as examining differential attributional patterns following achievement outcomes. Although these attributional patterns are important, Weiner's (1985) attributional model posits many relationships that have, by and large, gone untested or un-challenged by sport attribution researchers. For example, causal attributions are theorized to influence behavior through the mediation of expectancy and affect. As we shall see, only a handful of researchers have attempted to consider these relationships in sport. This is quite amazing when one considers that although emotion pervades sport it has rarely been studied in that environment (Silva & Hardy, 1984; Vallerand, 1983).

Therefore, in spite of the considerable body of sport attributional research that is available, there exist several voids in the literature that can be characterized as being due to poor measurement and inadequate or incomplete theory testing.

CAUSAL ATTRIBUTIONS, AFFECT AND SELF-PERCEPTIONS

One of the primary components of Weiner's (1985, 1986) attributional model is emotion. Affective reactions are proposed to mediate between causal dimensions and future behavior. One of the most obvious and ubiquitous features of any sporting event is the continual outpouring of emotions. Within the context of sport, the whole spectrum of affective reactions is displayed. Happiness, joy, pride, and gratitude are emitted in response to positive outcomes, whereas anger, frustration, and even shame may be demonstrated following negative outcomes. Such emotional reactions are considered important precursors of future behavior (Weiner, 1985). Unfortunately, emotion and its antecedents and consequences in sport and physical activity have largely been ignored (Vallerand, 1983). A small cadre of researchers have, however, assembled some interesting findings that link self-perception processes and emotions (e.g., Duncan & McAuley, 1989; McAuley, Duncan, & McElroy, 1989; McAuley et al., 1983; Vallerand, 1987). The following sections propose to examine how causal attributions in sport settings are related to such variables as emotion, perceptions of success, and self-efficacy (Bandura, 1977, 1986).

Causal Attributions and Emotion

Over the past 5 years McAuley and his colleagues have conducted a number of studies examining the relationship among causal dimensions and affective reactions to achievement outcomes. In an early study (McAuley, et al., 1983), we matched table tennis players by gender and ability following which they engaged in a competitive match played under normal rules. Causal attributions were assessed via the CDS (Russell, 1982) and an affect scale composed of four positive, four negative, and one surprise affect tapped the intensity of emotions experienced following outcome. Initial analyses revealed winners to be significantly more satisfied, proud, confident, and grateful, whereas losers experienced greater feelings of anger, depression, incompetence, and surprise.

In an effort to tease out the relationship between specific affects and causal dimensions, a series of separate multiple regression analyses were conducted for winners and losers. With respect to success affects, the three causal dimensions in combination accounted for 16% to 25% of the variance in these emotions. In his earlier models, Weiner (1979) suggests that the locus of causality dimension is primarily responsible for the generation of affects. Our findings ran contrary to this theoretical standpoint with the control, rather than locus of causality, dimension emerging as the most important predictor of affect. Such a pattern of results, suggesting that perceptions of control lead to more positive emotional reactions, were consistent with those reported by Forsyth and McMillan (1981) in academic settings. Analyses of the attribution–affect relationship within the failure condition were nonsignificant. This rather simple and straightforward investigation was illuminating from several perspectives. First, subjects apparently cared about their performance, demonstrating affective reactions to the outcome. Second, successful outcomes appear to elicit more intense affective reactions, a finding that supports Weiner, Russell, and Lerman (1979). Finally, that controllability was responsible for evoking affects suggests that settings such as sport contests, involving interpersonal competition and ego involvement, may increase the salience of the control dimension.

Expectancy Disconfirmation and Emotion

Expectancy disconfirmation has been shown to be a particularly strong antecedent of attributional search (Wong & Weiner, 1987) and it seems reasonable to assume that increased likelihood of causal search might result in more intense affective reactions following outcomes. In an effort to follow up on the McAuley et al. (1983) study, we conducted a laboratory study examining causal attributions and affective reactions following disconfirming outcomes on a bicycle ergometer task (McAuley & Duncan, 1989). Specifically, we were interested in extending previously reported studies in the academic and sport domains which suggest that all three causal dimensions are related to affective reactions (e.g., Forsyth & McMillan, 1981;McAuley et al., 1983; Vallerand, 1987).

Male and female undergraduate students were matched by gender and randomly assigned to one of two expectancy disconfirming conditions: (a) high expectancy with failure outcome and (b) low expectancy with success outcome. The bicycle ergometers were wired, via a manipulation panel, to a portable digital scoreboard which was able to register simultaneously scores and time remaining in each trial for the two bicycle ergometers. The electronic panel allowed the experimenter to manipulate the total score displayed, which was accomplished by setting the bias on the equipment so that one of the bicycle ergometers registered only 60% of its revolutions. The scoreboard was placed directly in front of the subjects, allowing them to see their own and their opponent's score as it accumulated, as well as the time remaining in each competitive trial. A screen separated the bicycle ergometers so that the subjects could see each other only from the chest up, thus concealing apparent differences in pedaling.

Subjects were allowed three practice trials and then competed in a best-of-three trials competition. Assessment of expectancies for competition performance following trials verified the success of the manipulation with subjects receiving bogus feedback expecting to win less trials in the future and expecting to perform less well. Thus, we were able to manipulate a high-expectancy and low-expectancy group. In the competition phase of the experiment we manipulated the outcome so as to disconfirm expectations, that is, high-expectancy subjects lost in competition and low-expectancy subjects won.

Following competition, causal attributions were assessed via the CDS (Russell, 1982). Affective reactions to the disconfirming outcome were also assessed by having subjects indicate the extent to which they had experienced the following achievement-related affects: depression, disappointment, guilt, shame, anger, incompetence, gratitude, satisfaction, surprise, pride and confidence.

Multivariate analyses of variance revealed both groups to make internal, unstable, and controllable attributions for outcome with discriminant function coefficients clearly indicating that the stability dimension was the dependent variable contributing most to the overall multivariate effect. A discriminant analysis examined the differential effects of the two conditions on affective reactions. Structure coefficients revealed subjects with low expectations who won to be significantly more satisfied and proud, whereas those subjects whose high expectations were disconfirmed exhibited significantly greater feelings of displeasure, incompetence, and anger. Hierarchical multiple regression analyses examined the relative proportion of variance accounted for in each affect by each causal dimension uniquely, and in combination with the other dimensions. As expected, the most dramatic findings occurred in the causal dimension–negative affect relationships. Unexpected outcomes, especially when they are negative, produce more intense affective reactions than do expected or positive outcomes. In combination, causal dimensions accounted for between 4.1% and 40% of the variance in negative affects with the locus of causality and stability dimensions maximizing depression, displeasure, guilt, shame, incompetence, and surprise.

These data suggest that competitive motor tasks, even in a controlled laboratory setting, can be affectively involving. Several aspects of the attribution–affect relationship as proposed by Weiner (1985, 1986) are supported by this study. First, satisfaction appeared to be the most powerful discriminating affect between conditions followed by pride and displeasure. Weiner et al. (1979) have discriminated between outcome-dependent and attribution-dependent affects with the former being a direct result of the outcome and requiring no cognitive processing, whereas the latter are generated as a result of causal search. Although satisfaction is generally considered to be an outcome-dependent affect, Weiner (1986) has suggested that it may also be a self-related attribution-dependent affect, serving to bolster self-esteem or self-worth through self-satisfaction. In this study, satisfaction was not related to causal dimensions, therefore appearing to be outcome-dependent. That certain affects are influenced by causal dimensions whereas others are not affirms that emotions can be differentiated into outcome-dependent and attribution-dependent affects.

The results of this study, however, are somewhat at odds with those reported by McAuley et al. (1983), who found affective reactions to be more strongly manifested following success than failure. This apparent inconsistency in the attribution–affect relationship can perhaps be explained by the nature of the situations. In the McAuley et al. (1983) study subjects were matched by ability, maximizing the challenge of the situation and creating similar expectancies of winning or losing. This contrasts markedly to the manipulation of expectancy in the McAuley and Duncan (1989) study in which expectancies for future outcomes were either positive or negative due to a previous history of success or failure, respectively. It appears therefore, that in cases where expectations are very strong with respect to future outcome and are subsequently disconfirmed, negative outcomes produce more pronounced affective responses. Conversely, when there is some doubt as to what the outcome might eventually be, that is, the situation is optimally challenging, then successful outcomes result in stronger affective reactions. Whether this interpretation of the outcome–attribution–affect relationship is completely accurate remains to be determined empirically in the sport literature.

Finally, these data also support Weiner's (1985) contention that all three causal dimensions can predict a variety of different affective reactions to achievement outcomes, and are consistent with past research (Forsyth & McMillan, 1981; McAuley et al., 1983; Vallerand, 1987). However, what appears cl ar, based on even a limited number of studies, is that the relationship between individual causal dimensions and individual affects is dependent on the environmental context of the outcome.

Self-perception, Attributions, and Emotion

Many studies in the sport attribution literature have made the erroneous assumption that absolute outcomes, for example, winning, and losing, are analogous to the perceived or cognitive outcomes of success and failure. In some ways this error parallels the problem discussed earlier of researchers assuming that their interpretation of subject's phenomenology, with respect to attributions and causal dimensions, is accurate and similar to that of the respondents (Rejeski & Brawley, 1983). Employing Maehr and Nicholls's (1980) conceptual framework of success and failure being psychological states, Spink and Roberts (1980) have demonstrated that perceived and absolute outcomes are not isomorphic, suggesting that the relationship between causal ascriptions and perceived success is as important as the relationship between causal ascriptions and the absolute outcome.

McAuley (1985) examined these relationships in a sample of female intercollegiate gymnasts competing in a tournament. Subjects made causal attributions for their performance in each of four Olympic events: vault, floor exercise, balance beam, and uneven parallel bars. A commonality analysis was conducted to determine the relative influence of perceptions of success and absolute success (actual score) on each causal dimension for each event. With the exception of floor exercise, causal dimensions for all events were significantly influenced by perceptions of success rather than actual score. Perceptions of success were particularly influential in the formulation of stable attributions for vault, beam, and bar, as well as in internal and controllable attributions for vault. One of the primary attributes of a successful gymnast at any level, from high school to Olympic competition, is consistency, Consequently, perceiving one's performance as successful may be indicative of the perception that consistency has been achieved, hence the stability of attributions. The findings from this study are consistent with those of Maehr and Nicholls (1980) and Spink and Roberts (1980), suggesting that perceptions of success are important antecedents of causal ascriptions.

The focus of the chapter thus far has been a series of studies that have attempted to consider the relationships among causal attributions, perceptions of

success, and affective reactions to sport and physical activity achievement outcomes. However, there exists virtually no data in this domain that have demonstrated a causal relationship among these variables as theorized by Weiner
(1985). To this end, we employed structural equation modeling techniques to
determine the relationships among perceptions of performance, causal dimensions, and affective reactions in two situations: following a term-long gymnastics
class and following a performance of a required gymnastic routine (Duncan &
McAuley, 1989).

Toward the end of the term, subjects in the gymnastics class documented their
perceptions of personal performance during the term as well as causal attributions
for and affective reactions to their performance. Similar procedures were employed 1 week later, at which point subjects had just completed the performance
of their required floor exercise routine. The same measures, as outlined previously, were assessed with respect to the performance of their routine. More
than two thirds of the subjects perceived themselves to have performed moder-
ately to extremely well, indicating a positive performance, so we chose to con-
centrate only on the positive affects. A positive affect score was created by
summing the affects of pleased, competent, satisfaction, pride, and gratitude.

We then attempted to fit the data to the model conceptualized by Weiner
(1985) and shown in Fig. 3.1.

As can be seen, perceptions of class performance were hypothesized to influence the causal dimensions of locus of causality, stability, and control. Stability
was then hypothesized to influence expectancy for future performance in their
routine, whereas all three dimensions impact upon affective reactions to class
performance. In turn, affect and expectancy were hypothesized to mediate perceptions of performance following the routine. The goodness of fit index for this
model was not particularly good, .77, χ^2 (12) = 70.21. Modification indexes
suggested that the relationships among the variables could be better explained by
deleting a number of nonsignificant paths in the model and including paths from
perceptions of class performance to affect and expectancy and from affect to
expectancy. The respecified model and its path coefficients are shown in Fig.
3.2.

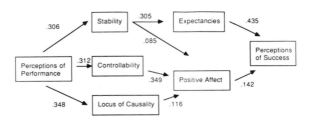

FIG. 3.1. Weiner's Model Showing the Relationship Between Perceptions, Causal Dimensions, Expectancies, and Affective Reactions.

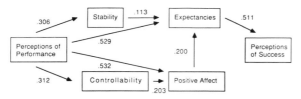

FIG. 3.2.   Respecified Model. All Path Coefficients With the Exception
of the Stability-expectancy Path ($p = .08$) are Significant ($p < .05$).

We then compared this respecified model with a null or completely independent model and to Weiner's (1985) original model (Fig. 3.1). Coefficient delta
(Bentler & Bonett, 1980), a measure of goodness of fit, was calculated for each
model comparison. The comparison of Weiner's model with the null model
rendered a value of delta = .468, indicating that the model could be substantially
improved. The respecified model, however, provided a considerably more accurate approximation of the data, with delta increasing to .971. Clearly, the respecified model, which includes direct paths from perceptions of performance
success to affect and expectancy, and an indirect path from affect to perceptions
of routine success through expectancy, can be interpreted as being the model
most able to reproduce the original correlations.

These data confirm that the relationship among causal attributions, expectancies, affect, and cognitions regarding behavior are quite complex. Outcome
perceptions regarding past performance played an important role in formation of
future perceptions of performance through the mediation of affect and expectancy. As predicted by Weiner (1985) controllable attributions were also related to
future perceptions of performance through an affect–expectancy mediation. That
different attributions take on more or less importance in different circumstances
is once again abundantly clear. What is also clear is that causal attribution
processes are related to indexes of future behavior (success cognitions) and that
this relationship is, as theorized by Weiner (1985), subject to the mediation of
affective reactions and future expectations. Future studies in the sport and physical activity domain are called for to utilize similar causal modeling techniques
and examine the relationships between attributions and other indexes of sport
behavior.

Causal Attributions and Self-efficacy

The final study to be reported in this chapter is a preliminary investigation that
attempts to link the causal attribution process and self-efficacy cognitions (Bandura, 1977, 1986). Bandura (1986) has argued that, in addition to influencing
overt behavior and performance, self-efficacy cognitions also provide information from which causal attributions are formed. Efficacy cognitions represent

individual convictions that one possesses the capabilities to complete successful-ly the task at hand. Measures of self-efficacy are often composed of multiple items representing difficulties or barriers to be surmounted in the accomplish-ment of the task. Past mastery experiences are particularly potent sources of efficacy information. Highly efficacious children have been shown to attribute failure to lack of effort, whereas less efficacious children ascribe failure to a lack of ability (Collins, 1982). Although Weiner (1979, 1985) theorizes attributions to influence future behavior partly through expectations, Bandura (1986) suggests that the relationship may be more complex, and that efficacy cognitions play an important role in the attribution process. That is, percepts of personal efficacy, as well as achievement outcome, act as a source of information from which causal ascriptions are derived. These attributions in turn, are proposed to influence future performance through the mediation of subsequently formed efficacy ex-pectations.

We conducted a laboratory-based study with children as subjects (McAuley, Duncan, & McElroy, 1989), to examine the proposed efficacy–attribution rela-tionship in an exercise/motor performance setting. We employed a methodology detailed earlier in this chapter, in which subjects participated in a bicycle ergometer competition with efficacy expectations being manipulated as a func-tion of electronically biasing one competitor's score on the ergometer. The chil-dren were manipulated into high and low self-efficacy groups and engaged in competition; then they made causal attributions for their performance. As the-orized by Weiner (1979, 1985), children's perceptions of actual performance success influenced their causal ascriptions. Children who perceived themselves to be more successful made more stable and controllable attributions for their performance. When this perception of performance was statistically controlled, greater efficacy expectations resulted in more stable and controllable attributions. These results constitute some preliminary evidence to suggest that how one cognitively processes information concerning personal capabilities plays an important role in shaping children's thinking (Bandura, 1986). Although such research represents an initial attempt to link two prominent theoretical ap-proaches to motivated behavior in the sport domain, it goes without saying that much work lies ahead if we are to establish a temporal causal link between efficacy cognitions and causal ascriptions.

FUTURE DIRECTIONS AND APPLICATIONS

It is only in the last 5 years or so that the sport attribution literature has begun to venture beyond its previously limited scope. However, many researchers are still content to investigate the attribution process in sport from a rather superficial level. This final section seeks to challenge the sport attribution researcher by suggesting some possible directions that might help us more fully understand the attribution process and its role in sport behavior. Although there are many issues that can be raised with respect to future applications, space permits us to identify only a few. However, we suggest that these may be the most fertile areas of study, capable of a substantial yield.

Attributions and Emotion

We have developed a line of research over the past 5 years that has sought to test the various associations suggested by Weiner's (1985) model, particularly with respect to the attribution–emotion relationship. Our work, combined with that of Vallerand (1987), provides a foundation for further testing of this relationship. It is no secret that emotions are generated as a function of sport performance. Furthermore, we know that causal attributions are related to various emotions; the specifics of which appear dependent on the situation. The time has come to determine how affective reactions are related to future behaviors in sport. If certain causal ascriptions predict certain affects, which in turn, are related to behavior, then changing maladaptive or dysfunctional attributions and, consequently, emotional reactions may serve to reduce learned helpless-type behaviors (Dweck, 1975; Försterling, 1985). At early stages of learning in sport, children are apt to attribute failures to lack of ability, and consequently experience such feelings as incompetence, frustration, and possibly shame, resulting in discontinued participation in that sport. Helping that child realize that ability in sport comes as a product of increased and sustained effort may serve to instigate renewed challenge and determination, resulting in the child's continuing to strive for success rather than giving up entirely. Much research has been directed at learning more about participation motives in children and youth sports (e.g., Gill, Gross, & Huddleston, 1983). Examining these reasons for discontinued involvement from an attributional perspective may provide further insights into the participation motivation process.

Exercise Psychology and Attributions

Over the last few years, sport psychologists have begun to broaden their horizons with respect to defining sport and physical activity operationally. Many individuals are currently actively engaged in the application of psychological theory to explain and understand a rapidly expanding phenomenon: exercise and physical fitness. The U.S. Department of Health and Human Services (1979, 1980) has identified exercise and physical fitness as one of the 15 behavioral interventions likely to reduce death and disease, making this a particularly attractive area to study from a psychological perspective. One of the most commonly studied and perhaps, least understood aspects of exercise is the problem of sustaining adherence to prescribed programs once they have begun. Indeed, well-documented statistics indicate that the attribution rate in exercise programs approximates 50% within the first 6 months (Dishman, 1982; Morgan, 1977, Oldridge, 1982), which parallels the compliance dilemma in modern medicine, one of the most serious problems encountered in disease control and health promotion (Epstein & Cluss, 1982). Interestingly, much of this exercise adherence/attrition research is concerned with the basic attributional question, "why?". That is, it is concerned with why people adhere to or drop out of programs. However, despite some promising attributional approaches to other health behaviors in the literature, such as smoking cessation (Eiser, Van der Plight, Raw, & Sutton, 1985), no empirical reports exist that document the role of the attributional process in exercise behavior. Clearly, how individuals perceive their reasons for ceasing to exercise, in causal dimensional terms, will impact upon future attempts to engage in this important health behavior.

Developmental Research

Sport participation among youths and children continues to increase at a rapid rate in this country. Sport is, in fact, a very important part of the socialization process. Brawley (1984) has argued that it is impossible to have a developmental psychology of attributions if those attributions that occur in play, sport, and physical activity environments are not more thoroughly studied.

Unfortunately, very little sport attribution research exists that is developmental in nature. Bird and Williams (1980) conducted one such study examining the relationship between attributions and sex roles as a function of increasing age. Although young subjects (7 to 12 ys) of both sexes offered similar attributional explanations for the outcomes of sport scenarios, older males (13 to 18 ys) attributed performance to effort, whereas females were more likely to use luck as a causal ascription. Although several studies have assessed attributional patterns among children in sport and athletic situations, the Bird and Williams study remains the single developmental attempt to explore this seemingly fertile area of inquiry.

Such attributional constructs as effort, ability, and perceived control are interpreted differently as a function of age. Effort has been identified as the most commonly perceived cause of outcome in young children with ability emerging as an important causal ascription as the child becomes older (Nicholls, 1984). From an affective perspective, young children (6 years old) have been shown to respond to attributional cues with outcome-dependent affects (e.g., happy/sad) whereas older children (10 years old) infer such affects as gratitude and guilt (attribution-dependent) from the same attributional cues (Weiner, Kun, & Benesh–Weiner, 1980). Research in the academic achievement domain has been successful in establishing developmental patterns with respect to causal attributions and their consequences. If attribution theory in sport is to expand its knowledge base further, it cannot continue to ignore developmental patterns in causal ascriptions.

Measurement and Model Testing

The development of the Causal Dimension Scale (Russell, 1982) was an important progression in the measurement of causal attributions allowing researchers to tap more credibly the subject's phenomenology by including the subject as an active agent in the attribution process. Although there are some problems with this measure, it has been demonstrated to be superior to other commonly employed measures (Russell, McAuley, & Tarico, 1987). However, much of the sport attribution research continues to rely on the researcher's ability to classify accurately causal attributions along causal dimensions. The most obvious problem with this methodology is perhaps the classification of the attribution "ability." Employing Weiner's (1979) $2 \times 2 \times 2$ taxonomy of causal dimensions, many researchers would classify this attribution as internal, stable, and uncontrollable. Subjects, however, invariably perceive ability in sport to be controllable and unstable. That is, ability in sport can be improved with effort and time. Unfortunately, if the attribution is not correctly classified, it becomes difficult to test the tenets of Weiner's model.

Even in those cases which do make the effort to measure carefully the constructs, complete testing of the model has been limited. Given the diverse array of achievement situations available in sport and physical activity, this domain provides an excellent arena for testing and, if necessary, extending and respecifying Weiner's (1985) model.

SUMMARY

In addressing the application of attribution theory in sport and physical activity, we elected to provide a brief review of some of the sport attributional literature of the 1980s, directing the reader to Rejeski and Brawley (1983) for a more general overview. In taking this approach, we discover more shortcomings than advances, questions than answers, problems than solutions. We maintain that poor measurement and incomplete testing of Bernard Weiner's (1985) attributional model of achievement motivation and emotion have, by and large, left us with a rather superficial knowledge of the attribution process in sport. To this end, McAuley and his colleagues (Duncan & McAuley, 1987, 1989; McAuley, 1985; McAuley & Duncan, 1989; McAuley, et al., 1989; McAuley et al., 1983) as well as researchers such as Vallerand (1987) and Spink and Roberts (1980) have attempted to investigate some of the more complex aspects of the attribution process. The relationship between causal dimensions and affective reactions to sport achievement outcomes has been explored, with attributions clearly active in the generation of emotion but with different dimensions taking on more important roles as a function of different situations. Moreover, differential patterns emerge with respect to absolute (win/loss) outcome versus perceived outcome

(Spink & Roberts, 1980). Furthermore, McAuley and Duncan, (1989) have shown attributions to predict cognitions regarding behavior through the mediation of affect and expectancy but in a slightly different manner to that suggested by Weiner (1985).

We suggest that the attribution–emotion link is in need of considerably more investigation in the sport science research. To do so, accurate measurement of constructs is crucial, as is a more thorough testing of the tenets of Weiner's model in more diverse sport settings. The growing interest in exercise and fitness as integral parts of sport and health psychology provides a new and exciting area within which to explore the attribution process. Although the extant sport psychology literature contains a great deal of information with regard to psychological processes and children's sport participation, there is a dearth of developmental sport attribution literature. This void must be filled if we are to understand better how age groups differently ascribe causality.

In closing, Weiner's theoretical model has been one of the most enduring and systematically tested social psychological models in the psychology of sport and physical activity. Clearly it is a model that can be further tested, applied, and used to understand sport behavior more fully.

ACKNOWLEDGMENT

Preparation of this article was facilitated by a grant to the senior author from the National Institute on Aging, R29 AG070907. Correspondence should be addressed to Edward McAuley, University of Illinois, Department of Kinesiology, Louise Freer Hall, Urbana, Illinois 61801.

REFERENCES

Auvergne, S. (1983). Motivation and causal attribution for high and low achieving athletes. *International Journal of Sport Psychology, 14,* 85–91.

Bandura, A. (1977). Self-efficacy: Toward a unifying theory of behavioral change. *Psychological Review, 84,* 191–215.

Bandura, A. (1986). *Social foundations of thought and action.* Englewood Cliffs, NJ: Prentice–Hill.

Bentler, P. M., & Bonett, D. G. (1980). Significance tests and goodness of fit in the analysis of covariance structures. *Psychological Bulletin, 88,* 588–606.

Bird, A. M., & Williams, J. M. (1980). A developmental-attributional analysis of sex-role stereotypes for sport performance. *Developmental Psychology, 16,* 319–322.

Brawley, L. R. (1984). Attributions as social cognitions: Contemporary perspectives in sport. In W. F. Straub & J. M. Williams (Eds.), *Cognitive sport psychology* (pp. 212–230). Lansing, NY: Sport Science Associates.

Bukowski, W. M. & Moore, D. (1980). Winners' and losers' attributions for success and failure in a series of athletic events. *Journal of Sport Psychology, 2,* 195–210.

Collins, J. (1982, March). *Self-efficacy and ability in achievement behavior*. Paper presented at the meeting of The American Educational Research Association, New York.

Dishman, R. K. (1982). Compliance/adherence in health-related exercise. *Health Psychology, 1*, 237–267.

Duncan, T. E., & McAuley, E. (1987). Efficacy expectations and perceptions of causality in motor performance. *Journal of Sport Psychology, 9*, 385–393.

Duncan, T. E., & McAuley (1989, April). *Cognition and emotion following sport performance: A causal model*. Paper presented at the national meeting of the American Alliance for Health, Physical Education, Recreation, and Dance, Boston.

Dweck, C. S. (1975). The role of expectation and attributions in the alleviation of learned help-lessness. *Journal of Personality and Social Psychology, 25*, 109–116.

Eiser, J. R., Van der Plight, J., Raw, M., & Sutton, S. R. (1985). Trying to stop smoking: Effects of perceived addiction, attributions for failure and expectancy of success. *Journal of Behavioral Medicine, 8*, 321–341.

Epstein, L., & Cluss, P. A. (1982). A behavioral medicine perspective on adherence to long-term medical regimens. *Journal of Consulting and Clinical Psychology, 50*, 950–971.

Forsyth, D. R., & McMillan, J. H. (1981). Attributions, affect, and expectations: A test of Weiner's three-dimensional model. *Journal of Educational Psychology, 73*, 393–403.

Förstering, F. (1985). Attribution retraining: A review. *Psychological Bulletin, 98*, 495–512.

Gill, D. L., Gross, J. B., & Huddleston,S. (1983). Participation motivation in youth sports. *International Journal of Sport Psychology, 14*, 1–14.

Harvey, J. H., Arkin, R. M., Gleason, J. M., & Johnson, S. (1974). Effects of expected and observed outcome of an action on the differential causal attributions of actor and observer. *Journal of Personality, 42*, 62–77.

Jones, E. E., & Davis, K. E. (1965). From acts to dispositions: The attribution process in person perception. In L. Berkowitz (Ed.), *Advances in experimental social psychology* (Vol. 2, pp. 219–266). New York: Academic.

Kelley, H. H. (1973). The process of causal attribution. *American Psychologist, 28*, 107–128.

Landers, D. L. (1983). Whatever happened to theory testing in sport psychology? *Journal of Sport Psychology, 5*, 135–151.

Maehr, M. L., & Nicholls, J. G. (1980). Culture and achievement motivation: A second look. In N. Warren (Ed.), *Studies in cross-cultural psychology*. New York: Academic.

Mark, M. M., Mutrie, N., Brooks, D. R., & Harris, D. V. (1984). Causal attributions of winners and losers in individual competitive sports: Toward a reformulation of the self-serving bias. *Journal of Sport Psychology, 6*, 184–196.

Martin, D. S., & Huang, M. (1984). Effects of time and perceptual orientation on actors' and observers' attributions. *Perceptual and Motor Skills, 58*, 23–30.

McAuley, E. (1985). Success and causality in sport: The influence of perception. *Journal of Sport Psychology, 7*, 13–22.

McAuley, E., & Duncan, T. E. (1989). Causal attributions and affective reactions to disconfirming outcomes in motor performance. *Journal of Exercise and Sport Psychology, 11*, 187–200.

McAuley, E., Duncan, T. E., & McElroy, M. (1989). Self-efficacy cognitions and causal attributions for children's motor performance: An exploratory investigation. *Journal of Genetic Psychology, 150*, 65–73.

McAuley, E., & Gross, J. B. (1983). Perceptions of causality in sport: An application of the Causal Dimension Scale. *Journal of Sport Psychology, 5*, 72–76.

McAuley, E., Russell, R., & Gross, J. B. (1983). Affective consequences of winning and losing: An attributional analysis. *Journal of Sport Psychology, 5*, 278–287.

Morgan, W. P. (1977). Involvement in vigorous physical activity with special reference to ad-herences. In L. I. Gedvilas & M. E. Kneer (Eds.), *National College Physical Education Association Proceedings*, (pp. 235–246). Chicago: University of Illinois–Chicago.

Nicholls, J. G. (1984). Achievement motivation: Conceptions of ability, subjective experience, task choice, and performance. *Psychological Review, 91,* 328–346.

Oldridge, N. B. (1982). Compliance and exercise in primary and secondary prevention of coronary heart disease: A review. *Preventive Medicine, 11,* 56–70.

Rejeski, W., & Brawley, L. (1983). Attribution theory in sport: Current status and new perspective. *Journal of Sport Psychology, 5,* 77–99.

Riordan, C. A., Thomas, J. S., & James, M. K. (1985). Attributions in a one-on-one sports competition: Evidence for self-serving biases and gender differences. *Journal of Sport Behavior, 8,* 42–53.

Roberts, G. C. & Pascuzzi, D. (1979). Causal attributions in sport: Some theoretical implications. *Journal of Sport Psychology, 1,* 203–211.

Russell, D. (1982). The Causal Dimension Scale: A measure of how individuals perceive causes. *Journal of Personality and Social Psychology, 42,* 1137–1145.

Russell, D., McAuley, E., & Tarico, V. (1987). Measuring causal attributions for success and failure: A comparison of methodologies for assessing causal dimensions. *Journal of Personality and Social Psychology, 52,* 1248–1257.

Silva, J. M., & Hardy, C. S. (1984). Precompetitive affect and athletic performance. In W. F. Straub & J. M. Williams (Eds.), *Cognitive Sport Psychology,* Lansing, NY: Sport Science Associates.

Spink, K. S., & Roberts, G. C. (1980). Ambiguity of outcome and causal attributions. *Journal of Sport Psychology, 2,* 237–244.

U.S. Department of Health and Human Services. (1979). *Surgeon General's Report: Promoting health-preventing disease, 1990 objectives for the nation.* Washington DC: Public Health Services, National Institutes of Health.

U.S. Department of Health and Human Services. (1980). *Promoting health and preventing disease.* Washington DC: Public Health Services, National Institutes of Health.

Vallerand, R. J. (1983). On emotion in sport: Theoretical and social psychological perspectives. *Journal of Sport Psychology, 5,* 197–215.

Vallerand, R. J. (1987). Antecedents of self-related affects in sport: Preliminary evidence on the intuitive-reflective appraisal model. *Journal of Sport Psychology, 9,* 161–182.

Weiner, B. (1972). *Theories of motivation: From mechanism to cognition.* Chicago: Rand McNally.

Weiner, B. (1979). A theory of motivation for some classroom experience. *Journal of Educational Psychology, 71,* 3–25.

Weiner, B. (1985). An attributional theory of achievement motivation and emotion. *Psychological Review, 92,* 548–573.

Weiner, B. (1986). *An attributional theory of motivation and emotion.* New York: Springer–Verlag.

Weiner, B., Kun, A., & Benesh–Weiner, M. (1980). The development of mastery, emotions, and morality from an attributional perspective. In W. A. Collins (Ed.), *Minnesota Symposium on Child Psychology* (Vol. 13, pp. 103–130). Hillsdale, NJ: Lawrence Erlbaum Associates.

Weiner, B., Russell, D., & Lerman, D. (1979). The cognition-emotion process in achievement-related contexts. *Journal of Personality and Social Psychology, 37,* 1211–1220.

Wong, P. T. P., & Weiner, B. (1981). When people ask "why" questions and the heuristics of attributional search. *Journal of Personality and Social Psychology, 40,* 650–663.

4 Explanatory Style in the Classroom and on the Playing Field

Christopher Peterson
University of Michigan

Explanatory style is a cognitive personality variable reflecting individual differences in how someone explains the causes of bad events (Peterson & Seligman, 1984). Some people explain events by pointing to factors within themselves that are chronic and pervasive ("I'm a loser"), whereas other people explain bad events in terms of circumscribed causes outside themselves ("it was a fluke"). We refer to the former as optimistic or efficacious, and to the latter as pessimistic or helpless (Peterson, Seligman, & Vaillant, 1988). According to theory and research, pessimistic individuals are more likely than their optimistic counterparts to respond with passivity and low morale to actual bad events.

Explanatory style was first discussed within the context of the learned helplessness model of depression, as a way of explaining the variation in people's responses to uncontrollable events (Abramson, Seligman, & Teasdale, 1978). Not surprisingly, therefore, most investigations of explanatory style have examined its relationship to depression (Sweeney, Anderson, & Bailey, 1986). However, my purpose in this chapter is to show that the notion of explanatory style applies more broadly than just to psychopathology. I'll describe lines of research that explore the relationship of explanatory style first to one's performance in the classroom, and second to one's performance on the playing field.

THE THEORY OF LEARNED HELPLESSNESS AND EXPLANATORY STYLE

Here I wish to provide some background on learned helplessness. There is by this time quite a body of literature, in which several discrete lines of work have emerged (Peterson, 1985). My organization is chronological, starting with the first studies of learned helplessness in animals, moving to learned helplessness as studied in people, and finally discussing applications of helplessness ideas to actual failures of adaptation.

Learned Helplessness in Animals

Twenty years ago, animal-learning researchers at the University of Pennsylvania discovered and explained the helplessness phenomenon among dogs (Overmier & Seligman, 1967; Seligman & Maier, 1967). Dogs were immobilized in a hammock and given a series of random shocks that they could neither avoid nor escape. Twenty-four hours later, the dogs were placed in a shuttlebox where the simple response of crossing a barrier in the middle would terminate the shock.

The dogs did not learn this simple escape response. Indeed, they rarely initiated any escape attempts at all. When they did occasionally move to the other side of the box, they did not repeat their actions during the next trial, suggesting that the dogs did not attend to the course of events. Further, the dogs showed few signs of overt emotionality. Dogs that were not exposed to uncontrollable shocks the day before encountered no difficulty in learning how to escape shocks in the shuttlebox. This set of deficits—motivational, learning, and emotional—is collectively called the *learned helplessness phenomenon.*

The original researchers proposed a cognitive interpretation of the phenomenon they produced in the laboratory (Seligman, 1975). According to their account, helplessness in animals results from their learning during exposure to uncontrollable shocks that responses and outcomes are independent. This learning is represented as an expectation that future responses and outcomes will be independent of each other as well. When generalized to new situations, such as the shuttlebox, this expectation of helplessness produces the observed deficits.

Learned helplessness is not a product of the physical trauma of bad events. Animal studies typically use a yoking procedure to create two groups of animals exposed to physically identical shocks, with the critical difference being that one group has control over their onset or offset while the other group does not (Maier & Seligman, 1976). Relative to animals exposed to no shock whatsoever (controllable or uncontrollable), only animals in the second group display helplessness deficits, and only animals in the second group show physiological effects of the shocks. Whether or not shocks are controllable is *not* a property of the shocks per se, but of the relationship between the animal and the shock. Uncontrollability is therefore not something that can be reduced below a psychological level. Helplessness must have a cognitive representation.

Learned Helplessness in People

Researchers next investigated the learned helplessness phenomenon by using people. Their studies closely followed the animal procedures, exposing people to events that could or could not be controlled (such as bursts of noise delivered through headphones), and seeing the effect on their performance of tasks that indeed could be mastered (such as unscrambling anagrams). Many human studies showed that uncontrollable events did indeed disrupt their subsequent performance (e.g., Hiroto & Seligman, 1975), but it was also apparent that human helplessness was more complicated that the original hypothesis implied (see reviews by Miller & Norman, 1979; Roth, 1980; Wortman & Brehm, 1975).

Abramson et al. (1978) thus revised helplessness theory (as applied to people) to take into account human cognitive capacities. Although a person's expectation remained critical in producing helplessness, Abramson et al. addressed the determinants of this expectation. Whereas the original helplessness theory assumed that the route from uncontrollable events to an expectation of helplessness was simple and automatic, the reformulated theory proposed that other factors intervened. To give a full account of learned helplessness, one must incorporate these other factors, particularly the individual's causal interpretation of the original uncontrollable events.

The new theory suggests that when a person encounters bad events that elude control, one asks oneself "Why?" The answer affects subsequent reactions, not only whether helplessness ensues, but also the nature of any helplessness that is produced. Three dimensions of a person's causal explanations are important.

First, if the person points to an *internal* cause of the bad events ("I made a mistake"), self-esteem falls. This is not the case if an *external* cause is implicated ("the day was windy"). Second, if the person explains bad events with a *stable* cause ("it runs in the family"), then deficits are long-lasting. This does not happen if the event is attributed to an *unstable* cause ("the circumstances were unusual"). Third, if the person offers an explanation in terms of *global* factors ("it's the human condition"), then helplessness is pervasive. An explanation in terms of a more *specific* cause leads to accordingly circumscribed deficits ("I've never gotten the hang of that one task").

People most at risk for helplessness following uncontrollable events are those who explain them using internal, stable, and global causes. The actual characteristics of the events obviously influence the sort of explanations a person offers, but so too does his or her habitual tendency to explain events in one way or another. Peterson and Seligman (1984) call this individual difference *explanatory style,* and with all other things being equal, people explain bad events in a characteristic way.

Learned Helplessness Applications

By reformulating helplessness theory along attributional lines, Abramson et al. not only increased its fit to the laboratory data, but also extended its scope by introducing personality factors. In its original version, it spoke only to the "main effects" of bad events. When explanatory style was added, it allowed psychologists to *predict* who was at particular risk following uncontrollability (i.e., those who offered internal, stable, and global explanations). It also helped them to *explain* why these people were disrupted (i.e., because their causal explanations determined their expectations of helplessness), and to *intervene* in a helpful way with people exhibiting helplessness (i.e., by changing their causal explanations with cognitive therapy techniques; Seligman, 1981).

As the term learned helplessness has come to be understood, we use several criteria to recognize the phenomenon (Peterson, 1985). First, learned helplessness is present when a person displays *inappropriate passivity:* failing through lack of mental or behavioral action to meet the demands of a situation where effective coping is possible. Second, learned helplessness follows in the wake of *uncontrollable* events. Bad events per se do not cause learned helplessness. Trauma may of course produce unfortunate reactions, including passivity, but trauma-induced helplessness is not of the "learned" variety. Third, learned helplessness is mediated by particular *cognitions,* which are acquired during a person's exposure to uncontrollable events and then inappropriately generalized to new situations.

In evaluating applications of learned helplessness ideas, we should measure the application against these criteria. The closer and more extensive the match, the more sensible an application in terms of learned helplessness theory. Seligman, Maier, and Peterson (in preparation) have identified more than two dozen suggested applications in the research literature, but have concluded that most are middling examples, meeting some of the criteria some of the time. As I focus in this chapter on educational and sport applications, I invite you to be skeptical. Do *these* applications fare well?

THE MEASUREMENT OF EXPLANATORY STYLE

Attributional Style Questionnaire

We have developed two ways to measure individual differences in explanatory style. The first technique is a self-report questionnaire called the Attributional Style Questionnaire (ASQ; Peterson et al., 1982). This questionnaire takes about 15 minutes to complete. Here are its instructions and a sample set of items:

> Several events will be described for you. When each event is described, vividly imagine it happening to you. Although events have many causes, I want you then to think of the one major cause of this event if it happened to you. I'll ask you what this cause is, and then I'll ask you several questions about the cause you provide.
> For instance . . .
> "You have been looking for a job unsuccessfully for some time."
> What is the *one major cause* of this event?
> Is this cause something about you, or something about other people and circumstances? If this cause is only something about you, rate it a 7. If this cause is only about other people and circumstances, rate it a 1. From 1 to 7, is this cause something about you?

Is this cause something that will last a long time, or something that will last only a short time? If this cause will last forever, rate it a 7. If this cause will last only a short time, rate it a 1. From 1 to 7, is this cause long-lasting?

Is this cause something that affects a lot of situations in your life, or something that affects only looking for a job? If this cause affects a lot of situations, then rate it a 7. If this cause affects only looking for a job, then rate it a 1. From 1 to 7, is this cause something that affects a lot of situations in your life?

In its original form, the ASQ presented a respondent with good and bad events involving the self. Internality, stability, and globality were averaged across events, separately for good and bad events, and across dimensions to give scores for one's explanatory style, ranging from pessimistic to optimistic.

Research consistently finds that causal explanations about bad events have more robust correlates than those for good events, and recent research therefore focuses on bad events (e.g., Peterson & Villanova, 1988; Robins, 1988; Sweeney et al., 1986). The ASQ possesses moderate reliability, although its internal consistency can readily be increased by including more events (e.g., Peterson & Villanova, 1988). Despite problems with reliability, the evidence for the validity of the ASQ is good (see review by Tennen & Herzberger, 1986).

The original ASQ was developed for administration to college students, and so the events about which it asks were chosen for their relevance to this population (Seligman, Abramson, Semmel, & von Baeyer, 1979). As explanatory style became a popular personality variable, researchers administered the ASQ to a variety of populations. In some of these groups, "undergraduate" events such as dating are not really pertinent, and thus the original ASQ is at risk for irrelevance and of course for invalidity.

My solution has been to develop a variety of alternative ASQs, using the format of the original questionnaire, but choosing events of clear concern to the population being studied. So, in some of the studies I'll describe later that look at the relationship between explanatory style and academic performance, an Academic Attributional Style Questionnaire was employed. Its bad events are typical of those that befall students (see Table 4.1).

And I have similarly developed sport-specific Attributional Style Questionnaires, under the assumption that one good way to increase correlations between predictors (i.e., ASQ scores) and criteria is to increase the specificity of the predictors vis-á-vis the criteria (Ajzen & Fishbein, 1977). I have encountered no difficulty in creating these alternative measures (although let me warn any who wish to follow my lead that new events should be added only if they admit to a degree of causal ambiguity). An event that is explained in the exact same way by all respondents quite obviously cannot reveal individual differences. Similarly, "reality" may suggest a clear causal attribution for some bad events, and these explanations are not psychologically informative, at least if one's interest is explanatory style.

TABLE 4.1
Events on the Academic ASQ

You cannot get all the reading done that your instructor requires.
You fail a final examination.
You show up for class and find to your surprise that there is a quiz.
You are on academic probation.
You do not have high enough grades to switch to your desired major.
You cannot solve a single problem in a set of 20 assigned as homework.
You are dropped from the university because your grades are too low.
You cannot get started writing a paper.
You cannot find a book in the library.
The required textbook for a course is unavailable in the school bookstore.
You cannot understand the points a lecturer makes.

Content Analysis of Verbatim Explanations

The second technique for measuring explanatory style is a content analysis strategy that I developed. It is called the CAVE procedure (Content Analysis of Verbatim Explanations) and it has two steps (Peterson, Seligman, & Vaillant, 1988). First, a researcher reads through the written material until a bad event involving the writer is encountered, along with a causal explanation. The event and its explanation are copied onto an index card and identified by a code number only. Blind judges, usually three or four, rate each causal explanation using 7-point scales corresponding to its internality–externality, stability–instability, and globality–specificity.

Our studies repeatedly find that both steps in the procedure are reliable. Independent researchers agree 90% of the time about the presence or absence of a particular causal attribution (e.g., Peterson, Bettes, & Seligman, 1985). And with four raters, the reliability of rating each dimension approaches .90, as estimated by coefficient alpha (e.g., Peterson, Seligman, & Vaillant, 1988).

Let me give you an example of a representative causal explanation and how it is scored. Here is a quote recently extracted and rated by Peterson, Seligman, and Vaillant: "I cannot seem to decide firmly on a career . . . (because) . . . this may be an unwillingness to face reality" (1986, p. 25). The attributed cause of the bad event would be given a score of 7–5–5 (along the dimensions of internality, stability, and globality, respectively).

I should emphasize that causal explanations of bad events are ubiquitous in written and spoken material (cf. Weiner, 1986), meaning that the CAVE technique can be widely deployed. I should also note that given subjects prove consistent in the sort of causal explanations they spontaneously offer (Peterson, Seligman, & Vaillant, 1988).

Finally, the procedure has growing validity. The CAVE technique has been used most extensively in studies of physical health (Peterson, Seligman, & Vaillant, 1988) and depression (e.g., Peterson et al., 1985; Peterson, Luborsky,

& Seligman, 1983), but it has also proved useful in predicting other manifestations of helplessness, such as political failure (.e.g, Zullow, Oettingen, Peterson, & Seligman, 1988). Later in this chapter, I will describe several studies in which the CAVE procedure was used to score the explanatory style of professional athletes from quotes found in the sport pages.

WHY EXPLANATORY STYLE IS NOT SIMPLY A RISK FACTOR FOR DEPRESSION

As I noted earlier, explanatory style was originally proposed within the context of the learned helplessness model of depression, to account for why some people become depressed after experiencing an uncontrollable event, whereas other people do not (Abramson et al., 1978). According to the reformulated model, one's explanatory style is critical in determining these various reactions. Literally hundreds of investigations have looked at explanatory style as a risk factor and correlate of depressive symptoms.

But explanatory style applies much more widely than just to psychopathology, and the learned helplessness model explains why this should be so. Explanatory style determines the boundary conditions of *helplessness* following bad events. Stability of explanatory style affects the generality of helplessness across time. Globality of style affects the generality of helplessness across situation. And internality of explanatory style affects the involvement of loss of self-esteem in helplessness. To the degree that explanatory style relates to depression, it is only through the intermediary of learned helplessness—so says the theory. Few researchers have taken a close look at how helpless behavior might mediate between explanatory style and depression, but this does not distract from the theoretical point. The relevance of the point in the present context is that explanatory style should affect a variety of outcomes in which helplessness is arguably important, including academic and athletic performance.

EXPLANATORY STYLE AND ACADEMIC PERFORMANCE

I now want to describe eight separate studies linking explanatory style to academic performance. Let me start out by making some general points about this line of research. First, a considerable debt must be acknowledged to earlier investigators for showing that consideration of causal attributions sheds light on academic performance. Work by Bernard Weiner (1978) and Carol Dweck (1975) has been particularly influential on my own thinking.

Second, these studies are not fine-grained. Although the learned helplessness theory which generated them is a process account of cognition and motivation, the research has typically looked at the distant consequences of explanatory style. Stated another way, my colleagues and I have worked with questionnaires and not stopwatches. Loose ends exist, because we sacrificed the control afforded by the experimental laboratory to gain the ecological validity of the field setting.

Academic Study No. 1

I did not conduct the first study in this line of work. Rather, Leslie Kamen and Martin Seligman (1985) at the University of Pennsylvania administered the ASQ to students at Pennsylvania as they began the academic year. Among 175 upper-level students, pessimistic explanatory style was associated with a lower grade-point average by the end of the year ($r = -.19$, $p < .01$).

These investigators grew concerned over an obvious confound. Perhaps the third variable of "ability" contributed both to a pessimistic explanatory style and to poor grades; perhaps explanatory style had no necessary correlation with academic performance. To investigate this possibility, they obtained for each subject the information used by the university admissions office to forecast academic success: Scholastic Aptitude Test (SAT) scores, College Entrance Examination Board achievement tests, and a measure of high school class rank that took into account class size. Although these measures indeed predicted grade-point average among the subjects, explanatory style continued to show a significant relationship, even when these ability measures were held constant statistically. So, explanatory style contributed to academic performance above and beyond a student's level of scholastic ability.

Academic Study No. 2

I conducted the next study in collaboration with Lisa Barrett (Peterson & Barrett, 1987), while we were both at Virginia Tech. We administered the Academic ASQ to 87 students at the beginning of their first year at the university. We also asked our subjects to complete the Beck Depression Inventory (Beck, 1967), because we wanted to show that a relationship between explanatory style and subsequent grades was not due simply to the third variable of depression.

We obtained the grades of the students at the end of the year and replicated the finding of Kamen and Seligman (1985) that pessimistic explanatory style foreshadowed poor grades. This correlation remained significant when we partialed out their depression scores. And this correlation continued to be significant when we also partialed out SAT scores. By the way, the zero-order correlation between SAT and grades was .55 among these students, and the correlation between explanatory style and grades was .36 ($p < .001$).

Three things should be noted about this comparison. First, SAT scores and explanatory style were essentially independent of each other. Second, the Academic ASQ takes only about 15 minutes to complete. Third, white students and

Black students in our sample did not differ in their average explanatory style, and the ability of explanatory style to predict grades among these two groups was the same. These findings suggest strongly to me that explanatory style warrants consideration as a supplement or perhaps even a replacement for traditional means of forecasting college performance.

Let me mention another aspect of this study. By design, a large number of our subjects had not declared a major, the significance of which is that they received academic advising at a centralized office that logged in each visit. When we calculated the number of visits made to an adviser by our subjects, pessimistic explanatory style was associated with fewer visits ($r = -.29, p < .02$). And fewer visits were in turn associated with lower grades ($r = .25, p < .05$). These results suggest a path between explanatory style and academic performance consistent with the learned helplessness rationale that I've already provided. Finally, we asked our subjects at the time they completed the Academic ASQ to describe in their own words up to five of their academic goals for the coming year. We coded each goal as *specific* if it mentioned some concrete accomplishment (e.g., "I wish to transfer into the College of Business") or as *nonspecific* if it failed to be concrete (e.g., "I hope to do my very best"). The importance of this distinction is that researchers in organizational psychology have shown that specific goals are associated with greater motivation and achievement than are vague goals (e.g., Locke, Shaw, Saari, & Latham, 1981). We wondered if perhaps goal setting was under the sway of explanatory style, a straightforward prediction, granted the importance accorded to expectations by the helplessness model. And as we hypothesized, pessimistic explanatory style was correlated with vague goals ($r = .30, p < .005$), which were in turn associated with a lower grade-point average ($r = .25, p < .02$).

Academic Study No. 3

Susan Nolen–Hoeksema, Joan Girgus, and Martin Seligman (1986) investigated the relationship of explanatory style to academic performance in a longitudinal study of 168 elementary-school students in central New Jersey. At the beginning of a schoolyear, these students completed our children's version of the ASQ (Seligman et al., 1984). Their classroom teachers subsequently completed a checklist measure of various behaviors showing helplessness or its opposite in the classroom (Fincham & Cain, 1984). For instance, a helplessness item on this measure is "wants to do easy problems rather than hard ones," whereas an item showing an efficacious approach to schoolwork is "tries to finish assignments even when they are difficult." Also available were the children's scores on the California Achievement Test (CAT), a test of vocabulary, reading, and mathematics skills. The CAT was taken by the subjects 1 month after they completed the ASQ.

Consistent with the studies I have already described with university students,

Nolen–Hoeksema et al. found among grade-school students that a pessimistic explanatory style predicted poor academic achievement as indexed by the CAT ($r = -.26, p < .05$). Furthermore, pessimistic explanatory style was positively correlated with helpless behaviors as reported by teachers ($r = .50, p < .0002$) and negatively correlated with efficacious behaviors ($r = -.56, p < .0002$).

Nolen–Hoeksema et al. also measured depressive symptoms among their young subjects and found bidirectional influences over time among all of their measures: explanatory style, academic achievement, and depression. These results imply that a student who starts to perform poorly in school, for whatever initial reason, can then embark on several routes of continued poor performance. Perhaps pessimistic grade-school students become college students of ostensibly low ability.

Academic Study No. 4

The next study I want to describe was carried out at the University of Michigan during the summer of 1987 (Peterson & Colvin, 1987). Dawn Colvin and I recruited 40 summer school students who were taking only one class. Each student completed the Academic Attributional Style Questionnaire the first week of the term. They kept weekly logs for the next 4 weeks in which successes and failures in the class were noted, as well as attempts to bolster their performance. Specifically, we asked our subjects to indicate whether they had done such things in the past week as:

- Seek help from the professor
- Seek help from the teaching assistant
- Seek help from a tutor
- Seek help from their fellow students
- Study a supplemental textbook
- Study old tests and quizzes

We considered all of these to be active attempts to do well in the course.

In 3 of the 4 weeks, explanatory style predicted the number of active attempts reported by students following an academic failure (in week 1: $r = -.23, p < .10$; week 2: $r = -.29, p < .04$; week 3: $r = -.35, p < .02$; week 4: $r = -.08$, ns). Those with an optimistic explanatory style were more likely to take active steps to improve their performance than were their pessimistic counterparts. The significance of these results is that they suggest a possible pathway between explanatory style and academic performance, one consistent with learned helplessness theory.

Academic Study No. 5

Another study that took a look at what might transpire between pessimistic explanatory style and poor performance in the classroom was undertaken by Peter Villanova, James Kyger, and me when we were at Virginia Tech (Villanova, Peterson, & Kyger, 1988). We followed up on the Peterson and Barrett (1987) finding that I described earlier, implicating goal setting as a mediator of the relationship between explanatory style and academic performance.

So, in this subsequent study, we administered to 141 introductory psychology students the Academic ASQ just 1 week prior to their midterm examination in the course. We also asked them to specify letter grades that represented their goals for the test and for the course itself. Finally, we asked them to report on whether or not they perceived their available resources—such as the amount of time they could devote to study—were sufficient to allow them to achieve the goals they had set.

Overall, pessimistic explanatory style predicted lower goals for the overall course ($r = -.15, p < .05$), but not for the pending examination. When resource availability was taken into account, explanatory style was associated with both goals. Specifically, pessimistic students who also perceived insufficient resources set lower test and course goals than either optimistic students or pessimistic students with sufficient resources. We did not obtain performance measures in this investigation, but we speculate that the lowered goals set by pessimists in constraining circumstances indeed translated themselves into less than optimal performance.

Academic Study No. 6

Following up the study I just described, Villanova et al. (1988) conducted a replication and extension with 60 introductory psychology students at Virginia Tech. Again, pessimistic explanatory style coupled with scant academic resources predicted lower goals for a pending examination and for the course as a whole. Further, pessimistic explanatory style predicted a person's poor performance on the test ($r = -.39, p < .005$).

Subjects in this study were also asked to report how threatening they found their situation in introductory psychology and how they characteristically coped with academic threats. In particular, their use of problem-focused strategies was ascertained. Did they try to change the threat—by studying more, negotiating with the teacher, hiring a tutor, and so on? Recognize these constructs as borrowed from the stress and coping approach of Lazarus and Folkman (1984).

There was no overall relationship between explanatory style and coping, but when we took into account the students' perceptions of resource availability and threat, a clear pattern emerged. Those students with a pessimistic explanatory style *and* insufficient resources used fewer problem-focused coping strategies as the threat to them increased ($r = -.71, p < .005$). Optimistic students with insufficient resources were, in contrast, more likely to use problem-focused coping as the threat increased ($r = .70$, $p < .005$).

Academic Study No. 7

During the 1988 winter term at the University of Michigan, David Smith, Paul Pintrich, and I administered the Academic Attributional Style Questionnaire to 121 students in my abnormal psychology class, along with the Motivated Strategies for Learning Questionnaire (MSLQ; Pintrich et al., 1988), an inventory of individual differences in cognitive and motivational approaches to academic work (Peterson, Smith, & Pintrich, 1988). Table 4.2 presents the correlations between explanatory style and selected subscales of the MSLQ. Many were significant, and the overall pattern is coherent. As the learned helplessness model would lead one to expect, pessimistic explanatory style is linked with passivity and lack of perseverance in the academic realm.

And once again, pessimistic explanatory style foreshadowed a student's poor academic performance, correlating with his or her final grade in the course ($r = -.38$, $p < .001$). Indeed, this correlation was unchanged when SAT scores were held constant statistically *and* when college grade-point average prior to the school term was held constant.

TABLE 4.2
Correlations Between Explanatory Style and MSLQ Subscales

Subscale	r With Explanatory Style
Intrinsic goal orientation	−.29*
Extrinsic goal orientation	.28*
Self-efficacy	.00
Perceived competence	−.17*
Expectancy for success	−.06
Test anxiety	.13*
Rehearsal strategies	−.18*
Selection strategies	−.14*
Organization strategies	−.15*
Elaboration strategies	.05
Metacognition: planning	−.13*
Metacognition: monitoring	.13*
Metacognition: regulating	−.26*
Surface processing	−.07
Critical thinking	−.26*
Original thinking	−.14*
Time and study management	.08
Study environment management	−.17*
Help seeking	−.14*

*p < .05.

Academic Study No. 8

Before I describe the final study in this line of work, let me stop and draw some conclusions. First, pessimistic explanatory style bears a consistent relationship with academic performance. Second, this correlation apparently reflects the operation of several behavioral and/or motivational and/or cognitive processes presumable under the sway of explanatory style. Third, the relationship between explanatory style and academic performance occurs independently of the effect of SAT scores. Fourth, because explanatory style can be measured quite simply, we have available an easy way of identifying students at risk for less than optimal classroom performance.

But then what can one do? In a recent study, I have shown that the explanatory style of high school students can be changed for the better if these students receive a healthy dose of success coupled with challenge (Peterson, 1988a). In 1987, I met with teachers and administrators at a suburban New York high school who were undertaking an educational experiment. They were interested in the fate of average students, those who seemed lost in the shuffle and destined to pass through school without achievements. Could something be done to encourage these students to greater efforts, both in and out of the classroom?

To this end, a special program was developed for 34 students who fell in the gray region of the student body. These students were placed within their own class, and team taught by three instructors who coordinated their efforts in such a way so as to encourage the students to do more than just get by in their studies. It is difficult to sketch the whole of this special program, but in psychological language, its stated goal was to increase the efficacy of the students involved.

I coordinated the evaluation of this program, and we arranged for the students to complete, among other measures, the Academic Attributional Style Questionnaire at the beginning and end of the schoolyear. A comparison group of 23 students not in the special program similarly completed the questionnaire.

The results were clear-cut. At the beginning of the year, the students in the special program scored somewhat worse on the Attributional Style Questionnaire than did the comparison students, as would be expected, granted the criterion by which they were chosen. But by the end of the year, their explanatory style had changed for the better, and now was more optimistic than that of the comparison group ($p < .002$). Interestingly, the students in the comparison group had become somewhat more fatalistic as the schoolyear progressed. As so many educational critics have charged, a typical school can erode a student's will to do well. However, it also appears that special interventions can stem and even reverse this trend.

We will follow these students to see if the observed changes in explanatory style in turn lead to improvements in long-term academic success. But even at this juncture, I am excited about the possibility that explanatory style can be reliably changed by a sustained educational experience. To date, almost all the research concerned with pessimistic explanatory style has been descriptive, documenting the various consequences of this individual difference. Perhaps the way is now clear for studies that intervene and preclude these consequences. Stay tuned.

EXPLANATORY STYLE
AND ATHLETIC PERFORMANCE

In this section, I will describe five studies conducted by my colleagues and me that look at the relationship between explanatory style and athletic performance. This line of work is not as well developed as the one I just finished describing linking explanatory style to academic performance. Small sample size has plagued most of our studies in the athletic domain. Nonetheless, the underlying logic of these studies remains the same: Explanatory style influences how individuals—in this case athletes—respond to bad events. Those with a pessimistic style show passivity and poor morale. Those with an optimistic style show perseverance and good humor.

Athletic Study No. 1

Our first foray into athletics started in the sport pages (Seligman & Peterson, 1984). We used the CAVE technique to score causal explanations for bad events offered by players and coaches in the National Basketball Association. Specifically, during the 1982–1983 season, we extracted and rated all explanations found in the hometown newspapers for the five teams in the Eastern Conference: the Boston Celtics, the New Jersey Nets, the New York Knicks, the Philadelphia 76ers, and the Washington Bullets.

We aggregated our ratings across the personnel of the same team, thereby creating a composite style for each group. We then used these aggregate scores to array the teams from most optimistic to most pessimistic: Boston > New York > Washington > Philadelphia > New Jersey.

Does explanatory style relate to athletic performance? We looked to the records of these five teams during the following season (i.e., 1983–1984). There was no overall relationship between explanatory style and the percentage of games that a team won. A finer look at performance was needed, so we calculated how each team performed against the point spread in games immediately following a loss. The *point spread* is a highly reliable method of handicapping teams. It attempts to equate them on factors such as past record, skill, where the game is being played, injuries to key players, the toll taken by travel, and so on. Specifically, the point spread is an estimate of the number of points by which a particular basketball team should beat another team on a given occasion. We assume the point spread, as reported in newspapers, is valid because it keeps thousands of betting establishments—legal and otherwise—profitable by assuring more or less equal numbers of bettors on both sides of the spread.

At any rate, learned helplessness theory directed our attention to team performance following a loss, because it is in the wake of bad events that explanatory style should show its strongest relationship to performance. And when we looked at how the teams fared against the point spread following a loss, the teams were ordered in the exact same way that they were ordered by explanatory style, from Boston (which beat the point spread 68% of the time) to New Jersey (37%). The odds of finding this particular order by chance seem slim $= 1/5 \times 1/4 \times 1/3 \times 1/2 = .00833!$

We attempted to replicate these results for the next several seasons, but without the same success. In the study I just described, there was minimal turnover in player and coach personnel from the first year when explanatory style was measured, to the second year when performance was measured. In subsequent pairs of seasons, as any fans reading this well know, the Eastern Conference teams witnessed coaching changes, major trades, and serious injuries. Explanatory style continued to bear a rough relationship to performance against the spread, but our perfect predictions never again occurred. We regard the study as interesting but not definitive. The notion of an aggregate explanatory style deserves further investigation.

Athletic Study No. 2

When we were at Virginia Tech, Elizabeth Davis and I asked 104 university athletes how they responded to the frustration and failure they experienced during their athletic career (Peterson & Davis, 1983). Various sports were represented: men's football ($n = 50$), men's basketball ($n = 5$), men's baseball ($n = 16$), men's swimming ($n = 8$), women's basketball ($n = 10$), and women's swimming ($n = 15$). Each athlete completed an anonymous questionnaire describing the frequency with which he or she responded to setbacks by withdrawing and being passive (i.e., with helplessness). They also reported on the frequency with which they reacted to athletic disappointments by feeling depressed, by getting angry, by using drugs or alcohol, by starting fights, by engaging in vandalism on campus, and by giving up on their schoolwork. Next, each athlete rated his or her career as a success or failure, and indicated the degree of control perceived over the way his or her career had unfolded. Finally, after the format of the ASQ, each athlete provided and rated "the one major cause" of his or her career turning out as it had.

We analyzed the results just for the half of the subjects who perceived their career to be a failure. Within this group, a path analysis confirmed the path implied by the learned helplessness model: Internal, stable, and global explanations predicted a lack of perceived control over one's career, and lack of perceived control predicted a helpless reaction to setbacks on the playing field. Interestingly, helpless reactions then predicted all the other negative reactions about which we inquired, with the exception of anger. This last finding is surprising, because reactions such as starting fights and engaging in vandalism are hardly passive, at least in any overt way. Perhaps they represent a failure of self-control, an inability to restrain one's impulses.

Athletic Study No. 3

At the University of Michigan, 34 varsity athletes (on the men's and women's swimming, diving, and track teams) completed the ASQ and a questionnaire asking for their own assessment of their own resilience and motivation (Peterson, 1988b). Explanatory style, in particular the dimensions of stability and globality, was related to a number of these ratings: ability to overcome injuries ($r = -.29$, $p < .10$), ability to perform well following disappointing losses ($r = -.31, p < .10$), perception of control over the successes one experiences in one's athletic career ($r = -.45, p < .001$), and perception of one's self as motivated to do well ($r = -.38, p < .05$).

Athletic Study No. 4

Martin Seligman, Susan Nolen–Hoeksema, Nort Thornton, and Karen Moe Thornton (1988) conducted an intriguing study with swimmers at a west coast university. All athletes completed the ASQ. Then the swimming coaches had each swimmer swim a timed race. In each case, a false time was given to the swimmer, one considerably slower than what he or she had actually achieved. Following this feedback, the swimmer then swam a second timed race.

As we would expect from learned helplessness theory, explanatory style determined how the swimmers performed during the second race relative to the first race. Those with an optimistic style improved their performance, whereas those with a pessimistic style did worse.

Athletic Study No. 5

Finally, I'd like to mention a study in progress that I am conducting with Alan Reifman at the University of Michigan (Reifman & Peterson, 1988). We read the hometown sport pages for the Baltimore Orioles major league baseball team during their record-setting streak of losses at the start of the 1988 season. Causal attributions by the coaches, players, and managers have been extracted and rated with the CAVE procedure.

We are interested in several aspects of these ratings. First, do they become increasingly pessimistic as the streak progresses? Our casual inspection suggests yes, and this may provide a hint about the ultimate origins of explanatory style.

To date, we know a lot more about the consequences of a pessimistic style than we do about its determinants. One suspects, though, that repeated failure—such as that experienced by the hapless Orioles—is a fertile soil for the seeds of helplessness and pessimism.

Second, if pessimism gradually overtook the Orioles, did it bring in its wake baseball equivalents of learned helplessness, such as errors, passed balls, base-running mishaps, and called third strikes? If these covary with pessimism as shown in the attributed causes for the repeated losses, then we will have some support for Yogi Berra's adage that "90% of this game is 50% mental." In other words, perhaps the Orioles streak reflected not simply the decay of their minor league system but also a vicious circle of learned helplessness. To paraphrase Yogi, perhaps sometimes it can be over *before* it's over.

A CRITICAL EVALUATION

I've described 13 studies investigating the relationship between pessimistic explanatory style and poor performance, in academic and athletic domains. I would like to argue that these studies support a central premise of learned helplessness theory: that is, that explanatory style foreshadows poor performance because it engenders passivity in the face of setbacks. But is this argument really justified?

One way to evaluate these studies is in terms of the criteria by which one can judge the pertinence of learned helplessness to some phenomenon: the documentation (or not) of (1) maladaptive passivity; (2) uncontrollable events; and (3) mediating cognitions. Table 4.3 summarizes the studies described in this chapter with regard to these criteria.

As you can see, most of the studies, taken individually, are but middling examples of learned helplessness. All point to cognitions in the form of pessimistic explanations, but not all of the studies measure passive behavior. Indeed, even the studies showing that pessimistic students or athletes behave passively do *not* show that the "helpless" behavior is inherently maladaptive. Perhaps what I identify as helplessness is in some way instrumental. And not all of the studies show that explanatory style is engaged particularly when bad events are encountered.

Perhaps the studies are more impressive collectively. Results of the 13 investigations do converge in showing that pessimistic explanatory style leads to poor performance. These studies use markedly different samples, measures, and designs, yet they point to the same conclusion that learned helplessness in general and explanatory style in particular shed light on less than optimal performance (cf. Campbell & Fiske, 1959).

Two aspects of these studies, individually and collectively, continue to gnaw at me. First, I worry about third variables. In some but not all of the 13 studies, likely confounds were anticipated, assessed, and ruled out. But perhaps less

TABLE 4.3
Evaluation of Studies

Study	Descriptions
Academics	
1. (Kamen & Seligman)	sample: 175 college students passivity: yes (grades) uncontrollability: no cognitions: yes (ASQ)
2. (Peterson & Barrett)	sample: 87 college freshmen passivity: yes (grades; help seeking) uncontrollability: no cognitions: yes (ASQ)
3. (Nolen-Hokesema et al.)	sample: 168 elementary-school students passivity: yes (grades; teacher ratings) uncontrollability: no cognitions: yes (ASQ)
4. (Peterson & Colvin)	sample: 40 college students passivity: yes (coping) uncontrollability: yes (failure) cognitions: yes (ASQ)
5. (Villanova et al., Study A)	Sample: 141 college students passivity: no uncontrollability: yes (resources) cognitions: yes (ASQ)
6. (Villanova et al., Study B)	sample: 60 college students passivity: yes (grades; coping) uncontrollability: yes (resources) cognitions: yes (ASQ)
7. (Peterson, Smith & Pintrich)	sample: 121 college students passivity: yes (grades; MSLQ) uncontrollability: no cognitions: yes (ASQ)
8. (Peterson, 1988a)	sample: 57 high school students passivity: no uncontrollability: no cognitions: yes (ASQ)
Athletics	
1. (Seligman & Peterson)	sample: 5 NBA teams passivity: yes (losses against spread) uncontrollability: yes (loss) cognitions: yes (CAVE)
2. (Peterson & Davis)	Sample: 104 college athletes passivity: yes (self-ratings) uncontrollability: yes (setback) cognitions: yes (ASQ)
3. (Peterson, 1988b)	sample: 34 college athletes passivity: yes (self-ratings)

(*continued*)

TABLE 4.3
(*Continued*)

Study	Descriptions
	uncontrollability: yes (setback) cognitions: yes (ASQ)
4. (Seligman et al., 1989)	sample: 33 college swimmers passivity: yes (lap time) uncontrollability: yes (false feedback) cognitions: yes (ASQ)
5. (Reifman & Peterson)	sample: Baltimore Orioles passivity: ? uncontrollability: yes (losing streak) cognitions: yes (CAVE)

likely variables are lurking in the classroom or on the playing field. Maybe these are responsible for the apparent link between explanatory style and performance. Second, as I earlier acknowledged, the studies are not fine-grained. More constructs are deemed important in helplessness theory than are ever investigated at the same time. I really don't know if the specific process hypothesized by helplessness theory is operating or not.

CONCLUSION: SOME PITFALLS IN APPLYING ATTRIBUTION THEORY

In planning and conducting the studies I have described in this chapter, I have learned the hard way some important lessons about how one might sensibly go about applying attribution theory. Most of these lessons take the form of cautions, and I'd therefore like to warn readers about some possible pitfalls awaiting the applied attribution theorist.

Pitfall No. 1: Cross-sectional Studies

The days are probably long past when cross-sectional data can be used to buttress longitudinal claims. The majority of learned helplessness studies have been cross-sectional, as I suspect is true for the majority of applied attribution studies. If, as cognitive social psychologists, we wish to conclude that thoughts and beliefs determine behavior, we must show this to be the case over time.

Pitfall No. 2: Third Variables

Even a longitudinal demonstration of a link between attributions and subsequent behavior may prove very little if likely confounds are not ruled out.

Pitfall No. 3: Reality

In a rather ironic way, the biggest enemy of the applied attribution theorist is reality. Let me explain. Beliefs about causes are not entertained in a vacuum. I believe that many people's causal attributions about bad events are highly sensitive to the actual characteristics of these events. Stated more baldly, attributions are often accurate. This is good for the "naïve scientist" as he or she navigates the world, but it ends up making it difficult for a researcher to show that causal attributions matter above-and-beyond reality. Perhaps one virtue of the explanatory style construct is that it reflects the way people explain a variety of events, thereby canceling out considerations of reality and allowing psychological characteristics to become manifest.

Pitfall No. 4: Too Many Outcomes

I've elsewhere noted that explanatory style has an embarrassingly large number of correlates, which means that its specificity with regard to any one outcome is nil (Peterson, Seligman, & Vaillant, 1988). Other factors, as yet unspecified, must be incorporated into helplessness theory to explain why one pessimistic person becomes depressed, why a second pessimistic individual falls ill, why a third fails out of school, and so on. But the same criticism can be leveled at attribution applications in general.

Pitfall No. 5: Cognitions Other Than Causal Attributions

Let us not be attributional chauvinists. Causal explanations do not exhaust the thoughts that determine one's behavior. For instance, beliefs about the consequences of events, about their religious or philosophical significance, and about one's ability to cope with their aftermath are probably just as important as beliefs about the causes of events.

Pitfall No. 6: Blaming the Victim

For the most part, the applied attribution theorist has an upbeat message. If the ills of the world are due to particular ways of thinking, then remedies are simple and effective. But hidden in this message is the risk of blaming the victim for entertaining unproductive attributions. Social psychologists are too sophisticated to confuse scientific causality with moral responsibility, but if we are successful in applying attribution ideas, a less sophisticated group of individuals who hear what we have to say may start blaming "those kinds of people" for how they think. So, we should probably accompany our applications with some loud statements that the primary determinant of what and how people think is the social situation in which they have found themselves.

SUMMARY

According to learned helplessness theory, people act passively following a bad event, to the degree that they explain the bad event in pessimistic fashion with internal, stable, and global causes. Explanatory style is a personality characteristic that influences how someone explains an actual bad event. In this chapter, I described 13 studies linking pessimistic explanatory style to poor performance in the classroom and on the playing field. Individually, each study is less than perfect. Collectively, they converge in their support of learned helplessness theory, although we can still raise some criticisms about unmeasured third variables and a lack of close attention to hypothesized processes. I concluded this chapter by discussing some of the pitfalls that the attribution theorist must avoid in applying attributional ideas outside the experimental laboratory.

ACKNOWLEDGMENT

Some of the research that I describe in this chapter was supported by the Faculty Assistance Fund of the College of Literature, Science, and the Arts at the University of Michigan. A version of this chapter was presented at a symposium on Motivational and Cognitive Dimensions of Student Learning at the 96th annual convention of the American Psychological Association, Atlanta, August 12, 1988. I would like to thank Lisa M. Bossio for her editorial advice. Address correspondence to Christopher Peterson, Department of Psychology, University of Michigan, 580 Union Drive, Ann Arbor, MI 48109.

REFERENCES

Abramson, L. Y., Seligman, M. E. P., & Teasdale, J. D. (1978). Learned helplessness in humans: Critique and reformulation. *Journal of Abnormal Psychology, 87,* 49–74.

Ajzen, I., & Fishbein, M. (1977). Attitude–behavior relations: A theoretical analysis and review of empirical research. *Psychological Bulletin, 84,* 888–918.

Beck, A. T. (1967). *Depression: Clinical, experimental, and theoretical aspects.* New York: Hoeber.

Campbell, D. T., & Fiske, D. W. (1959). Convergent and discriminant validity by the multitrait-multimethod matrix. *Psychological Bulletin, 56,* 81–105.

Dweck, C. S. (1975). The role of expectations and attributions in the alleviation of learned helplessness. *Journal of Personality and Social Psychology, 31,* 674–685.

Fincham, F., & Cain, M. (1984). *The Pupil Behavior Checklist.* Unpublished manuscript, University of Illinois.

Hiroto, D. S., & Seligman, M. E. P. (1975). Generality of learned helplessness in man. *Journal of Personality and Social Psychology, 31,* 311–327.

Kamen, L. P., & Seligman, M. E. P. (1985). *Explanatory style predicts college grade point average.* Unpublished manuscript, University of Pennsylvania.

Lazarus, R. S., & Folkman, S. (1984). *Stress, appraisal, and coping*. New York: Springer.

Locke, E. A., Shaw, K. N., Saari, L. M., & Latham, G. P. (1981). Goal setting and task performance. *Psychological Bulletin, 90*, 125–152.

Maier, S. F., & Seligman, M. E. P. (1976). Learned helplessness: Theory and evidence. *Journal of Experimental Psychology, 105*, 3–46.

Miller, I. W., & Norman, W. H. (1979). Learned helplessness in humans: A review and attribution theory model. *Psychological Bulletin, 86*, 93–119.

Nolen–Hoeksema, S., Girgus, J. S., & Seligman, M. E. P. (1986). Learned helplessness in children: A longitudinal study of depression, achievement, and explanatory style. *Journal of Personality and Social Psychology, 51*, 435–442.

Overmier, J. B., & Seligman, M. E. P. (1967). Effects of inescapable shock upon subsequent escape and avoidance learning. *Journal of Comparative and Physiological Psychology, 63*, 23–33.

Peterson, C. (1985). Learned helplessness: Fundamental issues in theory and research. *Journal of Social and Clinical Psychology, 3*, 248–254.

Peterson, C. (1988a). *Explanatory style and academic performance*. Paper presented at the 96th annual convention of the American Psychological Association, Atlanta, GA.

Peterson, C. (1988b). [Explanatory style of elite athletes.] Unpublished data, University of Michigan.

Peterson, C., & Barrett, L. C. (1987). Explanatory style and academic performance among university freshmen. *Journal of Personality and Social Psychology, 53*, 603–607.

Peterson, C., Bettes, B. A., & Seligman, M. E. P. (1985). Depressive symptoms and unprompted causal attributions: Content analysis. *Behaviour Research and Therapy, 23*, 379–382.

Peterson, C., & Colvin, D. (1987). [Explanatory style and response to academic failure.] Unpublished data, University of Michigan.

Peterson, C., & Davis, E. R. (1983). *Reactions to athletic failure: Test of the learned helplessness reformulation*. Unpublished manuscript, Virginia Tech.

Peterson, C., Luborsky, L., & Seligman, M. E. P. (1983). Attributions and depressive mood shifts. *Journal of Abnormal Psychology, 92*, 96–103.

Peterson, C., & Seligman, M. E. P. (1984). Causal explanations as a risk factor for depression: Theory and evidence. *Psychological Review, 91*, 347–374.

Peterson, C., Seligman, M. E. P., & Vaillant, G. E. (1988). Pessimistic explanatory style is a risk factor for physical illness: A thirty-five year longitudinal study. *Journal of Personality and Social Psychology, 55*, 23–27.

Peterson, C., Semmel, A., von Baeyer, C., Abramson, L. Y., Metalsky, G. I., & Seligman, M. E. P. (1982). The Attributional Style Questionnaire. *Cognitive Therapy and Research, 6*, 287–299.

Peterson, C., Smith, D. A. F., & Pintrich, P. R. (1988). [Explanatory style and strategies for learning.] Unpublished data, University of Michigan.

Peterson, C., & Villanova, P. (1988). An Expanded Attributional Style Questionnaire. *Journal of Abnormal Psychology, 97*, 87–89.

Pintrich, P. R., et al. (1988). *Motivated Strategies for Learning Questionnaire (MSLQ)*. Unpublished manuscript, University of Michigan.

Reifman, A., & Peterson, C. (1988). [Causal explanations and the Baltimore Orioles losing streak.] Study in progress, University of Michigan.

Robins, C. J. (1988). Attributions and depression: Why is the literature so inconsistent? *Journal of Personality and Social Psychology, 54*, 880–889.

Roth, S. (1980). A revised model of learned helplessness in humans. *Journal of Personality, 48*, 103–133.

Seligman, M. E. P. (1975). *Helplessness: On depression, development, and death*. San Francisco: Freeman.

Seligman, M. E. P. (1981). A learned helplessness point of view. In L. P. Rehm (Ed.), *Behavior therapy for depression: Present status and future directions.* New York: Academic.

Seligman, M. E. P., Abramson, L. Y., Semmel, A., & von Baeyer, C. (1979). Depressive attributional style. *Journal of Abnormal Psychology, 88,* 242–247.

Seligman, M. E. P., & Maier, S. F. (1967). Failure to escape traumatic shock. *Journal of Experimental Psychology, 74,* 1–9.

Seligman, M. E. P., Maier, S. F., & Peterson, C. (in preparation). *Learned helplessness.*

Seligman, M. E. P., Nolen–Hoeksema, S., Thornton, N., & Thornton, K. M. (1989). *Athletic achievement and explanatory style.* Unpublished manuscript, University of Pennsylvania.

Seligman, M. E. P., & Peterson, C. (1984). [Explanatory style of NBA players.] Unpublished data, University of Pennsylvania.

Seligman, M. E. P., Peterson, C., Kaslow, N. J., Tanenbaum, R. L., Alloy, L. B., & Abramson, L. Y. (1984). Attributional style and depressive symptoms among children. *Journal of Abnormal Psychology, 93,* 235–238.

Sweeney, P. D., Anderson, K., & Bailey, S. (1986). Attributional style in depression: A meta-analytic review. *Journal of Personality and Social Psychology, 50,* 974–991.

Tennen, H., & Herzberger, S. (1986). Attributional Style Questionnaire. In D. J. Keyser & R. C. Sweetland (Eds.), *Test critiques* (Vol. 4). Kansas City, KS: Test Corporation of America.

Villanova, P., Peterson, C., & Kyger, J. E. (1988). *Explanatory style and academic goals.* Unpublished manuscript, Northern Illinois University.

Weiner, B. (1978). Achievement strivings. In H. London & J. E. Exner (Eds.), *Dimensions of personality.* New York: Wiley.

Weiner, B. (1986). *An attribution theory of motivation and emotion.* New York: Springer–Verlag.

Wortman, C. B., & Brehm, J. (1975). Responses to uncontrollable outcomes: An integration of reactance theory and the learned helplessness model. In L. Berkowitz (Ed.), *Advances in experimental social psychology* (Vol. 8). New York: Academic.

Zullow, H., Oettingen, G., Peterson, C., & Seligman, M. E. P. (1988). Explanatory style and pessimism in the historical record: CAVing LBJ, presidential candidates, and East versus West Berlin. *American Psychologist, 43,* 673–682.

II   APPLICATIONS TO MENTAL HEALTH

Causal search is most likely to be initiated following events that are negative, unusual, or unexpected—precisely the kinds of outcomes that are most often of concern to mental health professionals. This recognition of the importance of perceived causality has resulted in a growing body of application-oriented research on attributional approaches to clinical problems. In fact, the popularity of clinical issues as a domain of application for attribution theory is perhaps second only to that of achievement. The three chapters that follow are illustrative of the breadth of clinical phenomena addressed in this research.

Amirkhan (Chapter 5) applies attribution principles to the vast (but often contradictory) literature on stress and coping. One of the persistent problems in this literature is the lack of agreement among researchers on the relations among control beliefs, stress, and coping behavior. In some studies, for example, perceived control is an antecedent of effective coping, but in other investigations control appears to follow, rather than precede, effective responding. By utilizing the thought-to-action sequences specified by attribution theory, Amirkhan demonstrates how attribution principles are useful for analyzing the complex causal relations between thoughts about control, stress-related emotions, and relevant behavior such as coping.

In Chapter 6, López and Wolkenstein shift from self-perception to perception of others in the domain of clinical judgment. In the first part of the chapter, the authors review research on clinicians' attributions for patient disorders. Although this literature has focused mostly on the locus of causes (i.e., whether mental health professionals perceive their clients' problems as due to internal versus external factors), López and Wolkenstein demonstrate how the dimensions of stability and controllability are also important conceptual distinctions that aid our understanding of the clinical judgment process. For example, the perceived stability of causes relates directly to patient prognosis, whereas perceived controllability has linkages to therapeutic efforts (i.e., help giving). In the second part of the chapter López and Wolkenstein apply this dimensional analysis to family members' perceptions of the causes of mental illness among relatives. The authors interpret this research within an attributional framework that draws specifically on the linkages between perceived controllability of negative outcomes, emotional reactions of sympathy versus anger, and the family member's decisions to withhold or offer help (e.g., social support) to their relative. Thus an attributional approach to clinical judgment can incorporate both professional and laypersons' causal perceptions with the same set of interrelated constructs.

The final paper in this section by Försterling (Chapter 7) addresses the general area of attributional therapy. Attributional therapies are guided by the belief that causal thoughts influence actions. Thus changing a dysfunctional attribution such as self-perceived low ability to a more adaptive ascription such as self-perceived lack of effort should also be accompanied by a change in behavior. Within this general framework, Försterling describes a number of approaches to psychotherapy that are based on attributional principles. The reader may be surprised at the range of therapies amenable to causal analysis. Even some behavioral treatment programs based on classical conditioning paradigms have a degree of conceptual overlap with principles of attributional change.

5 Applying Attribution Theory to the Study of Stress and Coping

James H. Amirkhan
California State University, Long Beach

That stress leads to illness would seem a matter of common knowledge. Nearly everyone can recall a period of duress—a marital conflict, a blunder at work, a scrape with the law, or even the rapid approach of April 15—that ended with a headache, sore throat, or worse. When researchers set out to study the link between stress and illness, in fact, it was with the confidence of those who need only to confirm the obvious. In their optimism, they implicated stress as a major etiological factor not only in the psychosomatic disorders (such as hypertension and ulcers), but in a wide range of others, including infections (Dubos, 1965), chronic diseases (Dodge & Martin, 1970), and affective, neurotic, and even psychotic disturbances (Hinkle & Wolff, 1958).

It came as quite a shock, then, to find that the relationship between stress and illness seemed to evaporate under the light of empirical scrutiny. Though researchers attempted to relate all manner of environmental stressors to all manner of diseases, the correlations they found were often insignificant, and nearly always of low magnitude (e.g., Goldberg & Comstock, 1976; Holmes & Masuda, 1974; Rabkin & Struening, 1976; Rahe, 1975). Their frustration is evident in a question posed by one of their number:

> Why is it that disorders develop in so many people with very little prior exposure to stressors . . . [While] more than 25% of concentration camp survivors— despite long years of physical suffering, the constant threat of annihilation, and other stressors too rueful to describe—have survived their ordeals without evidence of psychiatric disorder or chronic physical disease? (Jenkins, 1979, p. 265)

The answer apparently is that people think and do different things between the advent of a stressor and the onset of illness. Individual differences in the perception of the stressor, for example, seem to ameliorate or exacerbate its impact on the person. Perceptions regarding the controllability of the event have been identified as particularly important, perhaps "more important determinants of the stress response than the magnitude of the stressful stimulus itself" (Cohen, Glass, & Phillips, 1979, p.142). Individual differences in the choice of a coping strategy likewise can affect the probability of stress-induced pathology. In fact, one group of researchers has gone so far as to claim "stress and adaptational outcomes are always mediated through coping processes that either increase or decrease the risk of disease, low morale, and poor social functioning" (Lazarus, Cohen, Folkman, Kanner, & Schaefer, 1980, p. 112).

Research over the past several years has substantiated the important role of both perceived control and coping behavior as moderators of stress-related illness. Some progress has also been made in identifying how these processes interrelate. But research remains far from specifying the precise placement of these factors in the causal chain linking environmental stress to personal pathology.

It will be argued here that attribution theory, particularly as conceptualized by Weiner (1979, 1985, 1986), could prove extremely helpful in explicating this chain of causality. While only a handful of studies have employed the attributional perspective in examining stress (e.g., Affleck, Allen, Tennen, McGrade, & Ratzan, 1985; Baumgardner, Heppner, & Arkin, 1986; Follette & Jacobson, 1987; Prohaska, Keller, Leventhal, & Leventhal, 1987; Rodin, Bohm, & Wack, 1982; Taylor, Lichtman, & Wood, 1984), there is evidence to suggest that such an application is appropriate. First, much of attribution theory evolved in the context of negative life events, as theorists speculated how perceived causes for personal, academic, and social failures might explain an individual's reactions to those events (see Weiner, 1974). Then, too, it has been shown that people are most likely to search for causal explanations in the aftermath of negative, unexpected, and sudden changes, the very types of events likely to evoke stress (Holtzworth–Munroe & Jacobson, 1985; Wong & Weiner, 1981). The fact that a large part of the cognitive work in a threatening situation is devoted to a causal search would in itself seem testimony to the importance of considering attributions as mediators of illness. However, studies have further shown that the attribution process involves classifying the perceived causes according to certain key dimensions—one of which is controllability, precisely the dimension independently identified by stress researchers.

Perhaps an even stronger argument for incorporating attribution theory into the study of stress is that, after years of carefully controlled laboratory experiments, attribution researchers have traced the pathways linking perceptions of an event to consequent affective and behavioral reactions (Weiner, 1979, 1986; Weiner, Russell, & Lerman, 1979). Specifically, the type of cause selected to explain an event has been shown to influence the emotions experienced (including shame, guilt, and loss of self-esteem), expectancies for future successes or failures, and the type and intensity of ensuing behavior. Clearly, these consequences are germane to anticipating the impact of stressful events, in that they pertain to unpleasant emotions, the degree of optimism about the efficacy of coping, the form of the coping response, and the likelihood of persistence in the face of failure. Recognition of these findings, which not only identify the important aspects of event perceptions but link these to specific stress-related consequences, could save stress researchers years of trial-and-error investigation.

In the following pages, an abbreviated history of stress research, particularly those findings relevant to the mediating processes of "thinking" and "doing," will be presented. This presentation has been organized into three broad sections, one focusing on the impact of control perceptions, one on the effectiveness of coping behaviors, and the third on the causal interplay of these processes. In a fourth section, potentially fruitful applications of attribution theory in this research will be discussed. As will be seen, the theory in some cases helps to make sense of contradictory findings in the stress literature, and in others serves to provide direction for future research endeavors.

"THINKING": THE INFLUENCE OF PERCEIVED CONTROL

Early speculations that beliefs about the controllability of stressors might moderate their impact sparked an enthusiastic response among stress researchers. Using Rotter's (1966) locus-of-control scale, or derivatives of it, they searched for the covariation between perceived control and symptoms that had been missing between life events and illness. Unfortunately, these renewed efforts proved no more successful.

In attempts to relate control to the degree of stress experienced, a number of studies indicated that individuals with greater personal control (i.e., internals) experienced less self-reported anxiety and strain; this relationship held in samples of college students (Hountras & Scharf, 1970) and patients awaiting surgery (Lowery, Jacobsen, & Keane, 1975). However, other investigations showed no differences between internals and externals in self-reported anxiety, using similar populations of college students (Houston, 1972) and presurgical patients (Auerbach, Kendell, Cottler, & Levitt, 1976). And still others revealed internal control beliefs to be associated with *more* stress, as assessed by self-report measures in patient samples (Cromwell, Butterfield, Brayfield, & Curry, 1977) and physiological measures in student samples (Houston, 1972).

Similarly confusing results were obtained in attempts to relate locus of control directly to indices of physical health. Following myocardial infarctions, for example, externals were found to spend more days in the coronary care unit, and to have higher temperatures and sedimentation rates while there (Cromwell et al., 1977). Yet others reported internals to require longer hospitalization following heart attacks (Garrity, 1973), or surgery (Johnson, Leventhal, & Dabbs, 1971).

Nor was the picture any clearer when psychiatric symptoms were considered. Externality was found to be associated with more severe depression (Ganellen & Blaney, 1984) and schizophrenia (Cash & Stack, 1973; Lottman & DeWolfe, 1972), even when the number of stressors experienced was controlled (Wheaton, 1985). However, no relationship was found between locus of control and contemplation of suicide (Lambley & Silbowitz, 1973), or clinical forms of anxiety (Wheaton, 1985). And the majority of studies found more internal than external beliefs in populations of substance abusers (Berzins & Ross, 1973; Calicchia, 1974; Goss & Morosku, 1970; Oziel, Obitz, & Keyson, 1972; Smithyman, Plant, & Southern, 1974).

In short, contradictory findings emerged over a wide range of stress and illness outcomes. If it is to be maintained that perceived control is an important moderator of stress, these findings can be taken to mean that locus of control is not an appropriate measure of this construct. Or it may be that, in their haste to incorporate control indices in their studies, stress researchers seized upon locus of control questionnaires without completely understanding their theoretical underpinnings. In fact, both seem to be true.

Rotter (1966) believed that generalized control beliefs, such as locus of control, exert an influence on behavior only in situations completely unfamiliar to a person. In all others, a person would have formed situation-specific control beliefs that take precedence over the more general ones. For example, unless one had never taken an exam before, perceived control over success on a midterm would likely be based on situational appraisals of the course content, professor, and previous quiz performance—rather than on global estimates of the efficacy of one's behavior in academic, social, political, and all other of life's arenas. In light of this, it is not surprising that locus of control has limited predictive power in terms of health outcomes; such generalized beliefs should only be influential in those stressful situations wholly novel to the person. And even in such situations, locus of control would influence only initial appraisals of the stressor, giving way to more situation-specific estimates of control with time (Folkman, 1984).

The need for more situational indices of control has been recognized in several, more recent investigations. Some researchers have attempted to develop "sphere-specific" measures, that is, pertaining only to perceived control over health-related experiences. Yet even these have proven too global to be of much predictive value; in their review of studies using such measures, Wallston and Wallston (1980) ended on a discouraged note: "it is much too simplistic to believe that health locus of control beliefs will ever predict very much of the variance in health behavior by itself" (p. 57).

The failure of even such middle-ground measures seems to underscore Rotter's (1966) admonition that general and situational estimates of control may not always correspond. In fact, one study (Parkes, 1984) has shown a lack of association between locus of control and more situation-specific appraisals, while another has demonstrated that general and situation indices can yield completely opposite patterns of perceived controllability. Rosenbaum and Palmon (1984) found that, among epileptics, health locus of control beliefs decreased (i.e., became more external) with increasing incidence of seizures, while estimates of situational control were highest in those with the most seizures. Such findings suggest that researchers should incorporate situation-specific measures of control, even if these entail using nonstandardized items.

The researchers who have used such measures have met with greater success in predicting health-related outcomes. For example, the degree of control that secondary students reported over typical anxiety-provoking situations related to the amount of anxiety experienced in such situations (Magnusson & Olah, 1983). Similarly, control over daily events was found to be associated with greater life satisfaction, and lower incidence of morbidity in several studies of the elderly (Rodin, Bohm, & Wack, 1982). In a study by the author (Amirkhan, 1984), nearly 1,000 randomly sampled community residents described recent stressors in their lives, and rated these on several dimensions of controllability. A composite "control over event" scale significantly predicted satisfactory resolution of these problems. Bandura (1986) speculated that perceived control over a stressor might have direct physiological consequences, making the individual more constitutionally resistant to its impact. He cited a study in which phobic subjects were assigned to fearful situations varying in controllability; those in the least controllable situation exhibited the highest heart rates and levels of catecholamine activity, in addition to the highest subjective ratings of distress. In a more detailed investigation of these physiological effects, Bandura and his colleagues (Bandura, O'Leary, Taylor, Gauthier, & Gossard, 1987) found that perceived control worked through both opoid and nonopoid neural mechanisms to buffer the impact of experimentally induced stressors.

However, even among studies using situation-specific control measures, confusing and contradictory results have emerged. In women with breast cancer, for example, it was found that a sense of personal control over the disorder related positively to adjustment—but so did a belief that others controlled the illness (Taylor et al., 1984). Delineating different types of control did nothing to clarify these findings: Cognitive control related positively to adjustment, informational control related curvilinearly, behavioral control had variable effects, and retrospective control did not relate at all. Equally confusing findings emerged from a study of child oncology patients (Worchel, Copeland, & Barker, 1987) in which a belief in others' control over the illness again predicted adjustment. Examining avenues of personal control, it was found that behavioral control was most strongly associated with adjustment, but ironically related to *poorer* adjustment. Cognitive and decisional control had weaker, though positive, effects; and informational control had no effect at all.

Such ambiguous findings may well be attributed to residual ambiguity in the definition of control itself. While progress has been made by narrowing general conceptions of control to more situationally specific ones, further specificity is still necessary. This apparently is not a matter of distinguishing the routes through which control may be exercised (cognitive, behavioral, etc.), since such distinctions have not proven useful in clarifying the consequences of control perceptions. Rather, it may be more important to specify, as Folkman (1984) so succinctly put it, "Control over what?" Folkman herself speculated that perceived control over the emotions engendered by a stressful event could have quite different consequences than control over situational aspects of the event. Likewise, Ganellen and Blaney (1984) suggested that the impact of perceived control over the occurrence of a stressor may be distinct from that of control over the event's outcome. And, the study of victims of breast cancer (Taylor et al., 1984) showed that those who assumed control for its occurrence suffered poor adjustment, while those who believed they had control over their recovery fared relatively well.

Ambiguity in the relationship between perceived control and illness may also be due to the fact that this relationship has been assumed to be linear. That is, the hypothesis common to a majority of these investigations was that maximal, rather than optimal, levels of control would be beneficial. Some critics (e.g., Ell, 1986; Folkman, 1984) have questioned this assumption, and some studies have provided disconfirmatory evidence. It may be recalled that among women with breast cancer, too little or too much informational control was found detrimental to adjustment. And a similar curvilinear relationship was revealed between "mastery" (a sense of personal control) and depression (Wheaton, 1985).

It is noteworthy that within attribution theory, guidelines for disentangling the contradictory findings regarding control and illness can be found. First, the theory suggests that the primary focus of control perceptions is neither on the occurrence of a stressful event per se nor its anticipated outcome, but rather on one's successes or failures in dealing with that event. The student failing a midterm is said to attend more to the causes of the poor performance than to the reasons for the test itself or the long-term implications for graduate school admission. Analogously, it is implied that in a stressful situation, such as divorce, a person will reflect not so much on the spouse's decision to leave, or the eventual impact on job and family, as the causes for the disagreements that precipitated the break-up. By specifying the focal point of control perceptions— including that suggested by attribution theory—in their measures, researchers might well alleviate some of the ambiguity in this body of findings.

A portion of this ambiguity, however, may be traced to the unidimensional nature of research hypotheses in this field. In addition to controllability, attribution theory indicates at least two other perceptual dimensions are critical to the prediction of an event's impact (Weiner, 1985, 1986). In contemplating the reasons for their respective failures, both the student and the ex-spouse would likely consider the *locus* of the cause ("Was it something about me?"), and its *stability* ("Was it something that can be changed?"), as well as its controllability

("Was it something that I can change?"). In that each dimension is said to contribute uniquely to an event's emotional and behavioral effects, the assessment of all three would seem necessary to anticipate accurately the full spectrum of consequences.

Finally, attribution theory may prove useful in reducing the confusion surrounding optimal levels of control. According to the theory, humans are fundamentally truth-seekers, regardless of how painful the truth might be, because accurate information maximizes their opportunities for adaptation (Weiner, 1985). Knowing the real reason for an academic or marital failure allows the individual not only to predict the likelihood of future repetitions of the event, but often to control recurrences through adjustments in behavior. The absolute level of perceived control, then, may not be as relevant to stress-related outcomes as the veridicality of those perceptions. The fact that both very low and very high levels of control have been linked to illness could be taken to indicate that such extreme beliefs are likely nonveridical, and hence maladaptive.

"DOING": THE INFLUENCE OF COPING

In many of the studies presented thus far, a second error was made in the application of Rotter's theory. Rotter (1966) believed generalized control to be one of several cognitive determinants of behavior. An appropriate application of locus-of-control scales in stress research, then, would be to the prediction of coping behaviors, rather than the more distal illness states. If differences in perceived control do relate to different types of coping, which in turn are differentially effective (sometimes ameliorating, but sometimes exacerbating stress), this could explain the inconsistencies found in control-to-illness correlations.

Discussion of the links between perceived control and coping, however, is problematic, due to a lack of consensus regarding the definition of coping. Common knowledge would seem to indicate that any efforts made to reduce stress should be considered coping; yet there has been considerable disagreement among researchers as to whether such a definition includes both palliative and problem-solving efforts, cognitive as well as behavioral responses, the defenses along with more conscious and logical processes (Folkman & Lazarus, 1980; Haan, 1977; Mechanic, 1974; Moos & Billings, 1982). Despite such disagreements, there is a tradition in the literature recognizing two distinct classes of behavior as comprising coping (Averill & Rosenn, 1972; Byrne, 1964; Folkman & Lazarus, 1980; Miller, 1987; Roth & Cohen, 1986). One is a set of efforts aimed at eliminating the stressor (perhaps modern derivatives of primitive "fight" tendencies), such as gathering information, planning courses of action, and enacting instrumental behaviors. The other is a group of responses focused on minimizing negative affect (perhaps related to ancient "flight" tendencies), which includes avoidance, in terms of both physical withdrawal and psychological escape through the use of distraction, fantasy, and denial. To these, the author's own factor-analytic investigations (Amirkhan, 1984, 1990) suggest the addition of a third category: Seeking social support. Derivative of primal tendencies to seek human contact in times of crisis, such a strategy makes sense in light of the voluminous literature documenting the benefits of social support. Furthermore, this strategy cannot be comfortably placed in either problem-solving or emotion-focused categories, since support is sometimes sought for advice and material aid, sometimes for distraction and comfort, and sometimes for other reasons altogether. In order to compare the results of the following studies, a taxonomy composed of all three categories—Problem Solving, Emotion-Focused, and Support Seeking—will be employed.

However, one other hindrance to interpretation of the findings must first be noted. In evaluating control-to-coping links, many researchers have failed to distinguish these concepts, assuming them to be melded in a unitary process (Husaini & Von Frank, 1985; Taylor et al., 1984; Worchel et al., 1987). It would seem more reasonable first to treat perceived control and coping responses as separate entities, allowing ties between them to be demonstrated empirically. Rotter (1966), in fact, considered control beliefs to be distinct antecedents of behavior, a perspective seen in attribution theory and many current theories of coping (e.g., Lazarus & Folkman, 1984; Moos & Billings, 1982).

Studies appropriately using locus of control to predict coping, rather than symptomology, have yielded only somewhat consistent results. One study found that children with internal beliefs used confrontative and instrumental strategies in stressful situations, while those with external beliefs turned to passive and avoidant strategies (Rothbaum, Wolfer, & Visintainer, 1979). These results were replicated in samples of children awaiting surgery (LaMontagne, 1984) and first-year nursing students (Parkes, 1984). Within adult patient populations, too, internals have been found to use more instrumental responses, particularly in terms of seeking information about their condition (Lowery & DuCette, 1976; Seeman & Evans, 1962; Wallston & Wallston, 1980). However, such findings did not generalize to patients with other disorders (Wallston & Wallston, 1980), or even to similarly diagnosed patients who had suffered the condition longer (Lowery & DuCette, 1976). Furthermore, inconsistencies have been noted in student populations. One study found that generalized control beliefs did not predict either problem-solving or avoidant strategies, though internals did make greater use of social supports (Grace & Schill, 1986). Yet others have shown no association between locus of control and social supports (Richman & Flaherty, 1985), or have found externals more likely to seek support (Husaini & Von Frank, 1985).

Even in these more correct applications of locus of control, then, there are contradictions. Once again, it may be that the generalized measure failed to depict accurately situation-specific control beliefs. In fact, studies utilizing more specific indices of control have produced less ambiguous findings. Persons suffering uncontrollable illnesses (arthritis and cancer) were found to use more avoidant strategies, while instrumental coping was more frequently used in conjunction with controllable disorders such as hypertension and diabetes (Felton & Revenson, 1984). Similar associations were found when control was measured in the context of marital conflicts (Elliot, Trief, & Stein, 1986) or problems common to a student population (Magnusson & Olah, 1983).

Other studies did not measure situational control per se, but rather used perceptions regarding the "changeability" of the event to predict coping. Persons who appraised stressors as changeable used more problem-directed and instrumental forms of coping (Folkman & Lazarus, 1980; Folkman, Lazarus, Dunkel–Schetter, DeLongis, & Gruen, 1986; Krantz, 1983; Vitaliano, Russo, Carr, Maiuro, & Becker, 1985), and also made greater use of social supports (Vitaliano et al., 1985). On the other hand, those who believed they "must accept" the stressful situation because of limited opportunities for change tended toward emotion-focused strategies (Folkman & Lazarus, 1980; Folkman et al., 1986). Limitations to this trend have been noted, however. Parkes (1984) found perceptions of changeability to be linked to coping responses only in persons with generalized internal loci of control, and not in externals. Another study found that emotion-focused forms of coping did not vary across changeable and unchangeable situations, though problem-focused strategies did. And even this weak effect held true only in major stressful events, not in more chronic "daily hassles" (Forsythe & Compas, 1987).

While measures of changeability no doubt tap situation-specific control beliefs, they still beg the question, "Control over what?" Some investigators have attempted to answer this question by measuring perceived control over the occurrence of stressful states. One study found that when asked to name the cause of their symptoms, elderly subjects who gave an uncontrollable cause (aging) were more likely to use passive, emotion-assuaging strategies, and less likely to seek medical treatment (Prohaska et al., 1987). Other studies, too, have linked control over a stressor's occurrence with active, problem-solving approaches (Baumgardner et al., 1986; Rodin et al., 1982), and lack of control to avoidant strategies (Rodin et al., 1982). Stone and Neale (1984) found control over occurrence to be negatively related to passive, emotion-focused forms of coping, but not related at all to direct, instrumental efforts. They speculated that direct action may be related to perceived control over the outcome, rather than the onset, of a stressful event. Using a composite scale of control over both outcome and occurrence, the present author indeed found links to problem-solving coping, but not to avoidance or use of social supports (Amirkhan, 1984). Though they have not wholly eliminated ambiguities in the findings, these studies underscore the necessity of delineating control beliefs according to their foci. Inclusion of the focus specified by attribution theory might have provided even greater clarification of control-to-coping linkages.

However, specification of the focal points of control beliefs will probably not, in itself, perfect the prediction of coping behaviors. Assessment of all the attributional dimensions would also be necessary; in fact, the theory indicates that dimensions *other* than controllability are germane to anticipating the form of the ensuing response (Weiner, 1985, 1986). Specifically, given a cause selected to explain a failure, the locus of that cause is said to influence the emotional aftermath of the event. Internal causes produce negative emotions linked to decrements in self-esteem (such as shame or guilt), which could exacerbate an already painful situation. The stability of the cause, on the other hand, influences expectations for recurrences of the failure, with unstable causes offering hope for more positive outcomes in the future. Together, these dimensions provide the "expectancies" and affective "values" that determine the likelihood of subsequent problem-solving behavior. Internal and unstable causes couple high negative affect with high expectancies for change, motivating efforts to reverse the failure. External and stable causes, however, produce resignation, hopelessness, and less instrumental (though perhaps more palliative) types of behavior.

Of course, the controllability dimension is also influential according to the theory, though more in determining the amplitude than the type of response. If the cause of a failure is perceived to be controllable, a greater intensity and persistence in behavior is said to ensue than following uncontrollable causes.

Some stress researchers have already attempted to link perceptions of control to the intensity, rather than the form, of coping efforts. Ganellen and Blaney (1984) proposed that persons seeing little opportunity to control a stressor would put less effort into coping. Similarly, low levels of control have been said to relate to lower motivation, and less persistence in coping (Baumgardner et al., 1986; Folkman, 1984). Parkes (1984) verified that the number of coping responses actually does vary as a function of appraisals of controllability. There is, however, a potential pitfall in this line of research: When individuals are compared in terms of the number of coping efforts, there is often an implicit value judgment that coping is uniformly beneficial ("the more, the better"). In opposition to such assumptions, many studies have shown greater intensity of coping effort to be associated with *more* pathology (Forsythe & Compas, 1987; Wheaton, 1985; Worchel et al., 1987).

Different control beliefs thus do seem to relate to different types, and different numbers, of coping behaviors; the question remains as to whether such behaviors are differentially effective. Assumptions about the benefits of coping have been shown to be dangerous, and empirical study shows them to be simplistic as well. Links between coping responses and outcomes have proven to be quite complex. Some studies have shown instrumental strategies to be generally superior to others (Altmaier & Happ, 1985; Felton & Revenson, 1984; Folkman et al., 1986), but others have shown no particular long-term benefits for problem-directed responses (Amirkhan, 1984; Gross, 1986; Krantz, 1983). The social support literature clearly indicates that utilization of such resources should be health promoting, yet this strategy has been linked to increased psychiatric symptomology (Aldwin & Revenson, 1987). And avoidant strategies, though they do nothing to eliminate the source of stress, have been demonstrated to reduce pain (Bandura et al., 1987) and anxiety (McMurray, Bell, Fusillo, & Morgan, 1986).

It seems clear, then, that no one form of coping is consistently beneficial or detrimental. Most current theories instead emphasize that the "fit" between a coping strategy and the type of stressor is the primary determinant of an adaptive outcome (Cameron & Meichenbaum, 1982; Lazarus & Folkman, 1984; Moos & Billings, 1982; Wheaton, 1985). People utilizing problem-solving responses in situations that are truly uncontrollable may experience fatigue and frustration, which increase vulnerability to illness. Conversely, deployment of emotion-focused strategies in controllable situations may delay, or prevent, instrumental attempts to remove the source of stress. Forsythe and Compas (1987), in fact, demonstrated that the match between type of coping and type of stressor is a more powerful predictor of psychological adjustment than the nature of the coping strategy itself.

These findings verify the attributional position regarding the importance of veridical appraisal of an event. They also provide a mechanism for explaining the detrimental consequences of extreme control beliefs. Very high (i.e., exaggerated) levels of control are paradoxically maladaptive because they may lead to an overapplication of the problem-solving strategy, beyond its range of effectiveness. By the same argument, the negative consequences of too little control could arise from the underutilization of instrumental responses, resulting in unnecessarily prolonged exposure to the source of stress. Thus, as intimated by attribution theory, it may not be the degree of perceived control per se that accounts for its curvilinear relationship with adjustment. Rather, it is that non-veridical assessments of the situation may lead to misapplications of coping strategies, which in turn exacerbate stress reactions.

CONTROL AND COPING: CAUSAL CHRONOLOGIES

While it is important to distinguish control, coping, and outcome for the purpose of empirical investigation, it seems clear that they are complexly entwined in stressful episodes. Researchers have reported that highly intracorrelated clusters of control perceptions, coping responses, and symptoms make it difficult to discuss one process without consideration of the other two (Aldwin & Revenson, 1987; Magnusson & Olah, 1984). Unfortunately, in attempting to specify the causal relations within such clusters, unjustified assumptions once again have been made.

In this case, it seems that early investigations may have erred by too closely following, rather than by misinterpreting, Rotter's (1966) theory. The time-line of his theory is clearly prospective, in that current perceptions are identified as determinants of future behaviors. Most locus-of-control studies, in reality, only correlated these beliefs with existing illness states or coping patterns. However, when it came to interpreting these correlations, it was assumed, in line with Rotter's theory, that the control beliefs had preceded the choice of coping strategy or the emergence of symptoms. Clearly, such conclusions were unjustified; perceptions of control could just as well have been the result of coping or illness experiences.

A number of current theories of coping endorse the prospective chronology (e.g., Cameron & Meichenbaum, 1982; Lazarus & Folkman, 1984; Moos & Billings, 1982). The assumption is that the advent of a stressor is immediately followed by appraisals of the event; these situation-specific beliefs then influence the choice of coping response, which in turn determines the event outcome. Longitudinal studies have verified parts of this causal model. For example, it has been shown (using both general and situation-specific measures) that control beliefs can precede coping behaviors (Husaini & Von Frank, 1985; Krantz, 1983). Time 1–Time 2 comparisons have also been used to show that coping behavior precedes affective and pathological outcomes (Felton & Revenson, 1984; Husaini & Von Frank, 1985).

But theorists have also questioned the rigid unidirectionality implicit in this model. Monitoring the successes and failures of coping efforts, it has been argued, could cause shifts in control perceptions (Fleming, Baum, & Singer, 1984); or, as expressed by Folkman (1984), "Control expectancies are outcomes as well as antecedents" (p. 848). Consistent with this argument is the finding that beliefs regarding the controllability of the stressor's occurrence do not emerge right away, but rather late in the coping episode (Taylor et al., 1984), perhaps after a period of monitoring coping effectiveness. There is also Ell's (1986) suggestion that utilization of social supports alters an individual's beliefs about the controllability of a stressor. And a number of studies have demonstrated that training in coping skills precipitates changes in control perceptions (Altmaier & Happ, 1985; Bandura, 1986; McMurray et al., 1986).

Further evidence that coping may precede control in the causal chronology arises from path analyses of correlational data. In an investigation of the health and life satisfaction of a group of elderly subjects (reported in Rodin et al., 1982), perceived control was found to be strongly related to activity but the only significant correlate of the outcome variable. Similarly, the author (Amirkhan, 1984) found that perceived control was significantly associated with both problem solving and a positive outcome, though problem solving itself did not relate to the event outcome. Assuming the traditional chronology, both studies tested path models in which control was placed prior to behavior and outcome. The results of these tests can be summarized diagramatically as:

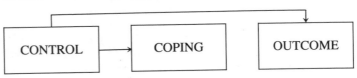

This sequence, however, is not logical: There appears no reason that control beliefs should lead to coping since the beliefs themselves more consistently influence the outcome than do the coping activities. A more palatable model, describing the same pattern of associations, would have been:

In this sequence, it is clear that coping efforts are rewarded with changes in perceived control, which in turn diminish the degree of stress experienced. Such a model is compatible with conceptualizations of "mastery" and "self-efficacy" as mediators of the coping-to-outcome relationship (Bandura, 1986; Elliot et al., 1986).

In short, there is evidence that parts of the traditional model are correct: Control and coping processes both seem to precede the onset of stress and illness. However, the relationship between control and coping is debatable. Some findings support the prospective chronology, in which control perceptions are antecedents to coping; yet, there is also support for a retrospective sequence, in which control beliefs are built upon assessments of past coping performance. Rather than arguing for one perspective or the other, it would seem wise to heed Folkman's (1984) admonition, and acknowledge reciprocity between control and coping—a bidirectional causal sequence, integrating prospective and retrospective chronologies.

Interestingly, attribution theory offers just such an integration. In part retrospective, the theory indicates that people review their past behaviors and outcomes in the causal search process. And it does make sense that the victim of a violent crime, for example, would reflect back on his or her failure to take precautionary measures. Yet the theory is also clearly prospective, in that the type of cause chosen will dictate future emotions, expectancies, and behaviors. It is obvious that the victim will experience bad feelings resulting from the assault itself, and attribution theory recognizes such "outcome-dependent affects" (Weiner, 1985, 1986). But knowing the attribution for the failure, and how this cause was viewed in terms of locus, stability, and controllability, allows for a much more fine-grained and comprehensive prediction of the victim's reactions. Specifically, it can be anticipated whether the bad feelings will be compounded with loss of self-esteem, whether the person will come to expect future victimization, and whether he or she will become resigned to such recurrences or fight energetically to prevent them.

That attribution theory recognizes bidirectional causality between perceptions and behaviors is probably not coincidental. The theory's assumption that humans seek truth to maximize adaptation seems to demand acknowledgment of such reciprocity. In a stressful situation, for example, it is unlikely that veridical information could accrue from initial impressions of the situation itself. Rather, input regarding the success or failure of deployed coping behaviors would also seem necessary. If prior coping efforts had not worked to alter the situation or its emotional concomitants, such information would be valuable in adjusting perceptions, and ensuring a shift to more appropriate strategies.

APPLYING ATTRIBUTION THEORY

After years of research into control, coping, and stress, the lessons learned have been that situation-specific control beliefs have greater predictive power than more general ones; that perceived control should also be specified in terms of its focus; that consequences of control should be measured both in terms of coping behaviors and stress-related outcomes; and that the veridicality of control assessments may be more relevant to adaptation than the absolute degree of control perceived. Furthermore, control, coping, and stress-related outcomes should be considered distinct processes, and linkages among them (including bidirectional ones) established empirically, rather than by assumption. It is ironic that all of these hard-earned lessons had been anticipated by attribution theory. Not only does the theory endorse these viewpoints, but suggests others that could prove useful in pointing future stress research in maximally productive directions.

To review the attributional perspective, and emphasize its applicability to stress research, consider what must surely be among the most trying of stressful events: Imagine that you had just been diagnosed as having a serious form of cancer. Under such negative and perhaps unanticipated circumstances, it is likely that you would seek a causal explanation. However, you would probably not dwell on the cause of the illness itself, which would no doubt be attributed to some vaguely understood physiological processes explained by the physician. Rather, you would probably reflect on the causes of the actions that brought you to such a state—your failure to quit smoking, for example. Your search for the cause of this failure would be an objective process, in the sense that self-serving rationalizations would be bypassed in order to reach a veridical explanation. Yet your search would also be highly subjective, in that you would decide for yourself which among several possible causes seemed most plausible. Having decided on a cause, you would then typify it according to the attributional dimensions, a process that is also highly idiosyncratic and often unconscious. If the cause was perceived to be internal, unstable, and controllable (such as "I just didn't try hard enough to quit"), it is likely you would suffer considerable negative affect though you would also have hope for a reversal of the failure and consequently the disease process itself. In this case, highly motivated, persistent and instrumental forms of coping would be expected. On the other hand, had you selected a more external, stable, and uncontrollable cause (e.g., "Life's pressures make it impossible to give up smoking"), there would still be considerable stress (though unencumbered by feelings such as guilt or shame) coupled with an attitude of resignation. Ensuing coping would likely be less effortful, and aimed at assuaging the emotions rather than reversing the situation. In either case, your retrospective analysis of past performance would influence your present feelings and activities, and ultimately the future outcome, including the possibility of a remission.

Perhaps unintentionally using the attributional perspective, some early studies focused on the perceived causes of illness, and specifically the consequences of attributions to "self." One such study found that cancer victims who blamed themselves for their condition experienced more distress, used less problem solving and more avoidant forms of coping than those who blamed external circumstances (Abrams & Finesinger, 1953). However, positive consequences of self-blame were also reported: Fully 50% of disabled accident victims saw themselves as responsible, and yet exhibited superior adjustment to others who saw the tragedies as random events (Bulman & Wortman, 1977). It was felt that self-blame, for all its emotional side-effects, might impart a feeling of control over the event that is missing if external, capricious forces are blamed (Chodoff, Friedman, & Hamburg, 1964).

More contemporary studies, deliberately incorporating attribution theory, have also produced contradictory results. Taylor and her associates (1984) found that 95% of breast cancer victims generated attributions for their condition, though these specific causes did not predict their level of adjustment. When the researchers grouped the causes into broad categories, however, "self" attributions were found to relate curvilinearly to adjustment, with high and low levels of self-blame proving maladaptive. In another study, epileptics were asked to choose among several possible causes for their seizures, and also rate the degree to which they blamed themselves, others, or the environment. In this case, no relationship with adjustment was found for either the specific attributions or the self-blame and other ratings (Rosenbaum & Palmon, 1984). And among mothers of chronically ill children, most were found to attribute the illnesses to environmental factors and adjust well, while the minority who blamed their own behaviors seemed more distressed (Affleck et al., 1985).

It may appear, then, that attribution theory has done little to rid stress research of ambiguous findings. But the contradictory results may once again have been due to errors made in the application of a theory.

First, all of the studies assessed attributions for the occurrence of the stressful event, rather than utilizing the focus specified by the theory.

Second, the studies attempted to link level of adjustment directly to the cause that had been selected, while the theory indicates that it is the dimensions underlying a cause that dictate the consequences. While some studies did try to typify the causes, they did so according to dimensions other than the attributional. Furthermore, the classifications were performed by the experimenters, ignoring the theory's admonition that the process is idiosyncratic. Perhaps some subjects perceived "self" to be an internal, stable, and uncontrollable cause (e.g., genetic makeup), while others saw it as an internal, unstable, and controllable cause (e.g., lack of effort in following a regimen). Such idiosyncratic interpretations could have produced the differential affective reactions documented in these studies.

Third, most of the studies focused only on such emotional reactions, while the theory directs attention toward both affective and behavioral consequences of attributions.

Other investigations, applying attribution theory with greater fidelity, have in fact produced more consistent results. One study of college students found attributions linked to the choice of coping strategies (Baumgardner et al., 1986, Study 1). Those who attributed typical adolescent problems to internal, unstable, and controllable causes (such as lack of effort) did tend to use instrumental responses, and were said to persist longer in their coping efforts. Another study, using a similar population, found attributions to be tied to both coping behaviors and affective reactions (Wack, 1981, as reported in Rodin et al., 1982). College students were asked to keep a diary of daily stressors, and rate the cause of each event on attributional dimensions. Causes perceived as controllable were once again found linked to active, instrumental coping responses. Events seen as having more stable and global causes, however, were rated more "bothersome" (creating feelings of frustration and helplessness), and produced avoidant forms of coping (withdrawal and the use of distraction).

Perhaps these studies fared better because they allowed subjective categorization of the causes, and they examined behavioral, not just affective, consequences. However, they still erred in focusing on perceived causes for the occurrence of the stressor, rather than for previous outcomes. A series of recent investigations were more accurate in this regard, although, as will be seen, they erred in other ways.

Seligman (1986) looked for cross-situational consistencies in attributions for success and failure, and labeled these as "explanatory styles." Citing longitudinal evidence, he showed that those who tend to attribute failures to internal, stable, and global causes are particularly at risk for later helplessness and depression, as well as physical morbidity and even mortality. Altmaier and Happ (1985) demonstrated that explanatory style is linked to coping behavior as well as health outcomes. They found that training people in problem-solving modes of coping produced high expectancies for future success and an immunity to learned helplessness. These effects were said to be mediated by changes in attributional style: Those who had gone through coping training more consistently used skill and effort attributions, a pattern unaffected even by occasional failure experiences.

Others outside the helplessness camp have also found evidence for a personological style in explaining past outcomes, and have linked this to both coping and health. Bandura (1986) argued that persons with high "self-efficacy" tend to attribute success to internal factors and failures to aspects of the situation. Self-efficacy was shown to relate to instrumental coping, persistence in coping, and increased tolerance for pain. Similarly, self-described "problem solvers" were found to attribute success to internal, and failure to external, causes more consistently than other people (Baumgardner et al., 1986, Study 2). In general, problem solvers made more use of effort and ability attributions, which was taken as evidence of a greater sense of personal control over life events. They were also said to have "fewer personal problems, greater motivation to approach and solve problems, fewer depressive symptomologies, fewer dysfunctional thoughts, and higher self-esteem" (p. 637).

Contrary to such findings, Follette and Jacobson (1987) reported that the supposedly maladaptive attribution of failure to internal, stable, and global causes was associated with increased motivation to problem-solve. The contradiction in findings may have resulted from an error common to all of these studies: the failure to measure directly the controllability dimension. While categorization by locus, stability, and even globality was assessed, these dimensions cannot be assumed to reflect perceived controllability of the cause. Stupidity and chronic laziness, for example, may both be considered internal, stable, and global causes for failure, and yet the latter seems much more controllable. In that each of the attributional dimensions is said to contribute in a unique way to behavioral and affective reactions, overlooking any one dimension is bound to limit the predictability of those reactions.

Another problem common to these studies is their focus on characterological attribution styles. This problem parallels that encountered in investigations of generalized locus of control beliefs: Cross-situational styles are probably not very good indicators of situation-specific attributions, and the latter would seem far more relevant to the eventual outcome of that particular situation. In fact, it has been demonstrated that explanatory styles do not predict affective reactions to failure, while situation-specific attributions do (Follette & Jacobson, 1987). A focus on generalized attributional tendencies thus seems a step backwards in stress research.

Besides, it is debatable whether such styles actually exist. One study found so much variation in the attributions made by problem solvers as to "discourage a notion of general attributional style" (Baumgardner et al., 1986, p. 639). In addition, the assumption of such styles implies that people disregard characteristics of the situation in forming causal explanations, and must therefore often make nonveridical assessments of life events. This clearly violates a central tenet of attribution theory. Moreover, it has been argued here and elsewhere (e.g., Cameron & Meichenbaum, 1982) that such nonveridical appraisals are ultimately maladaptive, in that they lead to inappropriate coping and exacerbated stress reactions. It is difficult to see, then, how any cross-situational consistency in attributions, which precludes veridical assessment at least some of the time, could be claimed to be health enhancing (as in Altmaier & Happ, 1985; Rodin et al., 1982).

While none of the attributional investigations has been completely accurate in application of the theory, it is interesting that the closer approximations have provided the more replicable results. These studies show consistent relationships among attributions and affects, behaviors, and even symptoms. But even the more flawed of the studies are useful in pointing out ways in which the theory can be more precisely, and hopefully more productively, utilized in stress research:

First, attribution theory provides a specific answer to the researcher's question, "Control over what?" In the past, some have insisted that perceived control over a stressor's occurrence is the appropriate focus; and studies have in fact shown these perceptions to have predictive power (Baumgardner et al., 1986, Study 1), though perhaps limited (Stone & Neale, 1984). However, others have argued that control over the stressor's impending outcome is a more crucial focus (Cameron & Meichenbaum, 1982; Ganellen & Blaney, 1984; Stone & Neale, 1984; Taylor et al., 1984). Attribution theory indicates that it is neither of these, but rather perceived control over previous outcomes in the situation that is essential to the prediction of a stressor's impact. Perhaps the other foci are worthy of investigation, but they should not preclude assessment of control from the attributional perspective—as has most often been the case to date.

Second, attribution theory indicates that while all people are motivated to find veridical explanations for their experiences, the process is highly subjective and idiosyncratic. Subjects, then, should not be forced to choose among experimenter-provided causes, such as "self" or others, but instead be allowed to generate explanations of their own spontaneously. However, the exact causes generated are not so important as the way they are typified. Researchers must allow subjects to categorize their specified causes according to the attributional dimensions, since such classifications are said to be the most proximal predictors of affective and behavioral reactions.

Third, while most current stress research focuses only on controllability, attribution theory dictates that there are at least three critical dimensions underlying perceptions of a stressor. Perceived locus is important, as Rotter (1966) indicated, though not because it reflects controllability. Instead, this dimension is believed to dictate the affective value of an event, by determining the emotional overtones to the stress produced by the event itself. Perceived stability is also important, a fact that is becoming apparent in coping studies showing quite different reactions to chronic, recurring "hassles" as opposed to acute and temporary "life events" (Forsythe & Compas, 1987; Prohaska et al., 1987). The stability dimension is said to determine expectancies for a future successful outcome. Perceived controllability is, of course, an important dimension, as has been verified in the bulk of studies reviewed here. Attribution theory indicates that it is a dimension distinct from the other two, and thus should be assessed independently. While locus and stability perceptions provide the value and expectancy determinants of the type of coping response, perceived controllability is said to dictate the intensity and persistence of that behavior.

Fourth, the theory clearly considers the attribution process to be distinct from either antecedent events or behavioral and affective consequences. Some have proposed that the causal search is in itself a mode of coping (Folkman, 1984; Rodin et al., 1982), aimed primarily at assuaging unpleasant emotions aroused by the stressor (Folkman, 1984). Such interpretations contradict the basic premise of attribution theory, that people search for truth, whether or not it makes them feel better. And they also confound the process of searching for a cause with the consequences of the cause selected.

As has been argued previously, linkages among perceptions, coping, and stress-related outcomes should be explored empirically, rather than assumed. Attribution theory proposes a causal chronology that may serve as a starting point for such explorations. Perceived causes of previous successes or failures in dealing with a stressor are expected to influence future coping efforts and affective experiences in that stressful situation. This chronology is appealing, in that it synthesizes retrospective and prospective viewpoints. That is, it acknowledges that perceptions can both be built upon prior experiences, and serve as a foundation for future outcomes as well.

SUMMARY

The history of stress research is one characterized by contradiction. Even commonsense relationships, such as the one linking stressful events to illness, have eluded empirical verification. This is not to say that there have been no gains; in fact, control perceptions and coping strategies have been identified as mediating processes, and methodological lessons have been learned. However, these insights have been achieved at the tremendous expense of years of laborious, trial-and-error research. It has been argued here that attribution theory, particularly as advanced by Weiner (1979, 1985, 1986), might have curtailed expenditures in the past, and may still do so by providing direction for future studies.

The attributional perspective is entirely consistent with the hard-earned lessons gleaned from previous stress investigations. The theory endorses the idea of control as a critical dimension underlying the perception of stressors. And it indicates that situation-specific beliefs are most germane to the outcome of a stressful event, a fact that stress researchers have come to accept with the failure of generalized control measures. The theory also portrays humans as truth-seekers, bent on finding accurate explanations for their experiences—a perspective consistent with findings that veridical appraisals of stressors, and not exaggerated notions of control, are most adaptive.

Attribution theory also provides answers to conundrums facing future stress research. It specifies the aim of perceptual processes in times of duress as the search for causes to explain failure. And it indicates the crucial dimensions of these perceptions, acknowledging controllability, but identifying locus and stability as well. It directs researchers to look for specific consequences tied to these dimensions, all of which are relevant to the experience of stress: Negative affects, expectancies, coping behaviors, and persistence. Finally it provides a nonsimplistic model for the causal interplay of perceptions, affects, and behaviors. This model incorporates both the retrospective and prospective viewpoints seen in the stress literature, acknowledging complex relationships in which perceptions are both built upon prior stress experiences and influence future ones.

In the past, attribution researchers have been criticized for their ivory tower methodologies, giving very rational college subjects simulated experiences to tease apart the linkages between perceived causes and their varied consequences. Ironically, stress researchers may be accused of the opposite, focusing on *real* people in the midst of *real* experiences, yet lacking a strong paradigm to direct measurements. Perhaps a collaboration would prove mutually beneficial. Stress research could profit from the specific guidelines suggested by attribution theory, and attribution theory could gain from real-world tests of the linkages so carefully delineated in the laboratory.

REFERENCES

Abrams, R. D., & Finesinger, J. (1953). Guilt reactions in patients with cancer. *Cancer, 6,* 474–482.

Affleck, G., Allen, D. A., Tennen, H., McGrade, B. J., & Ratzan, S. (1985). Causal and control cognitions in parents' coping with chronically ill children. *Journal of Social and Clinical Psychology, 3,* 367–377.

Aldwin, C., & Revenson, T. A. (1987). Does coping help? A reexamination of the relation between coping and mental health. *Journal of Personality and Social Psychology, 53,* 337–348.

Altmaier, E. M., & Happ, D. (1985). Coping skill training's immunization effects against learned helplessness. *Journal of Social and Clinical Psychology, 3,* 181–189.

Amirkhan, J. H. (1984). *Stress, perceived control, and coping in a community sample.* Unpublished doctoral dessertation, University of California, Los Angeles.

Amirkhan, J. H. (in press). A factor analytically derived measure of coping: The Coping Strategy Indicator. *Journal of Personality and Social Psychology.*

Auerbach, S. M., Kendall, P. C., Cottler, H. F., & Levitt, N. R. (1976). Anxiety, locus of control, type of preparatory information, and adjustment to dental surgery. *Journal of Consulting and Clinical Psychology, 44,* 809–818.

Averill, J. R., & Rosenn, M. (1972). Vigilant and nonvigilant coping strategies and psychophysiological stress reactions during the anticipation of electric shock. *Journal of Personality and Social Psychology, 23,* 128–141.

Bandura, A. (1986). *Self-efficacy and health.* Keynote address, annual meeting of the Society for Behavioral Medicine, San Francisco.

Bandura, A., O'Leary, A., Taylor, C. B., Gauthier, J., & Gossard, D. (1987). Perceived self-efficacy and pain control: Opoid and nonopoid mechanisms. *Journal of Personality and Social Psychology, 53,* 563–571.

Baumgardner, A. H., Heppner, P. P., & Arkin, R. M. (1986). Role of causal attribution in personal problem-solving. *Journal of Personality and Social Psychology, 50,* 636–643.

Berzins, J. I., & Ross, W. (1973). Locus of control among opiate addicts. *Journal of Consulting and Clinical Psychology, 40,* 84–91.

Bulman, R. J., & Wortman, C. B. (1977). Attribution of blame and coping in the "real world": Severe accident victims react to their lot. *Journal of Personality and Social Psychology, 35,* 351–363.

Byrne, D. (1964). Repression-sensitization as a dimension of personality. In B. A. Maher (Ed.), *Progress in experimental personality research* (Vol. 1). New York: Academic.

Calicchia, J. P. (1974). Narcotic addiction and perceived locus of control. *Journal of Clinical Psychology, 30,* 499–504.

Cameron, R., & Meichenbaum, D. (1982). The nature of effective coping and the treatment of stress related problems: A cognitive-behavioral perspective. In L. Goldberger & S. Breznitz (Eds.), *Handbook of stress: Theoretical and clinical aspects.* New York: Free Press.

Cash, T. F., & Stack, J. J. (1973). Locus of control among schizophrenics and other hospitalized psychiatric patients. *Genetic Psychology Monographs, 87,* 105–122.

Chodoff, P., Friedman, S. B., & Hamburg, D. A. (1964). Stress, defenses, and coping behavior: Observations in parents of children with malignant disease. *American Journal of Psychiatry, 120,* 743–749.

Cohen, S., Glass, D. C., & Phillips, S. (1979). Environment and health. In H. E. Freeman & L. G. Reeder (Eds.), *Handbook of medical sociology.* Englewood Cliffs, NJ: Prentice–Hall.

Cromwell, R., Butterfield, E., Brayfield, F., & Curry, J. (1977). *Acute myocardial infarction: Reaction and recovery.* St. Louis: C. V. Mosby.

Dodge, D., & Martin, W. (1970). *Social stress and chronic illness.* Notre Dame, IN: University of Notre Dame Press.

Dubos, R. (1965). *Man adapting.* New Haven, CT: Yale University Press.

Ell, K. O. (1986). Coping with serious illness: On integrating constructs to enhance clinical research, assessment and intervention. *International Journal of Psychiatry in Medicine, 15,* 335–349.

Elliot, D. J., Trief, P. M., & Stein, N. (1986). Mastery, stress and coping in marriage among chronic pain patients. *Journal of Behavioral Medicine, 9,* 549–558.

Felton, B. J., & Revenson, T. A. (1984). Coping with chronic illness: A study of illness controllability and the influence of coping strategies on psychological adjustment. *Journal of Consulting and Clinical Psychology, 52,* 343–353.

Fleming, R., Baum, A., & Singer, J. E. (1984). Toward an integrative approach to the study of stress. *Journal of Personality and Social Psychology, 46,* 939–949.

Folkman, S. (1984). Personal control and stress and coping processes: A theoretical analysis. *Journal of Personality and Social Psychology, 46,* 839–853.

Folkman, S., & Lazarus, R. S. (1980). An analysis of coping in a middle-aged community sample. *Journal of Health and Social Behavior, 21,* 219–239.

Folkman, S., Lazarus, R. S., Dunkel–Schetter, C., DeLongis, A., & Gruen, R. J. (1986). Dynamics of a stressful encounter: Cognitive appraisal, coping, and encounter outcomes. *Journal of Personality and Social Psychology, 50,* 992–1003.

Follette, V. M., & Jacobson, N. S. (1987). Importance of attributions as a predictor of how people cope with failure. *Journal of Personality and Social Psychology, 52,* 1205–1211.

Forsythe, C. J., & Compas, B. (1987). Interaction of cognitive appraisals of stressful events and coping: Testing the goodness of fit hypothesis. *Cognitive Therapy and Research, 11,* 473–485.

Ganellen, R. J., & Blaney, P. H. (1984). Stress, externality and depression. *Journal of Personality and Social Psychology, 46,* 326–337.

Garrity, T. F. (1973). Vocational adjustment after first myocardial infarction: Comparative assessment of several variables suggested in the literature. *Social Science and Medicine, 7,* 705–717.

Goldberg, E. L., & Comstock, G. W. (1976). Life events and subsequent illness. *American Journal of Epidemiology, 104,* 146–158.

Goss, A., & Morosku, T. E. (1970). Relation between a dimension of internal-external control and the MMPI with an alcoholic population. *Journal of Consulting and Clinical Psychology, 34,* 189–192.

Grace, G. D., & Schill, T. (1986). Expectancy of personal control and seeking social support in coping style. *Psychological Reports, 58,* 757–758.

Gross, A. R. (1986). Pain following surgical intervention for lower back pain. *Psychosomatic Medicine, 48,* 229–241.

Haan, N. (1977). *Coping and defending.* New York: Academic.

Hinkle, L. E., & Wolff, H. G. (1958). Ecological investigations of the relationship between illness, life experiences, and the social environment. *Annals of Internal Medicine, 49,* 1373–1388.

Holmes, T., & Masuda, M. (1974). Life change and illness susceptibility. In B. S. Dohrenwend & B. P. Dohrenwend (Eds.), *Stressful life events: Their nature and effects.* New York: Wiley.

Holtzworth–Munroe, A., & Jacobson, N. S. (1985). Causal attributions of married couples: When do they search for causes? What do they conclude when they do? *Journal of Personality and Social Psychology, 48,* 1398–1412.

Hountras, P. T., & Scharf, M. (1970). Manifest anxiety and locus of control in low-achieving college males. *Journal of Psychology, 74,* 95–100.

Houston, B. K. (1972). Control over stress, locus of control, and response to stress. *Journal of Personality and Social Psychology, 21,* 249–255.

Husaini, B. A. & Von Frank, A. (1985). Life events, coping resources, and depression: A longitudinal study of direct, buffering, and reciprocal effects. *Research in Community and Mental Health, 5,* 111–136.

Jenkins, C. D. (1979). Psychological modifiers of response to stress. In J. E. Barett (Eds.), *Stress and mental disorder.* New York: Raven.

Johnson, J. E., Leventhal, H., & Dabbs, J. M. (1971). Contribution of emotional and instrumental response processes in adaptation to surgery. *Journal of Personality and Social Psychology, 20,* 55–64.

Krantz, S. E. (1983). Cognitive appraisals and problem-directed coping: A prospective study of stress. *Journal of Personality and Social Psychology, 44,* 638–643.

Lambley, P., & Silbowitz, M. (1973). Rotter's internal-external scale and prediction of suicide contemplators among students. *Psychological Reports, 33,* 585–586.

LaMontagne, L. (1984). Children's locus of control beliefs as predictors of preoperative coping behavior. *Nursing Research, 33,* 76–85.

Lazarus, R. S., Cohen, J. B., Folkman, S., Kanner, A., & Schaefer, C. (1980). Psychological stress and adaptation: Some unresolved issues. In H. Selye (Ed.), *Guide to stress research.* New York: Van Nostrand–Reinhold.

Lazarus, R. S., & Folkman, S. (1984). *Stress, appraisal and coping.* New York: Springer.

Lottman, T. J., & DeWolfe, A. S. (1972). Internal versus external control in reactive and process schizophrenia. *Journal of Consulting and Clinical Psychology, 39,* 344.

Lowery, B. J., & DuCette, J. P. (1976). Disease-related learning and disease control in diabetics as a function of locus of control. *Nursing Research, 25,* 358–362.

Lowery, B. J., Jacobsen, B., & Keane, A. (1975). Relationship of locus of control to preoperative anxiety. *Psychological Reports, 37,* 1115–1121.

Magnusson, D., & Olah, A. (1983). *Predictive control, action control, coping style, and state anxiety: An analysis of individuals and situations.* Report No. 613, Department of Psychology, University of Stockholm.

McMurray, N. E., Bell, R. J., Fusillo, A., & Morgan, M. (1986). Relationship between locus of control and effects of coping strategies on dental stress in children. *Child and Family Behavior Therapy, 8,* 1–17.

Mechanic, D. (1974). Social structure and personal adaptation: Some neglected dimensions. In G. V. Coelho, D. A. Hamburg, & J. E. Adams (Eds.), *Coping and adaptation.* New York: Basic Books.

Miller, S. M. (1987). Monitoring and blunting: Validation of a questionnaire to assess styles of information seeking under threat. *Journal of Personality and Social Psychology, 52,* 345–353.

Moos, R. H., & Billings, A. G. (1982). Conceptualizing and measuring coping resources and processes. In L. Goldberger & S. Breznitz (Eds.), *Handbook of stress: Theoretical and clinical aspects.* New York: Free Press.

Oziel, J. R., Obitz, F. W., & Keyson, M. (1972). General and specific perceived locus of control in alcoholism. *Psychological Reports, 30,* 957–958.

Parkes, K. R. (1984). Locus of control, cognitive appraisal, and coping in stressful episodes. *Journal of Personality and Social Psychology, 46,* 655–668.

Prohaska, T. R., Keller, M. L., Leventhal, E. A., & Leventhal, H. (1987). Impact of symptoms and aging attribution on emotions and coping. *Health Psychology, 6,* 495–514.

Rabkin, J. G., & Struening, E. L. (1976). Life events, stress, and illness. *Science, 194,* 1013–1020.

Rahe, R. H. (1975). Epidemiological studies of life change and illness. *International Journal of Psychiatry in Medicine, 6,* 133–146.

Richman, J., & Flaherty, J. (1985). Coping and depression: The relative contribution of internal and external resources during a life cycle transition. *Journal of Nervous and Mental Disease, 173,* 590–595.

Rodin J., Bohm, L. C., & Wack, J. T. (1982). Control, coping, and aging: Models for research and intervention. In L. Bickman (Ed.), *Applied social psychology annual (Vol. 3).* Beverly Hills, CA: Sage.

Rosenbaum, M., & Palmon, N. (1984). Helplessness and resourcefulness in coping with epilepsy. *Journal of Consulting and Clinical Psychology, 52,* 244–253.

Roth, S., & Cohen, L. J. (1986). Approach, avoidance, and coping with stress. *American Psychologist, 4,* 813–819.

Rothbaum, F., Wolfer, J., & Visintainer, M. (1979). Coping behavior and locus of control in children. *Journal of Personality, 47,* 118–135.

Rotter, J. B. (1966). Generalized expectancies for internal versus external control of reinforcement. *Psychological Monographs, 80,* 1–28.

Seeman, M., & Evans, J. W. (1962). Alienation and learning in a hospital setting. *American Sociological Review, 27,* 772–783.

Seligman, M. (1986). *Explanatory style and health.* Keynote address, annual meeting of the Society for Behavioral Medicine, San Francisco.

Smithyman, S. D., Plant, W. T., & Southern, M. L. (1974). Locus of control in two samples of chronic drug abusers. *Psychological Reports, 34,* 1293–1294.

Stone, A. A., & Neale, J. M. (1984). New measure of daily coping: Development and preliminary results. *Journal of Personality and Social Psychology, 46,* 892–906.

Taylor, S. E., Lichtman, R. R., & Wood, J. V. (1984). Attributions, beliefs about control, and adjustment to breast cancer. *Journal of Personality and Social Psychology, 46,* 489–502.

Vitaliano, P. P., Russo, J., Carr, J. E., Maiuro, R. D., & Becker, J. (1985). The Ways of Coping Checklist: Revision and psychometric properties. *Multivariate Behavioral Research, 20,* 3–26.

Wallston, K. A., & Wallston, B. S. (1980). Health locus of control scales. In H. M. Lefcourt (Ed.), *Advances and innovations in locus of control research.* New York: Academic.

Weiner, B. (Ed.). (1974). *Achievement motivation and attribution theory.* Morristown, NJ: General Learning Press.

Weiner, B. (1979). A theory of motivation for some classroom experiences. *Journal of Educational Psychology, 71,* 3–25.

Weiner, B. (1985). An attributional theory of achievement motivation and emotion. *Psychological Review, 92,* 548–573.

Weiner, B. (1986). *An attributional theory of motivation and emotion.* New York: Springer–Verlag.

Weiner, B., Russell, D., & Lerman, D. (1979). The cognition-emotion process in achievement-related contexts. *Journal of Personality and Social Psychology, 37,* 1211–1220.

Wheaton, B. (1985). Personal resources and mental health: Can there be too much of a good thing? *Research in Community and Mental Health, 5,* 139–184.

Wong, P., & Weiner, B. (1981). When people ask "Why" questions, and the heuristics of attributional search. *Journal of Personality and Social Psychology, 40,* 650–663.

Worchel, F. F., Copeland, D. R., & Barker, D. G. (1987). Control-related coping strategies in pediatric oncology patients. *Journal of Pediatric Psychology, 12,* 25–38.

6 Attributions, Person Perception, and Clinical Issues

Steven Regeser López
Bonnie H. Wolkenstein
University of Southern California

Past clinical research with an attributional perspective has primarily addressed questions of self-perception (for a review see Harvey & Galvin, 1984). Perhaps the most notable example is that of the reformulated model of learned helplessness. Abramson, Seligman, and Teasdale (1978) posited that depression is the result of two factors: a belief that one's responses have no bearing on response outcomes, and the attributions one makes for this noncontingency or sense of helplessness. Recent attention to other clinical matters from an attributional perspective reflects the same emphasis on self-perception (Antaki & Brewin, 1982; Brewin, 1988; Försterling, this volume; Ickes, 1988). Much less attention has been given to questions of person perception, although there are exceptions (e.g., Bradbury & Fincham, in press; Jordan, Harvey, & Weary, 1988). In the present chapter, we aim to acquaint investigators and clinicians with the past and potential contributions in applying an attributional framework to the study of person perception within a clinical domain.

We examine two areas in which attribution theory has the potential to contribute to our understanding of person perception in a clinical context. First, we review research that examines the relationship between clinicians' attributions and their clinical judgment. Second, we examine the literature concerning the relationship between family members' views of the causes of their relative's mental disorder, and their affective reactions and levels of support. We specifically consider the available research that investigates the level of "expressed emotion" in the relatives of patients with schizophrenia.

The attributional perspective that we use draws largely from the work of Weiner and his associates (Weiner, 1985, 1986). This theoretical model begins with the assumption that a given outcome leads to a search for the cause of that

103

outcome. For example, clinicians seek to find out why patients have a given disorder or syndrome. Also, family members try to determine why their relative requires psychological treatment. The perceived causality, in turn, is related to specific psychological consequences. Among the attribution–consequence linkages are expectancy of behavior change, affective reactions (e.g., sympathy, anger, guilt), and help giving. We believe that these linkages are particularly relevant to clinical judgment and family members' interactions with significant others. Therefore, in addition to pointing out the significance of an attributional perspective to the study of person perception in clinical settings, we argue that Weiner's model has much to contribute to these areas of clinical research.

CLINICAL JUDGMENT

Underlying much of the clinical work with mental health patients are the judgments that clinicians make about their patients. Among the judgments are classifications (diagnosis and symptom recognition), predictions (response to treatment), and explanations (causes and reasons for the presenting problems). Clinicians use these judgments to form impressions about their patients and to formulate their interventions. Each type of judgment is intricately related to one another. For example, the clinical diagnosis (classification) can suggest the patient prognosis or likelihood of benefiting from treatment (prediction), and can suggest explanations for the disorder depending on the theoretical orientation of the therapist. In this chapter, we focus primarily on judgments of explanations, as attributions are typically explanations, although there will be some discussion of judgments of classification and prediction. Our review of the attribution and clinical judgment research is divided into two sections. The first section addresses the attribution literature that primarily considers whether clinicians make dispositional (internal) or situational (external) attributions. The second section focuses on the relationship between clinicians' attributions and their clinical judgments.

Locus Attributions

Research concerning attributions and clinical judgment focuses primarily on judgments of locus, or the internal/external locus domain. The most consistent finding among clinical judgment and attribution research is that professional helpers are more apt to make dispositional or internal attributions for the client's behavior, whereas laypersons are more likely to make situational or external attributions. Batson (1975) found that male seminary students, the professional helpers, perceived the problem of a pseudoclient presented in a taped interview as more dispositional than male undergraduate students. In a second study (Batson & Marz, 1979), advanced clinical psychology students (the trained professionals) again judged both situational and dispositional type problems to be more dispositional in nature than college students. These findings are consistent with a counselor analogue study that found college students, who took the role of a counselor, to attribute the client's problem to more personality-based factors than students, who took the role of a client or who assumed no particular role (Snyder, Shenkel, & Schmidt, 1976). It is important to note that there is no evidence at this time that this dispositional bias reflects error on the part of professional helpers (Batson, O'Quin, & Pych, 1982). Rather, professional helpers are more apt to implicate personal factors in understanding presenting problems than laypersons.

Batson and his colleagues (1982) propose that this dispositional bias is the result of several interrelated factors that reflect the therapist's role as an observer and as a helper. For example, as observers, therapists' attention is largely focused on the client and not the situation. As a result, therapists are more likely to collect information about the client than information about the environment. As helpers, clinicians are trained to expect dispositional problems, and they know that the available resources are largely oriented toward changing people. Thus, role characteristics of being an observer and a professional helper lead clinicians to view clients' problems as largely dispositional in nature.

Although clinicians are noted for their dispositional bias in general, there are some characteristics of mental health professionals that lead to attributions that are less person-based. One factor is the ethnic background of clinicians. Berman (1979) assessed Black and White therapists' attributions of problems presented by both majority and minority hypothetical patients. She found that Black counselors judged presenting problems of both groups of patients to be evenly split between person (internal) and societal (external) factors, whereas White counselors judged the same problems to be more person-oriented. Similarly, López (1983) found that Hispanic therapists, relative to Anglo therapists, judged an adolescent's gang-related problem to be caused by more external factors, irrespective of the adolescent's ethnicity.

A second therapist characteristic related to the use of the locus attributions is theoretical orientation. Research indicates that therapists who are trained in a particular theoretical orientation incorporate the attributions that the theory supplies. For instance, Snyder (1977) reanalyzed data from Langer and Abelson's (1974) study and found that psychodynamically oriented clinicians were more inclined to judge the problem as more person-based, relative to behaviorally oriented clinicians. Plous and Zimbardo (1986) replicated this finding, although they examined causal explanations for the presenting problems. Theoretical orientation has also been found to affect clinicians' attributions for the patient's responsibility for the problem cause and for the problem solution. Relative to therapists from cognitive-behavioral, family systems and eclectic orientations, psychodynamic therapists judged the patient to be less responsible for both the cause and solution of the presenting problem (McGovern, Newman, & Kopta, 1986).

Taken together, the available research suggests that a clinician's ethnicity and theoretical orientation may influence locus attributions. It is of interest to consider why these factors might alter clinicians' use of attributions. Drawing from what Batson and associates identified as potential sources of the dispositional bias, it seems possible that ethnic and theoretical background are likely to alter the therapists' role perspectives as observer and as helper. Considering ethnicity, Black and Hispanic therapists may be able to move out of the role of the observer and consider the client's perspective more than White therapists. Or perhaps minority clinicians are able to bring to their training a healthy respect for the role environmental factors play in shaping client's presenting problems, thereby altering the typical helper-role perspective. Similarly, theoretical orientation may also shape the role perspective of the helper away from the usual dispositional bias. For example, therapists from a behavioral tradition may learn to emphasize environmental factors, whereas therapists from a psychodynamic tradition may learn to focus on intrapsychic factors.

A final aspect of the locus attribution research that we will consider is the relationship between locus attributions and clinical judgments, such as treatment recommendations and level of maladjustment. Batson (1975) examined the relationship between attribution-related judgments and treatment referrals. He found that when helpers judged the problem to be personal in nature, referrals were more likely made to services oriented toward changing the person, such as a psychiatric hospital. On the other hand, when the problem was viewed as situational in nature, referrals were most likely made to organizations that dealt with the community, such as a social service agency. With regard to the relationship between attributions and judgments of maladjustment there are mixed findings. Synder (1977) found a positive correlation between ratings of maladjustment and locus of the problem. Specifically, the more the problem was judged to be an internal or person-based problem, the more clinicians judged the interviewee as maladjusted. López (1983) and Wolkenstein and López (1988), however, found no consistent relationship between clinicians' locus causal attributions and judgments of severity and need for treatment.

Critique. The general attribution and clinical judgment literature has a number of limitations. First of all, there is great diversity in conceptualizing and operationalizing attributions in clinical judgment settings. Therapists' locus attributions have been defined as (a) attributions of the client's responsibility for both the cause and the solution of presenting problems (Brickman et al., 1982; McGovern et al., 1986); (b) attributions of the problem, not the cause of the problem, as residing within the client or within the situation (Batson et al., 1982; Berman, 1979; Snyder, 1977); and (c) attributions of the client's problems viewed as being *caused* by dispositional or situational factors (Plous & Zimbardo, 1986; Snyder et al., 1976).

Each of these ways of conceptualizing and studying attributions contributes to identifying the many ways attributions are relevant to clinical judgment. However, adhering to these divergent formulations hinders the development of a clear, comprehensive body of research within any one conceptualization. For example, in examining the effect of clinicians' theoretical orientation on their attributions, Snyder (1977) found that psychodynamic therapists judged the presenting problem as more person-oriented (internal) and less situation-oriented (external) than did the behavioral therapists. Plous and Zimbardo (1986) found the same pattern for clinicians' perceptions of the *causes* of the presenting problem. Although these findings are parallel, the type of judgment may be different. In the former, the clinician is likely to categorize the problem as either personal or situational. In the latter, the clinician provides an explanation for the problem. Although there are occasions when problem description and problem explanation reflect the same dimension, there are also occasions when the problem is categorized in one direction (e.g., internal) and the causes of the problem are viewed as lying in the other direction (external). For example, the decompensation of a patient with schizophrenia is likely to be viewed as an internal problem, yet the cause of the decompensation could be perceived as either external (life stressors) or internal (failure to take medication). It may be particularly important to bear this distinction in mind when considering the potential consequences of such perceptions.

A second limitation of the available research is that it primarily concerns judgments of locus: locus of the problem's causality, locus of the problem, and locus of responsibility. This likely reflects the prominence that internal/external attributions have had historically in the nonclinical study of attributions. Nevertheless, there are other causal dimensions: stability, controllability, intentionality, and globality. These other dimensions have received little attention and might prove to be particularly significant to the clinical judgment process. A final limitation of the available research is that little attention is paid to uncovering the nature of the relationship between attributions and clinical judgments. Identifying the types of causal ascriptions clinicians use is of value. However, of most importance is how those attributions relate to clinical judgments and related therapist–patient interactions.

An Attributional Model of Clinical Judgment

We believe that Weiner's attribution theory has relevance for clinical decision making and has the potential to contribute to the available attribution and clinical judgment literature. Contrary to past research, which focused on locus attributions, Weiner's model considers two other causal dimensions, stability and controllability, and therefore has the potential to broaden the attributional perspective used in the study of clinical judgment. *Stability* refers to the perceived variability (unstable) or permanency (stable) of the causes of behavior. To use a clinical judgment example, an antisocial personality disorder would be considered a stable cause of violent behavior, whereas experimenting with phenacyclidine (PCP) would be considered an unstable cause of violent behavior. The *controllability* dimension considers the degree to which the causes are perceived to be under the control of the individual. The causes of alcoholism are frequently perceived to be subject to volitional control, whereas the causes of posttraumatic stress are not perceived to be subject to volitional control. In this section, we review Weiner's model as it applies to clinical judgment, and we discuss the beginning research efforts in this area.

The main advantage of applying Weiner's theory to the study of clinical judgment is that perceived causes along the aforementioned dimensions have been found to be related to important psychological consequences. The consequences of causes categorized according to their stability and controllability are probably most applicable to clinical judgment. Stability has been shown to be clearly linked to the expectancy of behavior change, or, in clinical terms, prognosis. If the causes of the presenting problem are thought to be stable, then the patient's prognosis will likely be considered poor. On the other hand, if the causes are perceived as unstable, the prognosis will likely be much better. Referring back to the example of violent behavior, one would expect the person with an antisocial personality disorder (a stable cause) to continue to become violent, whereas one would expect the person who experimented with PCP (an unstable cause) to become violent much less frequently, depending on the further use of drugs.

There is both direct and indirect evidence that the stability–expectancy of change linkage applies to the clinical arena. López (1983) presented six case summaries based on actual patients to 96 mental health professionals and assessed their perceptions of the causes of the presenting problems and related psychological consequences. The case summaries represented a range of presenting problems: psychosis, marital problems, rape trauma, a gang-related problem, male sexual dysfunction, and parent–child conflict. López found that clinicians' attributions of stability for five of the six cases were significantly related to their prognostic ratings. As clinicians perceived the causes of the problems to be unstable, they viewed the patients' prognoses in a more positive light.

Indirect evidence of the stability–prognosis is also found in Perlick and Atkins's (1984) study of age bias. Clinical psychologists were presented with an audiotaped clinical interview in which the patient's age was manipulated (75 and 55 years old). Clinicians were more likely to implicate organic causes for the elderly patient's depressive symptoms and functional causes for the middle-aged patient with identical symptoms. Further, the evaluators judged the elderly patient as being less likely to benefit from antidepressant medication than the younger patient. These findings are consistent with the stability–expectancy of change linkage. Organic causes are likely to be perceived as more stable causes than functional causes. Responsiveness to medication is an expectancy judgment similar to prognosis. It may have been that the more the clinicians viewed the depressive symptoms as organic in nature, the less they expected the patient to respond to medication. Together, the López (1983) and Perlick and Atkins (1984) studies provide evidence that clinicians' attributions of the stability of their patients' presenting problems are related to their expectations that the patients' mental health status will improve.

The consequences of the controllability dimension also appear to be related to clinical judgments. Weiner (1980) demonstrated that help in a nonclinical setting may be offered more readily to those persons whose problems are perceived to have been caused by uncontrollable rather than controllable factors. For example, a man who stumbled and fell because he was blind (an uncontrollable cause) was more likely to elicit a willingness to help than a man who fell because he was drunk (a controllable cause). Weiner's research further established that affective responses appear to mediate people's desire to help; feelings of pity are elicited for the blind person whereas feelings of anger are elicited for the drunk person. Given these and related data, Weiner (1980) argued for a cognitive-affective model of help giving. The potential helper first assesses the cause of the person in need of help, then has an affective response which is linked to the perceived cause and, finally, depending on the specific cognitive–affective linkage, the potential helper is more or less likely to assist the one in need.

Although clinicians are taught to be objective and not to let affective reactions interfere with their evaluations, it is naïve to ignore the fact that patients do elicit affective responses from clinicians. If so, the cognitive-affective model of help giving might also apply to the clinical judgment process. Clinicians may feel more pity or sympathy for clients whose presenting problems are judged to be less controllable than clients whose problems are judged to be more controllable. As a result, more help may be provided to those patients with problems perceived to be less controllable. For example, a therapist may be more inclined to help a marital couple whose problems stem from the death of a child (an uncontrollable cause) than a marital couple whose problems stem from both partners' extra-marital affairs (controllable causes).

In the only test of this second attributional linkage, López (1983) found an interesting twist to the controllability–affective reaction–help-giving linkages. Contrary to Weiner's attribution theory, judgments of the controllability of the perceived causes were virtually unrelated to the therapists' reports of their affective reactions and their interest in providing help. However, ratings of help giving were related to affective ratings; help was negatively correlated with anger and positively correlated with empathy. This represents at least part of the cognitive–affective–help linkage. Although controllability attributions were found to be in general unrelated to affective reactions and help giving, stability judgments and prognosis were related to help giving. These findings suggest that in a mental health setting, professionals' desire to help their patients is related to their perceptions that (a) the patient's problem is due to unstable factors and (b) the patient will respond to treatment. In other words, clinicians appear to be more inclined to help those who they believe can benefit from therapeutic efforts.

Although the controllability-based model of help giving is not supported by this research, evidence does support an attributional model of help giving, one that is based on stability attributions and prognostic judgments.

The potential strengths of Weiner's attributional model are twofold. The model considers causal dimensions other than locus, and calls attention to specific linkages between attributions and important psychological consequences (i.e., expectancies, affective reactions, and help giving). The beginning research in applying this framework to clinical judgment suggests that it has considerable utility.

Critique. Weiner's model was derived from an achievement domain. Although there is ample evidence of its generalizability to other settings, it is important to be open to aspects of the model that might require some modification for the clinical judgment domain. Several issues arise when attempting to apply this model to the clinical arena. First, in the achievement domain, a more limited number of attributions may be used to explain success or failure than clinicians use to explain a given presenting problem or set of problems. In the clinical judgment setting, clinicians are likely to entertain multiple causal hypotheses. For example, the etiology of a patient's panic disorder could include any of the following causal factors: a biological vulnerability, childhood separation anxiety, a learned fear of panic symptoms, cognitive distortions (fear of dying or "going crazy"), and marital stress. Investigators of attributions and clinical judgments need to be cognizant of the multiplicity of causal factors, and the implications this has for understanding the role of causal attributions in the clinical judgment process. One implication concerns the location of a specific attribution in the temporal causal sequence or causal chain. Kelley (1983) and Abramson, Metalsky, and Alloy (1988) describe the location of a given attribution as either distal, toward the beginning of the causal chain in the clinical judgment context, or proximal, toward the end of the causal chain and closest to the presenting problem. The more proximal attribution will likely be judged as having the greatest impact on the development of the presenting problem. Studies of attributions and clinical judgments would do best to examine first the effects of proximal attributions on clinicians' judgments.

A second consideration that likely reflects the use of multiple causes in clinicians' perceptions of presenting problems is whether the cause is viewed as necessary and sufficient for the occurrence of the presenting problem or if the cause is viewed as only a contributory factor to the presenting problem. This dimension is modified from Abramson et al.'s (1988) discussion of necessary, sufficient, and contributory causes in depression research. A contributory factor is not likely to have as great an effect on clinicians' judgments as is a necessary and sufficient cause. For example, if marital difficulties were viewed as the necessary and sufficient cause of a woman's panic attack, the clinician would likely view the problem much differently than if marital difficulties were only one of many contributing factors. In studying the relationship of attributions to clinical judgments, investigators might best attend to how attributions are viewed along the dimension of sufficient/necessary (primary) causes and contributory (secondary) causes. A specific attribution may be manipulated in an experimental study, but if the attribution is only a secondary causal factor, then the impact of the manipulation may be minimal or nonexistent.

A third factor that might be considered is the distinction between causes and reasons. Buss (1978) cogently argues that causal explanations and reason explanations differ from each other. Causes imply lawfulness, predictability, and antecedent–consequent relationships. Reasons imply justifying or appraising the action; these types of explanations help make an action understood by attaching *meaning* to the action. Clinicians are likely to use both types of causal and reason explanations. They are interested in identifying precipitating causal factors, elements that directly precede the onset of a disorder or presenting problem, and they are interested in explaining or demonstrating an understanding of the presenting problem. Again, reconsider the example of a woman with a panic disorder. Marital discord precipitates the panic episodes and the intense fears of "going crazy" or "dying" serve to heighten the panic. Both of these factors may be viewed as causal; these are the factors that precede the panic attack and are viewed as necessary to the episode. In contrast, the panic episode could be perceived as reflecting the patient's loss of control, low self-esteem, poor coping skills, and perhaps unresolved feelings toward her father for having abandoned her, all of which are reasons or explanations for the episode. None of these reasons individually or together *caused* the panic episode, but they all contribute to understanding and explaining the patient's presenting problem. The distinction between causes and reasons may be difficult to make because one therapist's reason may be another therapist's cause. Nevertheless, it is important to note this distinction because reasons may not function in the same manner as causal ascriptions.

A final consideration in using Weiner's attributional model is that it cannot explain all potential clinical judgments. Judgments of categorization, whether they be symptom recognition or diagnostic judgments, are not within the theory's range of convenience. Also, the theory is limited in explaining judgments of symptom, disorder, or problem severity, although Snyder did find that more internal attributions correlated positively with judgments of maladjustment. Weiner's theory does not offer an appropriate explanation for such a finding. Therefore, to examine the full range of clinical judgments, it will be important to draw from other conceptual frameworks to complement the theoretical basis offered by Weiner's model. López (1989) identifies other areas in social cognition and decision making that have the potential to contribute to the study of attributions and clinical judgment in particular, and the study of clinical judgment in general. Among these areas are the investigation of base rates, memory, and hypothesis testing.

Conclusion.   Clinical judgment is critical to the clinical work of mental health professionals. Therefore, research which can contribute to a better understanding of this person perception problem can eventually be used to improve clinicians' performance. Weiner's attribution theory has the potential to enhance our current understanding of clinical judgment. The theory provides a conceptual framework that builds on past attribution-clinical judgment research through its additional causal dimensions and noted psychological consequences associated with the given dimensions. Further research which addresses some of the aforementioned challenges in applying this theory to clinical judgment will contribute to the beginning efforts in applying this model.

FAMILIES' ATTRIBUTIONS OF A RELATIVE'S SERIOUS MENTAL DISORDER

In addition to considering clinicians' attributions for the patient's presenting problems, we believe that it is important to consider the family members' attributions for their relatives' presenting problems. There is a growing body of research that examines the relationship between the emotional atmosphere of families and the course of schizophrenia that is consistent with an attributional analysis, though no direct studies of the families' attributions have been published. Several investigations have found that schizophrenic patients are more likely to relapse when they return to families who have a critical, hostile attitude toward the patient and/or who are emotionally overinvolved with the patient. This critical, hostile tone, and emotional overinvolvement has been referred to as "expressed emotion" (Brown, Birley, & Wing, 1972). In this section, we summarize the key research which has established the relationship between expressed emotion and relapse. Recent reviews of this literature (Hooley, 1985; Koenigbsbert & Handley, 1986) have indicated that the mechanisms underlying the relationship between expressed emotion and relapse are poorly understood. We propose that attributions may be a critical mechanism in understanding this relationship. Specifically, we draw from Weiner's cognition–affect–helping model and argue that the attributions family members make for their relative's mental disorder is central to the way they feel toward the patient (sympathetic or angry) and the manner in which they may help the patient remain relatively symptom-free. Of particular importance to this model is the family members' perceptions of how much control the patient has for the cause of his or her disorder.

Expressed Emotion

Brown and his colleagues originally brought attention to the role of family attitudes in the relapse of schizophrenic patients. In a retrospective study, they observed that the likelihood of relapse for chronic male schizophrenic patients was related to living arrangement, particularly the presence of parents or wives (Brown, Carstairs, & Topping, 1958). In an attempt to understand this relationship, a prospective study was carried out with particular focus given to the emotional involvement (emotionality and hostility) of a key female relative (Brown, Monck, Carstairs, & Wing, 1962). Patients returning to homes in which the relative was designated as high in emotional involvement relapsed at a greater rate than those patients returning to homes in which the relative was designated as low in emotional involvement. This initial research pointed to the significance of the family's emotional atmosphere in the course of schizophrenia.

Further research was conducted to refine the assessment of the emotional climate of the household (Brown & Rutter, 1966), leading to the development of the Camberwell Family Interview (CFI), a reliable method to index relatives' emotional responses, or their *expressed emotion* (Brown, Birley, & Wing, 1972; Vaughn & Leff, 1976a, 1976b). The CFI is an open-ended interview which allows family members to discuss their feelings about the patient and his or her illness. Based on this interview, a rater assesses the number of critical remarks about the patient, the level of hostility, and the level of emotional overinvolvement, that together reflects the overall level of expressed emotion (EE).

Several studies have now demonstrated a significant association between the household level of expressed emotion as assessed by the CFI and the relapse rate of persons with schizophrenia. In a representative study of this relationship, Vaughn and Leff (1976a) found that 50% of the patients living with high-EE relatives relapsed within 9 months after their hospitalization, whereas 12% of the patients living with low-EE relatives relapsed within the same time period. This relationship is to some extent influenced by the patient's usage of medication and the amount of contact between patient and family member (Vaughn & Leff, 1976a). Patients living in high-EE households who maintain their medication regimen and who have fewer than 35 hours of contact per week with their family are less likely to relapse than those patients from households of high EE who do not regularly take their medication and who have greater amounts of contact with their family. Interestingly, medication and contact do not appear to influence the relapse rate of patients from low-EE households. The relapse rates of patients from low EE families were nearly identical for those who maintained their medication and for those who did not, as well as for those who had fewer than 35 hours of contact with their relative and for those who had greater than 35 hours of family contact. The findings of Vaughn and Leff replicated for the most part the original EE study of Brown et al. (1972) and have since been replicated cross-culturally (e.g., Karno et al., 1987) and for patients suffering from disorders other than schizophrenia, including depression (Hooley, Orley, & Teasdale, 1986; Vaughn & Leff, 1976a), manic bipolar disorders (Miklowitz, Goldstein, Nuechterlein, Snyder, & Mintz, 1988), and obesity (Fischmann–Havstad & Marston, 1984). Convincing evidence indicates that the hostile/critical posture of a family and/or their emotional overinvolvement with the patient increases the likelihood of relapse among schizophrenic patients and patients with other disorders.

Treatment Studies

An important limitation of the family studies is that they are correlational in nature: A causal relationship cannot be inferred between the household's level of expressed emotion and the patient's relapse. To examine the causal relationship of EE and relapse, investigators have developed treatment studies which attempt to reduce the level of EE and in turn attempt to lower the relapse rate. If the treatment reduces the household's level of EE and relapse rate, then one can more confidently accept the causal relationship between EE and relapse.

In a representative investigation, Hogarty et al. (1986) examined the effect of various treatment components for patients residing in families with high EE: family treatment, individual treatment–social skills training, combined family treatment and social skills training, and individual supportive psychotherapy. Each treatment contained a medication component as well. An important part of both the family treatment and social skills training was to reduce the level of expressed emotion in the household. In the family treatment, the investigators sought to educate the family members regarding the nature and course of schizophrenia and to teach specific management strategies to help cope with symptoms on a day-to-day basis. The social skills training attempted to enhance the patients' verbal and nonverbal social behavior and also to assist them to perceive and judge more accurately their social world. This was viewed by the investigators as serving as an indirect means of lowering the emotional climate of the families.

The findings of the Hogarty et al. (1986) study indicated that relative to the patients in the control condition of supportive therapy, the patients in the family treatment and social skills training relapsed much less. Moreover, patients in the combined family-social skills treatment had no relapses during the 1-year postdischarge period. Most importantly, an assessment of whether the interventions changed the household's expressed emotion revealed that there was no patient relapse in households that changed from high EE to low EE, suggesting that EE is indeed an important mechanism underlying relapse. Although Hogarty et al. (1986) and Falloon and associates (1985) make a valid argument that intervention studies do not conclusively demonstrate the causal relationship between EE and relapse, these studies, in conjunction with the family studies, provide consistent evidence of this relationship.

Attributional Analysis

There is little question that expressed emotion plays an important role in the relapse of patients with schizophrenia and other disorders. However, the specific mechanism that underlies this relationship, as noted earlier, is poorly understood. Drawing from the work of Weiner (1985, 1986), we propose that the attributions family members implicate for their patient's illness and symptomatology is central to the relationship between expressed emotion, particularly criticism and hostility, and relapse. Of particular interest in understanding the relationship between EE and relapse is the previously discussed cognitive–affective–helping model. High-EE family members may view the illness and related behaviors as within the personal control of the patient. As a result, they may feel anger and/or disgust toward the patient and offer little support or help. In contrast, low-EE family members may view the illness as outside the patient's volitional control, may feel sympathy or pity, and in turn may be more tolerant, helpful and supportive.

Although no research has prospectively examined the attributions that family members ascribe to the patient's behavior, there are two qualitative studies which provide evidence that attributions of controllability are indeed important. Vaughn and Leff (1981) conducted analyses of their family interview data to illuminate further the concept of expressed emotion. They identified four "characteristic attitudes or response styles" that discriminate between households of high and low expressed emotion. One such response style is whether the family views the patient as suffering from a legitimate illness. Vaughn and Leff report that high-EE relatives generally doubt that the patient is genuinely ill and believe that the patient is responsible for his condition. In contrast, low-EE relatives are portrayed as accepting the patient's illness. The differing response styles of high and low-EE relatives were also identified among Mexican American families. Jenkins, Karno, de la Selva, and Santana (1986) reported "some high-EE relatives, unlike those in low-EE families, more often doubted whether their family member was truly ill" (p. 45). These qualitative findings suggest that low-EE family members attribute the patient's problem behavior to mental illness, an uncontrollable factor, whereas high-EE family members attribute behavior to the patient's own volition, a controllable cause.

Further evidence that suggests attributions of controllability are significant in the relationship between EE and relapse concerns the study of symptomatology as it relates to families' views of the patient. In schizophrenia, two types of symptom clusters—positive and negative—have been identified (Andreasen & Olsen, 1982). Positive symptoms refer to behavioral excesses, specifically the florid symptoms of schizophrenia: hallucinations, thought disorder, and delusions. Negative symptoms refer to behavioral deficits, the affective flattening, limited communication, social withdrawal, and apathy. In one study, Vaughn (1977; as noted in Fadden, Bebbington, & Kuipers, 1987) examined the content of the critical comments directed toward the patient and found them to concern primarily behavior reflective of negative symptoms, that is, lack of communication, interest, and initiative. Family members were less frequently critical of positive symptoms. These findings suggest that relatives are likely to attribute positive symptoms to the patient's mental illness (uncontrollable) and negative symptoms to the patient's longstanding personality characteristics (controllable) (Falloon et al., 1985). In other words, family members are less critical when the patient exhibits clearly recognizable signs of psychosis (e.g., hallucinations and delusions) and more critical when the patient exhibits the less recognizable symptoms of schizophrenia, including apathy, limited communication, and social withdrawal.

Hooley, Richters, Weintraub, and Neale (1987) indirectly tested the symptom-controllability hypothesis suggested by Vaughn's work. Specifically, Hooley and associates hypothesized that spouses married to patients with schizophrenia or affective disorders would report greater marital satisfaction if the patient's predominant symptom pattern reflected positive symptoms than if their spouse's symptom pattern reflected negative symptoms. Although attributions were not assessed, these investigators expected that spouses would attribute the patient's problem behaviors to the patient's illness (an uncontrollable cause) given a symptom pattern of predominantly positive symptoms. Therefore the spouse would report marital satisfaction. Given predominantly negative symptoms, the spouse was expected to attribute the patient's problems to controllable causes and thus report marital dissatisfaction. The hypotheses were supported; spouse ratings of marital satisfaction were related to the positive/negative symptom profile of their patient-partners.

An examination of the family treatments devised to improve the emotional climate of families provides additional indirect evidence of the importance of attributions in the relationship between EE and relapse. A significant aspect of the family treatment of schizophrenia is the educational component concerning the nature and management of the disorder. This component is included in the interventions developed by three main groups of clinical investigators (Anderson, Hogarty, & Reiss, 1980; Falloon, Boyd, & McGill, 1984; Leff, Kuipers, Berkowtiz, Eberlein–Vries, & Sturgeon, 1982). Attention is given to correcting misperceptions of this disorder. For example, the evidence to support the biological basis of schizophrenia is presented, as is the view that families are not the cause of the disorder. These efforts strike us as attempting to reframe the attributions family members and patients themselves might use to understand schizophrenia, particularly family members' perception that the patient is responsible for his or her disorder. As noted by Hogarty and colleagues (1986), ". . . more direct efforts at formal education concerning the illness and its management might alter unilateral views of the patient as being either 'hopeless' or 'obstructional,' thereby reducing the understandable criticism, hostility, or emotional involvement. . . ." (p. 634). These psychoeducational efforts are consistent with current research on stigma, which suggests that education can lessen the perceived responsibility of the stigmatized person (Weiner, Perry, & Magnusson, 1988).

Although there is no direct evidence supporting the role attributions play in the relationship between expressed emotion and relapse, the available evidence suggests that attributions play an important role. Furthermore, it seems reasonable that the emotional climate of the household is related to the relatives' causal ascriptions. Qualitative data indicate that relatives with high levels of expressed emotion are more likely to express anger, disgust, and intolerance toward the patient (Vaughn & Leff, 1981; Jenkins et al., 1986). In contrast, relatives with low levels of EE are more likely to express sympathy, sorrow and tolerance (Vaughn & Leff, 1981; Jenkins et al., 1986). This is most consistent with Weiner's cognition–affect–helping model.

Our attributional analysis has focused exclusively on the critical and hostility components of expressed emotion. The hypothesized relationship between attributions and these components is clear given Weiner's theory. The attributional basis of emotional overinvolvement is less clear at this time. At the very least, the excessive involvement of the relative may be interpreted by the patient as indicating that he has no control over his illness and/or recovery and that he must depend on his relative. If the patient agrees, he learns to do nothing for himself. If he disagrees, he may feel resentment toward the significant other which will contribute to the heightened emotional tension that is associated with relapse. This brief analysis is speculative, however, it suggests that attributions and affect may play a role in understanding the emotional overinvolvement component of expressed emotion.

Future Directions

To advance an attributional perspective in the study of expressed emotion and relapse it is important to assess directly family members' causal ascriptions of the patient's problem behavior. This is the case for family studies that examine the relationship between EE and relapse, and for the intervention studies. Russell's (1982) Causal Dimension Scale, which measures the three dimensions of locus, stability, and controllability, may be particularly helpful as it has demonstrated reliability and validity. Furthermore, a more balanced assessment of the potential range of emotions expressed by the family member might be helpful. In addition to criticism, hostility, and emotional overinvolvement, the CFI also assesses warmth and positive remarks. However, to test the attributional model directly, assessments of pity, sympathy, and even likability will contribute to a more complete test of the attributional model. Also, the notion of help giving requires operationalization so that it can be directly assessed. If we can extrapolate from the family interventions, then perhaps help giving can be measured by effective communication, problem solving, and family coping. Some efforts have been made in this area (see Doane & Falloon, 1985). In addition, an important contribution could be made by identifying how relatives effectively negotiate the delicate balance of respecting the patient's desire for social distance and tolerating the problem behaviors, but still encouraging improvement in social functioning. We believe this to be the essence of help giving in the patient–relative relationship.

In future studies of attributions, expressed emotion, and relapse, two additional points might be considered. First, it is important that the investigator make efforts to distinguish between causal attributions of the disorder and causal attributions of the problem behaviors. The perception of the original cause of the disorder may be quite different than the perception of the day-to-day problem behaviors. As noted by Brewin (1988), causal ascriptions of present functioning may be more closely tied to the hypothesized psychological consequences than causal ascriptions of the onset of a given disorder. Second, although controllability appears to be central to the study of expressed emotion and relapse, family members' views of the stability of the causes of the problem behaviors may prove to be significant. Family members' perception of the illness' chronicity may be related to the sense of burden and perhaps expressed emotion. Studies which examine both stability and controllability should be able to identify the independent contributions of both causal dimensions to the family member's perception of their relative's serious mental disorder. Third, attention should be given to examining the processes that underlie emotional overinvolvement. Although an attributional analysis is not as apparent for this component of EE as it is for hostility and critical comments, we believe that attributions are likely to play a role.

CONCLUSION

Attribution theory has been applied to clinical psychology primarily from the perspective of self-perception. An examination of the role of attributions in clinicians' judgments of patients and in family member's views of relatives with serious mental disorders indicates that attribution theory has the potential to make important contributions in the person perception domain. The study of clinical judgment and perceptions of a family member's mental disorder are only two examples of a clinical issue with a person perception focus. Two other examples include the perceptions of spouses in marital relations (e.g., Bradbury, Fincham, & Grych, this volume) and parent's perceptions of their children's behavior (e.g., Affleck, McGrade, Allen, & McQueeney, 1985; Larrance & Twentyman, 1983). By highlighting the available research in clinical judgment and expressed emotion, we wish to encourage the application of an attributional framework to the further study of person perception problems of a clinical nature.

REFERENCES

Abramson, L. Y., Metalsky, G. I., & Alloy, L. B. (1988). The hopelessness theory of depression: Does the research test the theory? In L. Y. Abramson (Ed.), *Social cognition and clinical psychology* (pp. 33–65). New York: Free Press.

Abramson, L. Y., Seligman, M. E. P., & Teasdale, J. (1978). Learned helplessness in humans: Critique and reformulation. *Journal of Abnormal Psychology, 87*, 49–74.

Affleck, G., McGrade, B. J., Allen, D. A., & McQueeney, M. (1985). Mothers' beliefs about behavioral causes for their developmentally disabled infant's condition: What do they signify? *Journal of Pediatric Psychology, 10,* 293–303.

Anderson, C. M., Hogarty, G. E., & Reiss, D. J. (1980). Family treatment of adult schizophrenic patients: A psycho-educational approach. *Schizophrenia Bulletin, 6,* 490–505.

Andreasen, N. C., & Olsen, S. (1982). Negative vs. positive schizophrenia: Definition and validation. *Archives of General Psychiatry, 39,* 789–794.

Antaki, C., & Brewin, C. (Eds.). (1982). *Attributions and psychological change: Applications of attributional theories to clinical and education practice.* London: Academic.

Batson, C. D. (1975). Attribution as a mediator of bias in helping. *Journal of Personality and Social Psychology, 32,* 455–466.

Batson, C. D., & Marz, B. (1979). Dispositional bias in trained therapists' diagnoses: Does it exist? *Journal of Applied Social Psychology, 9,* 479–486.

Batson, C. D., O'Quin, K., & Pych, V. (1982). An attribution theory analysis of trained helpers' inferences about clients' needs. In T. A. Wills (Ed.), *Basic processes in helping relationships* (pp. 59–80). New York: Academic.

Berman, J. (1979). Individual versus societal focus in the problem diagnoses of black and white male and female counselors. *Journal of Cross-Cultural Psychology, 10,* 497–507.

Bradbury, T. N., & Fincham, F. D. (in press). Attributions in marriage: Review and critique. *Psychological Bulletin.*

Brewin, C. R. (1988). *Cognitive foundations of clinical psychology.* Hillsdale, NJ: Lawrence Erlbaum Associates.

Brickman, P., Rabinowitz, V. C., Karuza, J., Jr., Coates, D., Cohn, E., & Kidder, L. (1982). Models of helping and coping. *American Psychologist, 37,* 368–384.

Brown, G. W., Birley, J. L. T., & Wing, J. K. (1972). Influence of family life on the course of schizophrenic disorders: A replication. *British Journal of Psychiatry, 121,* 241–258.

Brown, G. W., Carstairs, G. M., & Topping, G. G. (1958). Post-hospital adjustment of chronic mental patients. *Lancet, 2,* 685–689.

Brown, G. W., Monck, E. M., Carstairs, G. M., & Wing, J. K. (1962). Influence of family life on the course of schizophrenic illness. *British Journal of Preventive and Social Medicine, 16,* 55–68.

Brown, G. W., & Rutter, M. (1966). The measurement of family activities and relationships: A methodological study. *Human Relations, 19,* 241–263.

Buss, A. R. (1978). On the relationship between reasons and causes. *Journal of Personality and Social Psychology, 36,* 1311–1321.

Doane, J. A., & Falloon, I. R. H. (1985). Assessing change in family interactions: Methodology and findings. In I. R. H. Falloon (Ed.), *Family management of schizophrenia* (pp. 153–170). Baltimore: Johns Hopkins.

Fadden, G., Bebbington, P., & Kuipers, L. (1987). The burden of care: The impact of functional psychiatric illness on the patient's family. *British Journal of Psychiatry, 150,* 285–292.

Falloon, I. R. H., Boyd, J. L., McGill, C. W. (1984). *Family care of schizophrenia,* New York: Guilford.

Falloon, I. R. H., Boyd, J. L., McGill, C. W., Razani, J., Moss, H. B., Gilderman, A. M., & Simpson, G. M. (1985). Family management in the prevention of morbidity of schizophrenia: Clinical outcome of a two-year longitudinal study. *Archives of General Psychiatry, 42,* 887–896.

Fischmann–Havstad, L., & Marston, A. R. (1984). Weight loss maintenance as an aspect of family emotion and process. *British Journal of Clinical Psychology, 23,* 265–271.

Harvey, J. H., & Galvin, K. S. (1984). Clinical implications of attribution theory and research. *Clinical Psychology Review, 4,* 15–33.

Hogarty, G. E., Anderson, C. M., Reiss, D. J., Kornblith, S. J., Breenwald, D. P., Javna, C. D., & Madonia, M. J. (1986). Family psychoeducation, social skills training, and maintenance chemotherapy in the aftercare treatment of schizophrenia: I. One-year effects of a controlled study on relapse and emotion. *Archives of General Psychiatry, 43,* 633–642.

Hooley, J. M. (1985). Expressed emotion: A review of the critical literature. *Clinical Psychology Review, 5,* 119–139.

Hooley, J. M., Orley, J., & Teasdale, J. D. (1986). Levels of expressed emotion and relapse in depressed patients. *British Journal of Psychiatry, 148,* 642–647.

Hooley, J. M., Richters, J. E., Weintraub, S., & Neale, J. M. (1987). Psychopathology and marital distress: The positive side of positive symptoms. *Journal of Abnormal Psychology, 96,* 27–33.

Ickes, W. (1988). Attributional styles and the self-concept. In L. Y. Abramson (Ed.), *Social cognition and clinical psychology* (pp. 66–97). New York: Guilford.

Jenkins, J. H., Karno, M., de la Selva, A., & Santana, F. (1986). Expressed emotion in cross-cultural context: Familial responses to schizophrenic illness among Mexican-Americans. In M. J. Goldstein, I. Hand, & K. Hahlweg (Eds.), *Treatment of schizophrenia: Family assessment and intervention* (pp. 35–50). New York: Springer–Verlag.

Jordan, J. S., Harvey, J. H., & Weary, G. (1988). Attributional biases in clinical decision making. In D. C. Turk & P. Salovey (Eds.), *Reasoning, inference, and judgment in clinical psychology* (pp. 90–106). New York: Free Press.

Karno, M., Jenkins, J. H., de la Selva, A., Santana, F., Telles, C. A., Lopéz, S., & Mintz, J. (1987). Expressed emotion and schizophrenic outcome among Mexican-American families. *Journal of Nervous and Mental Disease, 175,* 143–151.

Kelley, H. H. (1983). Perceived causal structures. In J. Jaspars, F. Fincham, & M. Hewstone (Eds.), *Attribution theory and research: Conceptual, developmental and social dimensions* (pp. 343–369). New York: Academic.

Koenigsbert, H. W., & Handley, R. (1986). Expressed emotion: From predictive index to clinical construct. *American Journal of Psychiatry, 143,* 1361–1373.

Langer, E. J., & Abelson, R. P. (1974). A patient by any other name. . .: Clinician group difference in labeling bias. *Journal of Consulting and Clinical Psychology, 42,* 4–9.

Larrance, D. T., & Twentyman, C. T. (1983). Maternal attributions and child abuse. *Journal of Abnormal Psychology, 92,* 449–457.

Leff, J., Kuipers, L., Berkowitz, R., Eberlein–Vries, R., & Sturgeon, D. (1982). A controlled trial of social intervention in the families of schizophrenic patients. *British Journal of Psychiatry, 141,* 121–134.

López, S. (1983). *Ethnic bias in clinical judgment: An attributional analysis.* Doctoral dissertation, University of California, Los Angeles. *Dissertation Abstracts International, 44,* 2516B.

López, S. R. (1989). Patient variable biases in clinical judgment: A conceptual overview and some methodological considerations. *Psychological Bulletin, 106,* 184–203.

McGovern, M. P., Newman, F. L., & Kopta, S. M. (1986). Metatheoretical assumptions and psychotherapy orientation: Clinician attributions of patients' problem causality and responsibility for treatment outcome. *Journal of Consulting and Clinical Psychology, 54,* 476–481.

Miklowitz, D. J., Goldstein, M. J., Nuechterlein, K. H., Snyder, K. S., & Mintz, J. (1988). Family factors and the course of bipolar affective disorder. *Archives of General Psychiatry, 45,* 225–231.

Perlick, D., & Atkins, A. (1984). Variations in the reported age of a patient: A source of bias in the diagnosis of depression and dementia. *Journal of Consulting and Clinical Psychology, 52,* 812–820.

Plous, S., & Zimbardo, P. G. (1986). Attributional biases among clinicians: A comparison of psychoanalysts and behavior therapists. *Journal of Consulting and Clinical Psychology, 54,* 568–570.

Russell, D. (1982). The causal dimension scale: A measure of how individuals perceive causes. *Journal of Personality and Social Psychology, 42,* 1137–1145.

Snyder, C. R. (1977). "A patient by any other name" revisited: Maladjustment or attributional locus of problems? *Journal of Consulting and Clinical Psychology, 45,* 101–103.

Snyder, C. R., Shenkel, R. J., & Schmidt, A. (1976). Effect of role perspective and client psychiatric history on locus of the problem. *Journal of Consulting and Clinical Psychology, 44,* 467–472.

Vaughn, C. E. (1977). Patterns of interactions in families of schizophrenics. In H. Kataschnig (Ed.), *Schizophrenia: The other side.* Vienna: Urban & Schwarzenberg.

Vaughn, C. E., & Leff, J. P. (1976a). The influence of family and social factors on the course of psychiatric illness: A comparison of schizophrenic and depressed neurotic patients. *British Journal of Psychiatry, 129,* 125–137.

Vaughn, C. E., & Leff, J. P. (1976b). The measurement of expressed emotion in families of psychiatric patients. *British Journal of Social and Clinical Psychology, 15,* 157–165.

Vaughn, C. E., & Leff, J. P. (1981). Patterns of emotional response in relatives of schizophrenic patients. *Schizophrenic Bulletin, 7,* 43–44.

Weiner, B. (1980). A cognitive (attributional)–emotion–action model of motivated behavior: An analysis of help-giving. *Journal of Personality and Social Psychology, 39,* 186–200.

Weiner, B. (1985). An attributional theory of achievement motivation and emotion. *Psychological Review, 92,* 548–573.

Weiner, B. (1986). *An attributional theory of motivation and emotion.* New York: Springer–Verlag.

Weiner, B., Perry, R. P., & Magnusson, J. (1988). An attributional analysis of reactions to stigma. *Journal of Personality and Social Psychology, 55,* 738–748.

Wolkenstein, B. H., & López, S. R. (1988). *Underlying social cognitive processes of age bias in clinical judgment.* Paper presented at the annual meeting of the American Psychological Association, Atlanta, August.

7 Attributional Therapies

Friedrich Försterling
Universität Bielefeld

INTRODUCTION

Ideally, one would start a chapter about "attributional therapies" with a summary of studies that have analyzed the efficacy of therapeutic techniques derived from attribution theory, treating a vast amount of clinical problems and populations in different therapeutic settings. Unfortunately, studies in which "real" clients in various clinical settings receive "attribution therapy" still remain to be performed. However, attribution conceptions have addressed a number of other important questions of clinical psychology in many different and productive ways, possibly bringing the field a little closer to a "real" attribution therapy. This chapter describes some of these applications.

In fact, hundreds of studies have been published that cast different specific problems of clinical psychology in an attribution framework. For instance, research has investigated whether depressed individuals explain negative events in a different way than nondepressed individuals and whether attributions of internal arousal to a placebo reduces insomnia of college students in a therapy analogue study. Much of this work has already been summarized in review articles (see, for example, Brewin, 1985; Coyne & Gotlib, 1983; Försterling, 1985; Peterson & Seligman, 1984; Reisenzein, 1983; Ross & Olson, 1981). Therefore, the present chapter does not pursue the goal of exhaustively reviewing one specific area of clinical attribution research. Instead, a more general overview and classification of the research areas that have used attribution theory in clinical psychology will be provided and these attempts will be related to basic attributional theorizing and research.

I will first outline some of the clinically relevant basic attribution concepts, that is, Schachter and Singer's two-factor theory of emotions, Weiner's theory of emotion and motivation, Abramson, Seligman, and Teasdale's attributional approach to depression, and Kelley's covariation principle. Following the description of each of these approaches, it will be shown how they have been used to understand, predict, or alleviate different maladaptive states, such as underachievement, depression, anger, and avoidance behavior. Furthermore, it will be shown how attribution approaches have been used to develop and understand therapeutic intervention techniques.

I will also describe analogue studies that have "simulated" important aspects of the therapy process (i.e., diagnosis, intervention, and outcome evaluation) in the laboratory. These studies come closest to the goal of an attribution therapy: They not only demonstrate that certain attributions are related to different maladaptive behavioral or emotional reactions, they also introduce techniques for attributional change and analyze whether the change of attributions leads to changes in these reactions. In addition, concepts and findings of attribution research will be used to conceptualize approaches to psychotherapy that have developed independently of attribution theory (e.g., Beck's Cognitive Therapy and therapeutic procedures based on classical conditioning) in an attribution framework. In this context, elements of attribution theory and research will be pointed out that have not yet been used—but well could be used—to understand clinical phenomena.

Theories and studies addressing the question as to how naïve causal judgments develop are called attribution research whereas attributional research analyzes the behavioral and emotional consequences of causal ascriptions (see Kelley & Michela, 1980). Among the most influential models with regard to the antecedents of causal attributions is Kelley's (1967) covariation principle. With regard to the consequences of attributions, the two factor theory of emotions (Schachter & Singer, 1962), the attributional approach to motivation (Weiner, 1985, 1986), and depression and helplessness (Abramson, Seligman, & Teasdale, 1978) have sparked clinical research. We shall begin by reviewing clinical research that was guided by the theories about the consequences of attributions and then return to clinical implications of attribution (antecedent) research.

CONSEQUENCES OF CAUSAL ATTRIBUTIONS

The 2-factor Theory of Emotion

The first studies to apply attribution principles to questions of psychotherapy used the so-called misattribution paradigm. These studies were stimulated by Schachter and Singer's (1962) two-factor theory of emotion, which maintains that affects result from an interaction of physiological arousal and cognitive processes. More specifically, it was suggested that an individual's appraisal of a situation may lead to physiological arousal (e.g., increased heart rate) and an "emotional" cognition (e.g., "the situation is dangerous"). As a result of the interaction of arousal and thought, the individual is assumed to experience an emotional state. The arousal is thought to be responsible for the intensity, and the cognition for the quality of the affect. Hence the same physiological arousal can give rise to different feelings (e.g., joy or anger).

Clinical applications of this theory are based on the derivation that negative emotional states, such as anxiety, can be altered by providing individuals with "nonemotional" cognitive explanations for their arousal in emotional situations (see Reisenzein, 1983). For instance, Storms and Nisbett (1970) gave insomniacs a placebo and told them that it produced the arousal that they typically experienced while trying to fall asleep (e.g., increased body temperature). This procedure was designed to change the insomniacs' explanation of their arousal from an emotional (internal) one (e.g., "I sweat because I'm an insomniac") to an unemotional (external) one ("I sweat because I took an arousing pill"). As expected, Storms and Nisbett (1970) found that individuals who thought that they had taken an arousing pill needed less time to fall asleep than before.

In a second set of relevant studies (see, for example, Olson, 1988; Ross, Rodin, & Zimbardo, 1969), a salient nonemotional stimulus (e.g., noise) was presented while subjects were in an emotional situation (e.g., when reading a speech in front of a camera or while thinking that they would be shocked). Again, subjects who were led to believe that the noise produced their anxiety-relevant arousal (unemotional cognition) exhibited less fear-related behavior while thinking that they might be shocked or while holding a speech than participants who thought that the noise produced symptoms unrelated to anxiety (e.g., itching).

How can the applicability of misattribution approaches to clinical practice be evaluated? First, with regard to their effectiveness, there are somewhat ambiguous findings about the replicability of the effects (see Reisenzein, 1983; Ross & Olson, 1981): In some settings misattribution seems to work, in others it does not. Secondly, although research has demonstrated that misattribution can be used to alleviate anxiety in certain conditions, it has not yet been proven that clinically relevant levels of anxiety are connected with a specific habit of attributing arousal to a certain source. There are no studies that suggest that certain populations that report suffering from the relevant symptoms (e.g., speech-anxious individuals) differ in their attribution of arousal from less anxious populations. Hence, misattribution research has conducted "therapy" before providing evidence that the postulated mechanisms actually are responsible for the symptoms (e.g., before having conducted a "diagnosis"). Finally, misattribution invariably employs deception which might render it as unethical and unpractical for therapeutic applications, and, in addition, might not appear believable to the subject. However, there is a second research tradition that links attributions to behavioral consequences that might not suffer from some of the shortcomings of the misattribution paradigm.

Weiner's Theory of Motivation

A second prominent research program relating causal attributions to behavioral consequences was carried out by Bernard Weiner and colleagues (see Weiner, 1985, 1986; Weiner et al., 1971). Weiner assumes that success and failure in achievement settings give rise to a search for causal attributions. Ascriptions of failure to stable causes (e.g., lack of ability or task difficulty) decrease subsequent expectancies of success, whereas attributions of failure to internal causes (e.g., lack of effort) maximize negative esteem-related emotions following the outcome. Weiner and colleagues have furthermore demonstrated that individual differences in achievement behavior result from differential causal attributions for outcomes: Low achievement strivings are associated with a preference for stable and internal attributions for failure. This attributional pattern leads individuals to give up easily following failure (due to the decreased success expectations) and to avoid subsequent achievement tasks (because of the associated negative affects). High achievement strivings, on the other hand, appear to be associated with a preference to make variable attributions for failure (see, for example, Weiner & Potepan, 1970).

According to Weiner's model, achievement strivings can be enhanced if individuals with a tendency to make internal stable attributions for failures (e.g., to lack of ability) are taught to make variable attributions (e.g., to lack of effort or chance) for failure instead. Studies that are guided by this assumption can be labeled attributional retraining studies (see, for a summary, Försterling, 1985). Note the important difference that attributional retraining studies aim to change cognitions about success and failure, whereas misattribution research aims to change cognitions about internal arousal. In addition, attributional retraining is based on research that had already demonstrated individual differences in attributions (i.e., between individuals high and low in achievement motivation) before designing the training programs. Misattribution research, by contrast, has not yet demonstrated (but merely assumed) that individual differences in a certain symptom (e.g., speech anxiety) are related to differential patterns of arousal attribution.

In attributional retraining studies, participants are selected on the basis of their attributional style, their behavior, and or by self-reports on cognitive, affective, or behavioral characteristics (e.g., Andrews & Debus, 1978; Wilson & Linville, 1982). For instance, Andrews and Debus selected subjects who exhibited (motivational) performance deterioration following failure. In a second step, an attributional intervention was performed with these subjects. For instance, Andrews and Debus (1978) used an operant technique. Children had to work on tasks and following each failure they were asked to make an attribution for the outcome that was positively reinforced when it was desired (i.e., a "lack of effort" attribution). Most of the attributional retraining studies, however, rely on persuasion. Without receiving a specific rationale, the subject is told by the

126

experimenter that a certain cause was responsible for the outcome. (This cause was naturally the one that was identified as "desirable" by the respective theory.) However, informational techniques can be used as well. Wilson and Linville (1982) provided their subjects with antecedent distinctiveness and consensus (see the following section on the antecedents of attributions) information that was designed to lead to the desired attribution. Subjects were told that other individuals also experienced failure (consensus) and that they were able to overcome that failure over time (consistency).

In a last step, attributional retraining studies evaluate their "effectiveness." In a review of 15 of these studies (Försterling, 1985), I concluded that the training influences a significant amount of behaviors and cognitions in the expected directions. For instance, Andrews and Debus (1978) found that their "attributionally retrained" subjects used the desired attributions more frequently as a consequence of the training and that they also improved in performance at an arithmetic task.

Learned Helplessness

In their influential attributional analysis of learned helplessness and depression, Abramson et al. (1978) propose that individuals who experience uncontrollability ask *why* they were unable to control a particular event. The answer to this "why question" (the causal attribution) should then influence the subsequent expectancy of controllability and thus influence whether and to what extent individuals might experience helplessness or depression. Abramson et al. (1978) classify causal attributions on three dimensions: locus of control, stability, and generality. Each of these dimensions is supposed to be responsible for different aspects of the symptoms of helplessness that can occur following an aversive event.

The dimension of locus of control determines whether or not doubts about self-esteem arise in connection with the experience of noncontingency. Abramson et al. (1978) introduce the example of a participant in a psychological experiment who is not able to control the occurrence of an aversive noise. If participants trace this failure back to internal factors, for example, their general inability to solve problems, this can lead to doubts about self-worth. On the other hand, if the participants manage to convince themselves that the experiment involves a problem that nobody is able to solve (an external attribution), no doubts about self-esteem occur.

According to Abramson et al. (1978), the dimension "stability over time" determines the temporal duration of helplessness. For example, suppose an individual attributes uncontrollability (such as losing a job) to stable factors such as own inability (internal) or the (general) economic situation (external). The symptoms of helplessness should last for a long time because our individual does not anticipate any change in his or her unfortunate situation (personal ability and economic conditions might be perceived as fixed).

In addition to the dimensions of locus of control and stability, Abramson et al. (1978) introduce the bipolar dimension of generality with the poles labeled "global" and "specific." If noncontingency is explained by a global factor, which is characterized by the perception that it does not just influence the original situation but also a wider range of other situations, the helplessness will consequently spread to a much larger area of life. If, for example, a participant in a psychomotor task experiences failure as being caused by a lack of intelligence (global), helplessness deficits should appear at subsequent dissimilar tasks (e.g., mathematical problems). However, if the failure is attributed to a special psychomotor skill that is only needed for that particular experimental task, there should be no negative effects due to noncontingency in other areas of life or with regard to other tasks.

Although the attributional analysis of learned helplessness has generated a vast amount of empirical research (see, for a review, Brewin, 1985; Coyne & Gotlib, 1983; Peterson & Seligman, 1984), attributional change studies guided by the reformulated concept have not yet been published. However, the initial— and frequently cited—training method that attempted to change causal attributions (Dweck, 1975) was based on derivations from the earlier model of learned helplessness that did not include attribution processes. Indeed, this study can be considered the first one to combine the attributional literature with learned helplessness research. Dweck and Repucci (1973) found that helpless subjects (children with impaired performance following failure) made fewer effort attributions for their successes and failures than did those who were not helpless. Guided by these findings and by the original model of learned helplessness, Dweck (1975) concluded that helpless individuals should be trained to make the same causal attributions as nonhelpless persons, that is, to ascribe success and failure to effort (an internal controllable factor). Note that the similarity in the retraining methods as introduced by Andrews and Debus (1978) and by Dweck illustrates the similarities between helplessness theory and achievement theory.

Additional Clinical Phenomena that Have Been Cast in an Attributional Framework

Weiner's theory and, to a limited extent, the attributional analysis of learned helplessness and depression, have stimulated the analysis of the role of causal attributions in clinically relevant fields other than achievement behavior and depression. However, this research has thus far concentrated on assessing rather than changing the attributions that might lead to different maladaptive states. For example, Anderson, Horowitz, and French (1983) and Peplau, Russell, and Heim (1979) investigated the attributions made by persons who complain that they are lonely; Weiner (1980) formulated the attributional conditions of helping behavior; McHugh, Beckman, and Frieze (1979) were concerned with the causal attributions made by alcoholics; and Eiser, Van der Pligt, Raw, and Sutton (1985) investigated the attributions individuals make for attempts to quit smoking. In addition, attributional frameworks have been used to conceptualize test anxiety (Arkin, Detchon, & Maruyama, 1982), the effectiveness of weight-reducing programs (Haisch, Rduch, & Haisch, 1985), and coping with critical life events such as reactions to accidents at work, rape, or illness (see Antaki & Brewin, 1982; Taylor, 1983). Mention should also be made of the analysis of the role of attributions in the reactions of hyperactive children to medicinal therapy (Whalen & Henker, 1976), clinical judgments (Weiner, 1975), marital distress (e.g., Fincham, this volume; Fincham, Beach, & Beaucom, 1987) (see for a summary, Weiner, 1980, 1986), and to questions of behavioral medicine (see for a summary, Michela & Wood, 1986).

The basic format of these studies consists of identifying individuals with a certain symptom (e.g., anger, marital distress, loneliness, or inappropriate coping behavior) and then to analyze differences in these individuals' attributions. For instance, it was found that members of maritally distressed couples attributed their spouses' negative behaviors (e.g., not doing the household chores) more to internal, global, and stable characteristics of the spouse than did members of nondistressed couples (e.g., Fincham, 1985). In addition, Brewin (1982) reports that industrial workers coped better with minor job injuries when they considered themselves to be personally responsible for the accident than when they thought they were not responsible. Furthermore, studies have revealed that individuals differing in test anxiety also differ in their attributions for success and failure: High test-anxiety subjects, compared with individuals low in test anxiety, for instance, use more internal, stable attributions for failure. It has also been shown that anger-prone individuals make more external, controllable attributions, compared with individuals who are less prone to feel angry (Försterling, 1984); and Eiser et al. (1985) found that unstable, as opposed to stable attributions, about the possible failures to quit smoking increase the likelihood that an individual arrives at the intention to give up smoking.

Although the (incomplete) list of studies summarized herein indicates the relevance of attributional concepts in clinical psychology, it certainly leaves open a great number of questions with regard to the "causality" of causal attributions for the respective "pathology" (see Brewin, 1985). Since most of the studies are correlational, it is not clear whether the attributions associated with a specific problematical reaction (e.g., anger or marital distress) are causes or consequences of the specific state or symptom under consideration. For instance, the finding that couples who experience marital distress make more stable attributions for partners' negative behaviors might reflect an accurate summary of the partners' past behavior. They might indeed have behaved consistently negative in the past, hence, the stable attribution can be conceived of as veridical. In addition, one might wonder whether the attributional change techniques described earlier can also be applied to modify these possibly maladaptive behavioral or emotional states (e.g., marital distress or test anxiety). Suppose these differences in attributions are veridical assessments of past events; they might be of a high functional value for the individual's long-range well-being. Hence, as the relevant research has not analyzed whether differences in causal attributions reflect veridical assessments of antecedent information or errors and biases, it is not clear whether an attributional change for these problems is justified.

ATTRIBUTION AND ATTRIBUTIONAL THEORIES AND THEIR RELATION TO MODELS OF PSYCHOTHERAPY

Thus far, we have described attempts to cast different psychological states that appear as worthy of change in an attributional framework, and to change the attributions with different retraining methods. However, there is an additional, quite different possibility for using attributional conceptions for therapeutic questions: They can be used to conceptualize theories and techniques of currently employed psychotherapy systems. Hence, attribution theory might be able to provide a unifying theoretical framework for the understanding of different psychotherapy systems (see Försterling, 1988; Seligman, 1981). We shall now illustrate this attempt, using the examples of therapeutic methods based on classical conditioning and Beck's Cognitive Therapy. (However, an attributional analysis would also appear applicable to other systems of psychotherapy, such as psychoanalysis or Rogerian therapy.) In order to cast psychotherapies in an attributional framework, however, we will need to refer to theories about the antecedents of attributions in addition to theories about their consequences. Therefore, we shall now describe some of the most important concepts with regard to antecedent attribution research.

CAUSAL ANTECEDENTS

The Covariation Principle

Guided by Heider (1958), Kelley (1967, 1973) assumes that individuals process observations that are relevant for the causal explanation of an event in a way that is similar to methods used by scientists. More specifically, he assumes that the effect will be attributed to the cause with which it *covaries*.

Kelley identified three classes of causal attributions for effects (such as success or failure) that are relevant in the field of social psychology: (1) Attributions to persons (e.g., ability), (2) to entities (e.g., task ease), and (3) attributions to circumstances (or "time", e.g., chance). According to the covariation principle, whether an effect is traced back to one of these three causal classes depends on which of these causes the effect covaries with.

Kelley (1967) labels the covariation information on the joint occurrence of effects and persons as consensus. Information on the joint occurrence of an effect and one or more entities is labeled distinctiveness, and consistency stands for the circumstances (points in time, modalities) under which an effect occurs. For instance, if an effect (e.g., a person's failure) only covaries with the entity (e.g., task) and not with the person or the circumstances, we tend to make entity (task) attributions: that is, when there is high distinctiveness (the person only failed at this specific task and not with others), high consensus (everybody fails at this task), and high consistency (he or she failed at this task all the time). However, we would tend to make a person attribution when the effect only covaries with the person and not with entities and time: If the effect (e.g., failure) is present when the person is present and not present in the other persons (low consensus) and if it does not vary systematically with different entities (person 2 fails equally at different tasks, i.e., there is low distinctiveness) and different points of time (high consistency).

Therapies Based on Classical Conditioning and Attribution Theory

Recent literature (Alloy & Tabachnik, 1984; Rescorla, 1988) indicates that there are parallels between classical conditioning and attribution processes. Both classical conditioning and attribution theories rely on the mechanism of covariation. In classical conditioning, common occurrences of a neutral and an unconditioned stimulus (UCS) result in the fact that the formerly neutral stimulus acquires the capability of evoking the reaction that the unconditioned stimulus used to evoke (the conditioned response, CR) and therefore becomes the conditioned stimulus (CS).

For example, suppose an individual is exposed to a loud noise (UCS) that triggers anxiety (UCR) whenever he or she enters an elevator (neutral stimulus). Suppose furthermore that subsequently, the elevator alone (CS) triggers the anxiety (conditioned reaction, CR). In this example, we have an effect that is in need of explanation (ringing of the sound) and a possible cause for the sound (the elevator). In addition, the occurrence of the noise covaries with the elevator, or, in Kelley's terminology, there is high consistency (the noise is always present when approaching an elevator) and there is high distinctiveness (the noise is only present when the possible cause is present: the elevator) and absent when the possible cause is absent (no elevator). Therefore, it would seem logical if the individual who wants to escape the stimulus that causes the anxiety (the noise) tries to avoid the perceived cause of it (the elevator). Hence, some aspects of the process of classical conditioning can be conceived of as an attribution process. In the present example, a formerly neutral stimulus that covaries with a UCS becomes a CS because the CS is present when the UCS is present and absent when the UCS is absent. As a consequence, the individual experiences the formerly unconditioned reaction (anxiety) when the cause for the stimulus that had originally triggered the anxiety (UCR) is present.

Recent literature has pointed to several additional aspects of the process of classical conditioning that have parallels with the attribution process. For instance, and most generally, Rescorla (1988) points out that more recent formulations conceive of conditioning "as a learning that results from exposure to relations of events of the environment. Such learning is a primary means by which the organism represents the structure of its world" (p. 152). A more specific parallel between the attribution and classical conditioning process can be found while looking at the concept of contiguity that was formerly regarded as sufficient for conditioning to occur. Rescorla states that conditioning would most likely not occur when a neutral stimulus occurs contiguously but uncorrelated with the UCS. For instance, when a rat receives an electric shock after having been exposed to a neutral stimulus, conditioning is not going to occur when the neutral stimulus is uninformative about the occurrence of the UCS. Thus, when the UCS occurs not only when the neutral stimulus is present but also when it is absent (the rat experiences the shock in the absence of the tone), conditioning is not likely to occur. However, when the shock only occurs when the light is present and does not occur when the light is absent conditioning is more likely (in Rescorla's words, the CS is not only contiguous but also *informative*). Hence, from an attribution standpoint there has to be covariation between a neutral stimulus and a UCS before conditioning occurs. The effect (UCS) has not only to be present when the cause (CS) is present, it also has to be absent when it is absent.

In line with this analysis, is the use of the technique of systematic desensitization in many behaviorally oriented psychotherapies. During the procedure of systematic desensitization, the client learns to approach the feared stimulus (the elevator) while being in a state of relative relaxation, hence, collecting the information that there is not a perfect covariation between the elevator and the occurrence of noise. It is learned that the effect (the noise and the accompanying anxiety) is *not* always present when the possible cause (elevator) is present. Hence, attribution conceptions (especially the covariation principle) are compatible with the concepts used within the area of classical conditioning (for a more detailed analysis of the parallels of [animal] learning and covariation detection see Alloy & Tabachnik, 1984; Brewin, 1988).

BELIEFS AND ATTRIBUTIONS

In many instances, however, the observer does not have all the information available as specified in the covariation principle (consensus, distinctiveness, and consistency) or might lack the opportunity or motivation to process them. In these cases the causal attribution of the focal event depends on the beliefs, expectancies, or schemata of the attributer (see Alloy & Tabachnik, 1984; Kelley & Michela, 1980; Meyer, 1988; Weiner, 1986). For instance, suppose a person holds the belief that he or she is not good at a specific task, that is, he or she estimates the chances of succeeding to be fairly low, and this person succeeds on the relevant task (focal event). Research has indicated (e.g., see Zuckerman, 1979, for a summary) that this person's (unexpected) success will most likely be explained by an unstable attribution (e.g., chance). However, had he or she expected to succeed at the task, the expected success would probably be traced back to a stable factor such as high ability (see Weiner, 1986, for a summary). Hence, our initial expectations determine our attributions of focal events.

However, studies have also indicated (see, for example, Weiner, Nierenberg, & Goldstein, 1976; Weiner, 1986, for a summary) that the way we change our expectancies in response to focal events (e.g., success or failures) is, at least in part, a function of the attribution we make for the event (e.g., for success and failure). If, for instance, success is attributed to good luck (a variable cause) we will not necessarily expect success again, whereas success attributed to high ability will make us more confident about its reoccurrence. Similarly, making stable attributions for failure will probably increase expectancy of future failure whereas attributions of failure to variable causes will not decrease our expectations to achieve success in a similar manner. Hence, low expectations of success might be considered a self-stabilizing system (see Meyer, 1983). If one expects to fail and fails, one tends to make stable attributions for failure and these (stable attributions), in turn, decrease success expectations even more. However, when one expects to fail but succeeds, one tends to attribute success to variable factors and, hence, success expectations are not increased.

In the same manner, high expectations of success have a tendency to perpetuate themselves. If one expects to do well and does so, one tends to attribute success to stable and failure to variable causes. Both of these attributions help to maintain high expectations in the face of failure and to increase expectations even more following success. Hence, low as well as high expectations have a tendency to function like self-stabilizing systems.

To summarize, attributions for a focal event are determined (at least) by two different processes: covariation information and prior expectancies. However, both processes are not independent of each other. The covariation information determines our attributions for a focal event and this attribution influences the impact that this event will have on our subsequent expectancies. However, the expectancies also determine how we attribute focal events, that is, covariation information. Obviously both, assimilation (of information to our expectancies) and adaptation (of the expectations to new data patterns) take place in this process. The prior expectancies determine how incoming information is assimilated and the incoming information determines how expectancies are adapted and or changed (see Bartlett, 1932; Piaget, 1952). We shall now demonstrate that the concepts that were introduced while analyzing the antecedents of attributions are quite compatible with the concepts employed by cognitive therapy theories.

AN ATTRIBUTIONAL ANALYSIS OF BECK'S
COGNITIVE THERAPY

In his analysis of the cognitive determinants and consequences of reactive depression, Beck (1967, 1976, 1985; Beck et al., 1979) uses the following constructs: cognitive triad, cognitive schemata, and faulty information processing. By cognitive triad he means the tendency of depressives to carry out unrealistic negative observations of their own person, the situation, and the future. The self is regarded to be inadequate and worthless, the situation and the environment are perceived to be unfair and bad, and the future is interpreted as being unalterably negative.

Beck uses the concept of the cognitive schema to explain the fact that depressives maintain this unrealistic view of their own person, the situation, and the future, despite contradictory positive information. Under cognitive schemata, he understands relatively stable representations of previous experiences (e.g., the conviction that one is a failure) that cause environmental information to be processed erroneously and in a way that generally disfavors the depressive. The schema-guided, incorrect processing of information is called "systematic thinking errors" or erroneous information processing. This leads to the maintenance of the cognitive triad and the cognitive schemata. Examples of erroneous information processing are maximization and minimization. Maximization refers to the depressive's tendency to attach especially high importance to bad events (e.g., failure), whereas minimization refers to the tendency to reduce the impact of positive experiences (e.g., success). For instance, the schema "I am a failure" could cause the depressed person to maximize the impact of not succeeding by attributing failure to personal factors (e.g., low ability) and to minimize the impact of success by attributing success to chance. Naturally, minimizing success and maximizing failure lead the depressive to maintain one's self-image as a loser. Another example of faulty information processing is the thinking error of "overgeneralization," which refers to the tendency to draw global negative conclusions from specific single events ("The fact that my fellow worker doesn't like me shows that I don't have any real friends"). Arbitrary inferences—a further thinking error of depressives—describes the tendency to extract single aspects from events and then to draw a negative conclusion ("Because my boss was unfriendly to me today he must be planning to fire me"). According to Beck, therapeutic changes of the cognitive triad can be attempted by scientifically examining the cognitive constructs of the depressed client, hence, treating his depressogenic cognitions as hypotheses that can be subjected to logical examinations and empirical tests. In addition, cognitive therapy is concerned with correcting the systematic thinking errors (e.g., maximization or overgeneralization) that seem to be characteristic for depressives. Frequently, new data are collected to test depressogenic thoughts. For instance, the client who claims that he or she manages nothing satisfactorily in life may be instructed to monitor his or her performances and could then engage with the therapist in deciding which activities are satisfactory and which ones are not. A more realistic view of the self, the environment and the future should then lead to the alleviation of the emotional disorder.

It seems evident that cognitive psychotherapy uses concepts that are comparable with the key concepts of attribution theory. Both approaches are concerned with cognitive determinants of human behavior and emotions, address humans in their capacity to be "naïve scientists" and assume that scientific thinking has functional value.

On a more specific level, Seligman (1981) points out that the cognitive triad that Beck considers to be responsible for reactive depression has the same meaning as the tendency to make internal, stable, and global attributions for failure. The tendency of depressives to make internal attributions for failure is characteristic of their negative view of themselves; the stability of the attributions for failures causes the future to also be perceived as hopelessly negative, and the globality of their causal thinking reflects the thinking error of overgeneralization. Hence, both attribution research and the clinical experiences of cognitive psychotherapists came to comparable insights with regard to the cognitive determinants of depression: the cognitive triad and internal, stable, and global attributions for failure.

A further similarity between attribution concepts and Beck's approach concerns the use of a structural component that summarizes past experiences and determines how new information is processed. In attribution theory, expectancies of success and failure that were acquired earlier in the individual's performance history determine how we interpret incoming information. Similarly, in Beck's theory there are cognitive schemata, possibly acquired early in childhood, that determine how information is processed. In addition, the cognitive consequences of low expectations of success (e.g., attributions of failure to internal, stable and attributions of success to external, variable causes) are comparable with the cognitive consequences of the depressogenic schemata as postulated by Beck. According to Beck, depressogenic schemata cause systematic "thinking errors" in the processing of new information. They consist of a minimization of successes and a maximization of failures which, in turn, maintain the perception of the depressive that negative states will remain and positive ones are not apt to occur (the cognitive triad). For instance, if depressed persons fail, they maximize failure by blaming themselves (rather than chance). This tendency has a clear parallel with the attributions for failure that are made when expectations for success are low. That is, expected failure is attributed to the person whereas unexpected success is attributed to chance (minimized). Notice again, that maximizing failure (attributing it to ability) and minimizing success (attributing it to luck) has a self-stabilizing effect on expectancies; that is, they will keep future success expectancies low.

Finally, the mechanisms that are used in Beck's therapy to foster psychological change resemble in many aspects the most fundamental mechanism that is assumed by attribution theorists to be responsible for the formation of causal attributions; that is, the "scientific" processing of covariation information. In cognitive psychotherapy the client is frequently led by the therapist to gather new information with regard to his causal beliefs. This information resembles in many instances Kelley's (1967) consensus, distinctiveness, and consistency principles (see Försterling, 1988).

For instance, therapists leading groups often demonstrate to their clients that internal stable attributions for failure are not correct by asking other group members about their experiences with regard to a certain entity. More specifically, a client insisted that failure to attain a desired job was entirely attributable to his lack of ability for job interviews. The therapist asked who of the other group members had been rejected after job interviews (most of them were) and hence demonstrated that there is high consensus. In addition, cognitive therapists would typically ask this client to search in his memory for other instances of job interviews at similar (consistency) or dissimilar (distinctiveness) jobs in order to examine the veridicality of the client's causal assumptions.

SUMMARY

This chapter has summarized how attribution theory has been used to cast selected questions of clinical psychology within a unifying theoretical framework. First, clinically relevant basic attribution models were described. Secondly, corresponding areas of clinical attribution research that have proven to be fruitful were summarized. It was demonstrated that attribution theory has generated a research program that has investigated the cognitive determinants of different maladaptive behaviors and emotions (e.g., depression, learned helplessness, and underachievement) and that it can provide tools to alter therapeutically these cognitions (attributional retraining). In addition, it was shown that influential approaches to psychotherapy, such as cognitive psychotherapy, as well as more traditional forms of behavior therapies that are based on classical conditioning paradigms can be conceptualized from an attributional perspective. The possibility that attribution theory might be able to bridge the differences between cognitive and behavioral, laboratory-based versus clinically invented therapies was pointed out. Throughout this chapter, it is argued that research about the antecedents of causal attributions has not yet been fully exploited in its applicability to clinical questions. A more comprehensive application of these theories could aid our understanding of additional aspects of psychotherapy and also help us to design further techniques for cognitive change.

REFERENCES

Abramson, L. Y., Seligman, M. E. P., & Teasdale, J. D. (1978). Learned helplessness in humans. *Journal of Abnormal Psychology, 87*, 49–74.

Alloy, L. B., & Tabachnik, N. (1984). Assessment of covariation by humans and animals. The joint influence of prior expectations and current situational information. *Psychological Review, 91,* 112–149.

Anderson, C. A., Horowitz, L. M., & French, R. de S. (1983). Attributional style of lonely and depressed people. *Journal of Personality and Social Psychology, 45,* 127–136.

Andrews, G. R., & Debus, R. L. (1978). Persistence and the causal perception of failure: Modifying cognitive attributions. *Journal of Educational Psychology, 70,* 154–166.

Antaki, C., & Brewin, C. (1982). (Eds.). *Attributions and psychological change: Applications of attributional theories to clinical and educational practice.* London: Academic Press.

Arkin, R. M., Detchon, C. S., & Maruyama, G. M. (1982). Roles of attribution, affect, and cognitive interference in test anxiety. *Journal of Personality and Social Psychology, 43,* 1111–1124.

Bartlett, F. C. (1932). *Remembering.* Cambridge, England: Cambridge University Press.

Beck, A. T. (1967). *Depression: Clinical, experimental, and theoretical aspects.* New York: Harper & Row.

Beck, A. T. (1976). *Cognitive therapy and the emotional disorders.* New York: International Universities Press.

Beck, A. T. (1985). *Anxiety disorders and phobias: A cognitive perspective.* New York: Basic Books.

Beck. A. T., Rush, A. J., Shaw, B. F., & Emery, G. (1979). *Cognitive therapy of depression.* New York: Guilford.

Brewin, C. R. (1982). Adaptive aspects of self-blame in coping with accidental injury. In C. Antaki & C. Brewin (Eds.), *Attributions and psychological change: Applications of attributional theories to clinical and educational practice.* London: Academic Press, pp. 119–133.

Brewin, C. R. (1985). Depression and causal attributions: What is their relation? *Psychological Bulletin, 98,* 297–309.

Brewin, C. R. (1988). *Cognitive foundations of clinical psychology.* Hillsdale, NJ: Lawrence Erlbaum Associates.

Coyne, J. C., & Gotlib, I. H. (1983). The role of cognition in depression: a critical appraisal. *Psychological Bulletin, 94,* 472–505.

Dweck, C. S. (1975). The role of expectations and attributions in the alleviation of learned helplessness. *Journal of Personality and Social Psychology, 31,* 674–685.

Dweck, C. S., & Repucci, N. D. (1973). Learned helplessness and reinforcement responsibility in children. *Journal of Personality and Social Psychology, 25,* 109–116.

Eiser, J. R., Van der Pligt, J. L., Raw, M., & Sutton, S. R. (1985). Trying to stop smoking: Effects of perceived addiction, attributions for failure, and expectancy of success. *Journal of Behavioral Medicine, 8,* 321–341.

Fincham, F. D. (1985). Attribution processes in distressed and nondistressed couples: 2. Responsibility for marital problems. *Journal of Abnormal Psychology, 94,* 183–190.

Fincham, F. D., Beach, S. R., & Baucom, D. H. (1987). Attribution processes in distressed and nondistressed couples. 4. Self–partner attribution differences. *Journal of Personality and Social Psychology, 52,* 739–748.

Försterling, F. (1984). Importance, causal attributions, and the emotion of anger. *Zeitschrift für Psychologie, 192,* 25–32.

Försterling, F. (1985). Attributional retraining: A review. *Psychological Bulletin, 98,* 495–512.

Försterling, F. (1986). Attributional conceptions in clinical psychology. *American Psychologist, 41,* 275–285.

Försterling, F. (1988). *Attribution theory in clinical psychology.* Chichester, New York: Wiley.

Haisch, J., Rduch, G., & Haisch, I. (1985). Längerfristige Effekte Attributiostheoretischer Massnahmen bei Übergewichtigen. *Psychotherapie, Psychosomatik und Medizinische Psychologie, 35,* 133–140.

Heider, F. (1958). *The psychology of interpersonal relations.* New York: Wiley.

Kelley, H. H. (1967). Attribution theory in social psychology. In D. Levine (Ed.), *Nebraska Symposium on Motivation*. Lincoln: University of Nebraska Press, pp. 192–238.

Kelley, H. H. (1973). The process of causal attributions. *American Psychologist, 28,* 107–128.

Kelley, H. H., & Michela, J. (1980). Attribution theory and research. *Annual Review of Psychology, 38,* 457–501.

McHugh, M., Beckman, L., & Frieze, I. E. (1979). Analyzing alcoholism. In I. Frieze, D. Bar-Tal, & J. S. Carroll (Eds.), *New Approaches to Social Problems*. San Francisco: Jossey-Bass, pp. 168–208.

Meyer, W.-U. (1983). Das Konzept von der eigenen Begabung als ein sich selbst stabilisierendes System (The self-concept of ability as a self-stabilizing system). *Zeitschrift für Personenzentrierte Psychologie und Psychotherapie, 2,* 21–30.

Meyer, W.-U. (1988). Die Rolle von Überraschung im Attributionsprozess. [the role of surprise in the process of causal attribution.] *Psychologische Rundschau, 39,* 136–147.

Michela, J. K., & Wood, J. V. (1986). Causal attributions in health and illness. In P. C. Kendall (Ed.), *Advances in cognitive-behavioral research,* (Vol 5). New York: Academic Press, pp. 179–235.

Olson, J. M. (1988). Misattribution, preparatory information, and speech anxiety. *Journal of Personality and Social Psychology, 54,* 758–767.

Peplau, L. A., Russell, D., & Heim, M. (1979). The experience of loneliness. In. I. Frieze, D. Bar-Tal, & J. S. Carroll (Eds.), *New Approaches to Social Problems*. San Francisco: Jossey-Bass, pp. 53–78.

Peterson, C., & Seligman, M. E. P. (1984). Causal explanations as a risk factor for depression: Theory and evidence. *Psychological Review, 91,* 347–374.

Piaget, J. (1952). *The origins of intelligence in children*. New York: International Universities Press.

Reisenzein, R. (1983). The Schachter theory of emotions: Two decades later. *Psychological Bulletin, 94,* 239–264.

Rescorla, R. A. (1988). Pavlovian conditioning: It's not what you think it is. *American Psychologist, 43,* 151–160.

Ross, L., Rodin, J., & Zimbardo, P. G. (1969). Toward an attribution therapy: The reduction of fear through induced cognitive-emotional misattribution. *Journal of Personality and Social Psychology, 12,* 279–288.

Ross, M., & Olson, J. M. (1981). An expectancy-attribution model for the effects of placebos. *Psychological Review, 88,* 408–437.

Schachter, S., & Singer, J. E. (1962). Cognitive, social and physiological determinants of emotional states. *Psychological Review, 69,* 379–399.

Seligman, M. E. P. (1981). A learned helplessness point of view. In L. P. Rehm (Ed.), *Behavior therapy for depression: Present status and further directions*. New York: Academic Press, pp. 123–141.

Storms, M. D., & Nisbett, R. E. (1970). Insomnia and the attribution process. *Journal of Personality and Social Psychology, 16,* 319–328.

Taylor, S. E. (1983). Adjustment to threatening events: A theory of cognitive adaptation. *American Psychologist, 38,* 1161–1173.

Weiner, B. (1975). "On being sane in insane places." A process (attributional) analysis and critique. *Journal of Abnormal Psychology, 84,* 433–441.

Weiner, B. (1980). A cognitive (attribution)–emotion action model of motivated behavior: An analysis of judgments of help giving. *Journal of Personality and Social Psychology, 39,* 186–200.

Weiner, B. (1985). An attributional theory of motivation and emotion. *Psychological Review, 92,* 548–573.

Weiner, B. (1986). *An attributional theory of motivation and emotion*. New York: Springer.

Weiner, B., Frieze, I. H., Kukla, A., Reed, L., Rest, S., & Rosenbaum, R. M. (1971). *Perceiving the causes for success and failure*. New York: General Learning Press.

Weiner, B., Nierenberg, R., & Goldstein, M. (1976). Social learning (locus of control) versus attributional (causal stability) interpretations of expectancy of success. *Journal of Personality, 44,* 52–68.

Weiner, B., & Potepan, P. A. (1970). Personality characteristics and affective reactions toward exams of superior and failing college students. *Journal of Educational Psychology, 61,* 144–151.

Whalen, C., & Henher, B. (1976). Psycho-stimulants and Children: A review and analysis. *Psychological Bulletin, 83,* 1113–1130.

Wilson, T. D., & Linville, P. W. (1982). Improving the performance of college freshmen: Attribution therapy revisited. *Journal of Personality and Social Psychology, 42,* 367–376.

Zuckerman, M. (1979). Attribution of success and failure revisited, or: The motivational bias is alive and well in attribution theory. *Journal of Personality, 47,* 245–287.

III

APPLICATIONS TO CONFLICT IN INTERPERSONAL AND INTERGROUP RELATIONSHIPS

International terrorism, racial and ethnic violence, divorce, labor strikes and courtroom litigation are just a few of the manifestations of conflict in our world. Considering the wide-ranging and costly implications for society, it is not surprising that psychologists have had a long-standing interest in understanding conflict, its antecedents and course of development. For many years the main theoretical approach to conflict focused on the resources possessed by the antagonists and each partner's control over the other. In contrast, the attribution approach taken by the four chapters in this section emphasizes cognitive and affective variables that provide the basis for overt conflict. The authors hold in common the belief that examining causal inferences is essential to understanding interpersonal or intergroup disputes. Yet the context within which such processes are examined differs for each chapter.

The marketplace provides the context in which Folkes explores conflict (Chapter 8). Discrepant causal inferences for product performance lie at the heart of many disputes between consumers and sellers of products and services. Different information used to make causal inferences, self-serving motivations, and the inherent complexity of understanding the causes of many product problems account for many of these differences. The chapter describes studies showing that causal inferences influence a variety of consumer reactions to product failure, including negative feelings toward sellers and demands for restitution and redress.

In contrast to the relatively new interest in consumer issues by psychologists, the study of conflict in family and spousal relationships has long been a concern of psychologists. Within the last decade, attribution theory has provided an innovative perspective on this field, with Fincham and his colleagues providing important contributions. In Chapter 9, Fincham, Bradbury, and Grych propose a model of the complex underlying cognitive processes fostering disagreements in close relationships. Further, they identify the nature of events that can instigate conflict, the psychological consequences of cognitive processing of the events, and the extent to which the parties engage in overt conflict behavior.

The organization provides the context in which Baron (Chapter 10) examines the initiation, persistence, and resolution of conflicts. Whereas the previous chapters emphasize covert cognitive processes, this chapter highlights interpersonal communication of reasons for negative actions. More specifically, it deals with attributions when employees negotiate over a firm's resources. The chapter reports several empirical studies stressing that the kinds of excuses that are delivered, as well as how and when they are communicated, influence reactions to provocation.

In contrast to the individual level of analysis appropriate for domains in the previously described chapters, Betancourt (Chapter 11) expands the use of attribution theory to disputes that involve groups and nations. Building and improving on previous attributional models of international conflict, he focuses on the consequences of causal inferences for group cooperation, competition, and aggression. The value of the attributional approach is demonstrated in his analysis of the Middle East tensions between the Israelis and Palestinians.

The variety of domains in which conflict is examined in this section provides evidence of the flexibility and range of attribution theory. Partly because the chapters focus on different types of relationships, quite different kinds of issues are at stake in the disputes examined by these authors. For some authors the issue is personal happiness and fulfillment in intimate relationships. For others the issues are job satisfaction and optimal work environments for employees, customer satisfaction, consumer rights and product liability litigation, or international cooperation and deterrence of aggression. Yet, the importance of examining causal attributions in initiating, aggravating, and ameliorating disputes is common to each.

8

Conflict in the Marketplace: Explaining Why Products Fail

Valerie S. Folkes
University of Southern California

> *Since 1982, over 800 deaths and 300,000 injuries have been associated with all terrain vehicles. In government hearings, safety groups have blamed the vehicle's design, but Honda, the largest manufacturer, faults the drivers.*
>
> —Sahagun, 1987
>
> *In litigation against A. H. Robins, many Dalkon Shield users accuse the I.U.D. of causing their infertility. Consequently, the firm was driven to bankruptcy, denying all the time that the I.U.D. was at fault.*
>
> —Richards, 1988
>
> *Many Ford drivers blame 300 deaths and over 5,000 injuries on the car's unsafe transmission. Ford has countered that these unjust accusations could cost the firm almost $600 million.*
>
> —Emshwiller and Camp, 1988

These incidents illustrate the high stakes that can be involved in conflicts based on different attributions for product failure. The costs can include consumers' deaths and injuries, companies' reputations, employees' jobs, and stockholders' losses. Whereas few of us have suffered so dramatically from a marketplace conflict, most can recall an incident when we disagreed about the cause of product performance. As consumers, we often recall confrontations with sellers about the reason for product failure. Perhaps you thought the stained shirt was the dry cleaner's fault, but the dry cleaner blamed you. Or you concluded that an appliance was defective but the store accused you of improper usage.

At the heart of many disputes between buyers and sellers lie discrepant causal inferences for product performance. Attribution theory can illuminate the sources of these conflicts and predict some of the consequences of the disputes. But causal inferences need not always be discrepant, nor do causal inferences have only consequences which aggravate disputes. Some consequences of causal attributions lessen the likelihood of conflict. This chapter discusses a number of empirical studies examining causal attributions for product failure, reasons for their similarities and dissimilarities for buyers and sellers, and the consequences of those attributions. Finally, means of reducing buyer–seller conflict are identified, based on the attributional analysis.

ATTRIBUTIONAL CONFLICT IN EXCHANGE RELATIONSHIPS

Many of the sources of attributional conflict and consequences of attributions to be discussed here will be applicable to behavior in other domains besides the marketplace. For example, causal inferences influence anger over product failure in a manner similar to their influence on anger over academic failure. However, differences between exchange relationships (e.g., consumer–firm relationships) and communal relationships (e.g., family and friendship relationships) mean that conflict will have a different focus and goal. In exchange relationships, reciprocity is carefully and constantly monitored to ensure that benefits given are equitable with benefits received (Clark, 1984). Product failure raises the possibility of an inequitable exchange. Causal attributions for product failure are a part of the monitoring of benefits. In contrast, benefits in communal relationships are given for the other's welfare, without regard for reciprocation (Clark, 1984). Causal attributions for events in communal relationships are not so closely linked with reciprocity. For example, a friend's compliment on one's appearance does not require immediate reciprocation. Nor do friends typically search for causes for the lack of immediate reciprocation. Although the roles of buyer and seller may at times be assumed by those in communal relationships (e.g., as when one sibling sells a possession to the other), the discussion here centers on buyers and sellers only in exchange relationships (e.g., firms selling goods to consumers).

THE ROOTS OF ATTRIBUTIONAL CONFLICT

When products fail, people are likely to feel the need for an explanation. Product failure is the kind of negative and unexpected event that has been shown to prompt causal search (Weiner, 1985). Having an explanation provides a feeling of mastery over one's environment and serves an adaptive function. In addition to these intrapersonal incentives for causal search, the public nature of many product failures leads to interpersonal pressures for explanation. Consider the explanation given on the CBS Evening News for a 1987 airline crash that killed 156 people.

> Dan Rather: We've all been told the plane can fly on one engine. If that's the case then why did it crash?
> Peter Van Sant: Well, that's the mystery right now, Dan. My best guess . . . is that it was a catastrophic failure of the engine, that it literally exploded. Pieces of hot metal went inside the plane, possibly damaging control surfaces so that the pilot couldn't have control of that airplane anymore.

CBS News, NBC, the *Wall Street Journal* and *USA Today* were among the media blaming the Pratt and Whitney engine for the disaster. As a consequence, the engine maker's stock fell by $2.50 a share, losing a total of $330 million (Carley, 1988). It seems only fair that company officials and stockholders should pay a high price for the destruction caused by a defective product; however, subsequent investigations found that the engine was not to blame. The airline crash news stories illustrate how problems with products often prompt premature causal attributions. The pressure to provide an explanation seems to have led otherwise more cautious reporters to go "into a frenzy to find a cause," according to FAA officials (Carley, 1988). Whereas the need for an explanation is common for airline disasters (Butcher & Hatcher, 1988), many other product failures may prompt individuals to seek causes, though not commonly on such a large scale.

The urgency to produce an explanation before the desired or even necessary information is gathered may sow the seeds for a variety of marketplace disputes. Publicly presenting even a tentative cause commits the explainer to that position. People often feel their credibility depends on maintaining a stated position. This is a particular concern for the seller because attributional errors may be perpetuated within a firm because of employees' desires to support fellow employees' position against outsiders. Customers may even come to be viewed as common adversaries (cf. Janis, 1972). Thus, interpersonal, as well as intrapersonal, factors may be important in initiating and sustaining attributional conflict with others. Let us turn now from the impetus to make a causal inference for product failure to the type of inferences made.

Self-serving Attributions for Product Failure

Several studies have examined the kinds of causes given for product failure by buyers and by sellers, and have found patterns suggesting self-serving biases. From the buyer's perspective, blame tends to fall on the seller. In a survey of Dutch households, 90% of respondents placed at least some blame for their dissatisfaction with clothing and appliance purchases on marketing institutions (Richins, 1980).

Sellers also want to present themselves in a positive light. For example, company executives have the opportunity to explain their firm's performance in their letters to shareholders. These communications influence stock prices and executive compensation. In an analysis of numerous letters across many industries, a pattern of self-serving biases emerged (Bettman & Weitz, 1983). External (environmental), unstable (temporary), and firm-uncontrollable reasons were given for poor performance (e.g., lower profits were attributed to unusual economic conditions), but internal (firm-related), stable (permanent), and firm-controllable reasons were more frequent for good earnings (e.g., high profits due to the firm's research and development efforts).

Financial incentives for self-serving attributions reach their apex in product liability litigation. With settlements running into millions of dollars, these court cases result from an inability to resolve buyer–seller conflicts. I have engaged in some exploratory research investigating the kinds of attributions made for product failure in such disputes. Fifteen consumer products liability cases in which jury verdicts were rendered between January, 1982, and July, 1983, in Los Angeles, Orange, San Bernardino, Riverside, and San Diego counties were examined.

In seven cases, the jury brought a verdict favoring the plaintiff (the consumer) and in eight cases the jury favored the defense (firms such as Sears, Upjohn Laboratories, and Coca Cola Bottling). Gross recoveries by the plaintiffs ranged from $20,000 to $ 6 million. When the reasons for product failure presented by plaintiffs and defendants were examined, clear differences emerged. In all 15 cases, the plaintiff (the consumer) accused the defendant (the seller) of being able to control the reason for product failure while maintaining lack of control over the cause of product failure. Defendants (sellers) uniformly presented themselves as lacking control over product problems. But attributions did not follow a completely self-serving pattern. In eight cases defendants (sellers) maintained the plaintiff (the buyer) had control over the cause of the problem, whereas in seven cases they agreed that the plaintiff lacked control over the problem's cause. This admittedly small sample suggests that in high-stakes disputes initiated by the buyer and requiring third-party mediation for resolution, buyers and sellers disagree about whether product failure is caused by the seller but may show some agreement about the buyer's role in causing the problem. Thus, disagreement over the seller's role rather than the buyer's role appears more influential in escalating these sorts of conflicts over product failure.

Discrepant Attributions from Different Information

Even when the incentives for discrepancies between buyers' and sellers' attributions are minimized, systematic differences emerge. In one field study consumers and vendors read descriptions of products failing and made attributions for product failure (Folkes & Kotsos, 1986). The consumers were divided between apparel shoppers in malls and drivers at service stations. Half read sce-

TABLE 8.1
Locus of Explanations for Product Failure

	Sellers		Buyers	
	Car Mechanics	Apparel Salesclerks	Drivers	Apparel Shoppers
Reasons for car breakdown				
Mechanic-related	20%	93%	80%	82%
Driver-related	40	—	—	—
Other (e.g., car replacement part)	40	7	20	18
Total	100%	100%	100%	100%
Reasons for split seams				
Manufacturer-related	62%	36%	76%	87%
Customer-related	38	64	18	13
Other	—	—	6	—
Total	100%	100%	100%	100%

narios describing a problem with recently purchased apparel while the remainder read about a problem with a car shortly after it was repaired. Regardless of the problem described, more than three quarters of the consumers perceived failure as seller-related. For example, apparel shoppers and service station customers who read a scenario describing split seams in recently purchased clothing attributed the problem to poorly made goods (see Table 8.1). They rarely accused the customer of buying the wrong size. Similarly, consumers attributed the car problem to the mechanic, rather than to the driver's actions.

In this study, vendors' attributions for the same product failures were also examined. Sellers were more likely to perceive failure as buyer-related but only for products they themselves offered. For example, apparel salesclerks were more likely to blame split seams on the purchaser (e.g., "the customer bought the wrong size," "the customer is too fat"). But clothing salesclerks reading about car problems attributed the problem to the mechanic to the same extent as apparel shoppers and drivers (Table 8.1). Similarly, few car mechanics believed a car problem occurring shortly after repair had anything to do with the mechanic. However, mechanics blamed apparel problems with split seams on the manufacturer more than the consumer. Therefore, when incentives for self-serving attributions are minimized, the role of seller does not in itself lead to different attributions, but selling a particular product does.

These discrepancies may be partly due to access to different information. Because failure incidents are more available in consumers' memories relative to their incidence, consumers appear to overestimate how commonly products fail. Failure becomes more accessible in memory partly due to its greater frequency as a conversational topic. People are more likely to relate negative rather than positive experiences with products to others (Day, 1980). Further, one's own colorful product failure experiences, as contrasted to the mundane occurrences when products work, lead product failure to be more available and so over represented (Folkes, 1988; Tversky & Kahneman, 1973). The more common problems are thought to be, the more likely are people to attribute the problem to the seller (i.e., if many others experience this problem, something must be wrong with the product itself; Folkes & Kotsos, 1986; Kelley, 1967). For example, estimates of how commonly problems occur shortly after having a car repaired are highly correlated with identifying the mechanic as causing the problem. Frequent problems are attributed to the mechanic.

In contrast, the seller's information leads to different attributional biases. People often do not complain to sellers about product failure (Day, 1980), so sellers do not receive complete feedback about product performance. It is not surprising that sellers believe the products they sell fail less commonly than do purchasers (Folkes & Kotsos, 1986). Unusual problems are attributed to the buyer (i.e., few customers experience this problem, so the problem must be caused by the purchaser's misuse of the product). For example, infrequent car repairs are associated with driver-related problems.

An additional source of confusion for the seller occurs when consumers' reactions to product failure exhibit high variance. A good example of diversity in consumer reaction can be seen among passengers waiting for delayed flights. A glance around the departure gate reveals that some passengers fume while others are unperturbed. This variance occurs partly because passengers infer different reasons for flight delays (e.g., some attribute the delay to mechanical problems while others attribute the same delay to bad weather; Folkes, Koletsky, & Graham, 1987). From the perspective of the complaint handler, lack of consensus in consumer response suggests a person attribution (e.g., the complainer is idiosyncratic or a crank; Kelley, 1967).

One source of product information that may be particularly credible for consumers, the media, may be systematically biased in the temporal stability of explanations for events. The media tend to give explanations that suggest change is not due to chance but will persist (Andreassen, 1987). Thus, financial news writers give stable or permanent reasons for a firm's stock price increase, leading readers to expect continued increases and so to purchase the stock. In a simulated stock market game, subjects read actual newspaper headlines giving reasons for stocks rising (e.g., gains in the stock due to a merger proposal) or falling (e.g., declines due to the entry of a new, major competitor in the industry). Compared with conditions when no reasons were given, reasons for prices falling led subjects to sell the stock, whereas reasons for gains led to purchases.

The Complexity of Explanations for Product Failure

Another important factor leading to discrepancies in attributions is the fundamental complexity of many causal judgments in the marketplace. Complex causal relationships may contradict common causal heuristics. For example, the representativeness heuristic holds that causes and effects should resemble each other (Kahneman & Tversky, 1982). The astronauts' deaths were consistent with the dramatic sight of the Challenger explosion. But people initially found it hard to accept that a minor piece of equipment, an o-ring, could be the cause of the disaster. Similarly, invisible causal agents, such as airborne chemicals, are difficult to link to concrete effects.

Because temporal contiguity is an important cue to causality, delayed effects are often not linked to causes. In a study of responsibility for accidents and other injuries, the time lag between the negligent act and the injury decreased the defendant's perceived responsibility (Johnson & Drobry, 1985). However, the extent of delay needed to reduce responsibility differed for various types of situations from a day to a year. When products have few immediately observable effects, but have minute effects that accumulate over many years causal relations may be particularly obscure. For example, the fluorocarbons in aerosol sprays can dramatically impact the ozone and weather over the long term but received widespread attention as a causal factor only with the particularly severe winter and drought of 1988. Delayed manifestation of the problem, such as has also occurred with asbestos and urea-formaldehyde, has presented the jurisprudence system with particular difficulties in judging responsibility (Dworkin & Sheffet, 1985). In short, the kinds of causal complexities discussed here make it easy for people to arrive at different causal inferences for the same event.

Influence of the Buyer–seller Relationship on Causal Inference

Aspects of the buyer–seller relationship can also influence attributional conflict. Buyer and seller can vary in interdependence, which influences attributional search. For example, the buyer might have many alternative sources from which to purchase goods or might be dependent on just one seller. Dependence increases search for attributions to explain the other's behavior (Berscheid, Graziano, Monson, & Dermer, 1976), and so may make one more willing to seek out the other's perspective. Consequently, attributional disagreements would be reduced. The buyer's or seller's expectation for future interaction also influences search for causes (Berscheid et al., 1976) and so can increase sensitivity to the nuances of the other's interpretations. Expecting future interaction may also lead to more caution in accepting the other's interpretation. Agreeing that a certain cause led to failure or that a cause implies certain responses can commit one to the same course of action in the future.

Lengthy history of the relationship, especially when it includes a variety of experiences and interactions, gives each partner more information to use when making attributions. Further, the attributions are likely to be held with more confidence. This can both aggravate and ameliorate conflict. When attributions are discrepant, opponent's positions would be less tractable than when positions are held with less confidence. Finally, a high degree of trust in the other may minimize causal search and the felt need to justify one's perspective, whereas distrust may instigate a thorough search with the main goal of that search being to reach an explanation that can be easily justified.

Summary

Only a few of the factors leading to differences between buyers' and sellers' attributions for product failure have been discussed here. Product failure is the kind of negative and unexpected event that has been shown to prompt causal search. One's own need for mastery and demands from others to explain an event can lead to premature explanations that sow the seeds of attributional conflict. Some disputes involve high stakes, financial and otherwise, that provide incentives for self-serving attributions. Different information used to make causal inferences and self-serving motivations can also account for many discrepancies. The inherent complexity of understanding the causes of many product problems due to lack of temporal contiguity and other factors permit different inferences to be drawn. Finally, characteristics of the buyer–seller relationship, such as expectation for future interaction, history of the relationship, and trust, can aggravate or ameliorate attributional conflict.

CONSEQUENCES OF ATTRIBUTIONS FOR PRODUCT FAILURE

Having identified some of the bases for similar and dissimilar attributions for product failure, we now turn to the consequences of these attributions. Central issues in the study of conflict are understanding the sources of such negative interpersonal feelings as anger and revenge, the resolution of conflict through such behaviors as restitution, redress, and apologies, and the kinds of behaviors leading to conflict avoidance. A number of studies examining consumer reaction to product failure link these constructs to certain underlying causal dimensions. Causes of product failure have been categorized by locus of causality, controllability and temporal stability, causal properties analyzed in a wide variety of other domains (Weiner, 1986). In this section I relate these causal dimensions to consequences that either increase or decrease buyer–seller conflict.

Locus of Causality and Remedying Product Failure

Locus of causality is probably the most fundamental distinction for understanding consequences of product failure. Whereas in most attributional research the internal/external terminology is sufficient (e.g., Weiner, 1986), possible confusion over whose perspective is taken makes a distinction between seller-related and buyer-related causes clearer. Locus influences beliefs about who should solve problems. People believe that problems should be solved by the source of the problem or causal agent; problems arising from consumers' actions should be solved by consumers, whereas problems arising from firms' actions should be solved by firms. In a survey of Salt Lake City households, those attributing the energy crisis to the general public favored the public's solving the problems by such actions as voluntary conservation, whereas those attributing the energy crisis to the oil companies more strongly favored government pressure on oil companies as a solution (Belk, Painter, & Semenik, 1981).

Because of the link between causing the problem and problem solution, locus of causality influences beliefs about restitution and redress for product failure (Folkes, 1984). In one study, consumers were presented with scenarios describing various product failures (e.g., a consumer who failed to lose weight while using a breakfast drink marketed as a weight-loss aid). Thus, for each product, eight different explanations were given for why the failure occurred. The causes each varied as to locus (buyer-related or seller-related), controllability (volitional or nonvolitional) and temporal stability (temporary or permanent). For example, a buyer-controlled, unstable reason for no weight loss while using the diet drink involved the buyer's lack of effort to reduce calories while going to holiday parties. The locus, controllability, and stability of the reason for product failure were varied orthogonally.

Locus influenced redress. When product failure was seller-related, the consumer deserved restitution, such as a refund. When product failure was buyer-related, the seller was not obligated to provide restitution. But product failure also damages the trust essential for the exchange relationship between buyer and seller. Seller-related product failure requires repair of this relationship. In the study just described, consumers felt that apologies are deserved when product failure is seller-related but not when product failure is buyer-related (Folkes, 1984). Research using children suggests that outcome may also be related to the need for apologies. More elaborate apologies are needed as the severity of the outcome increases (Darby & Schlenker, 1982).

From this analysis it is clear that conflict can arise when the seller makes buyer-related attributions for product failure but the buyer makes seller-related attributions (Table 8.2). For example, a tire store maintains that the driver misused the tires but the driver maintains the tires are defective. The consumer would feel a refund and an apology are deserved whereas the seller would not. But attributions differing in locus do not always lead to disputes. Conflict is unlikely when the seller makes seller-related attributions but the buyer makes buyer-related attributions. For example, an automobile manufacturer might announce a product recall but the consumer might attribute the problem with his or her car to lack of maintenance. Obviously, such a discrepancy will not fuel a dispute.

TABLE 8.2
Attributions Leading to Postpurchase Buyer–Seller Conflict

Attributional Discrepancy

Buyer's Attributions	Seller's Attributions	Consequences of Conflict
Seller-related	Buyer-related	Disagreement over whether seller should give refund and apology to buyer
Seller-related and controllable	Buyer-related or seller-related and uncontrollable	Disagreement over whether buyer should feel angry and vengeful toward seller
Seller-related and stable	Buyer-related or seller-related and unstable	Disagreement over whether buyer should expect future product failure and should accept replacement or exchange rather than refund

Control over Causes, Anger, and Retaliation

Causes also differ in controllability over outcomes (Weiner, 1986). For some actions a consumer "could have done otherwise" and so had volitional control over an outcome, while at other times the situation forces or constrains the consumer to follow a certain course of action. For example, in litigation over cigarettes' ill effects, plaintiffs maintain that their smoking was addictive and that they lacked control over stopping. Tobacco companies counter that smoking is a habit that the smoker chooses to indulge in and is under the user's control. Disputes over controllability are important because control influences evaluations of product hazard. Risks people voluntarily assume (e.g., snow skiing) are perceived as more acceptable than those perceived as imposed by firms (Rethans & Albaum, 1980).

Although sellers are often groups rather than individuals, firms can also be perceived as having varying amounts of control over their actions. For example, passengers perceive airline personnel problems, such as slow baggage handling, to be more firm-controllable reasons for flight delays than mechanical problems (Folkes et al., 1987). Research has primarily examined how consumers' perceptions of sellers' control over a problem (external locus) influences consumers' responses to product failure. When sellers are thought to have control over the cause of product failure, consumers feel angry and desire revenge more than when they are believed to lack control (Folkes, 1984; Folkes et al., 1987). When others volitionally cause us to suffer negative outcomes, we behave more punitively toward them than when constraints force a negative outcome (Hamilton, 1980; Weiner, 1986). A typical response to anger is "denial or removal of some benefit customarily enjoyed by the instigator" (Averill, 1983, p. 1148). The desire for revenge raises particular concerns when one considers incidents of consumer sabotage, such as product tampering.

In the case of marketplace conflict, anger appears to mediate partly the relationship between attributions and the desire to engage in conflict with the seller over the problem. These relationships were examined in a field study of 97 airline passengers waiting for delayed flights (Folkes et al., 1987). The passengers provided what they believed were the reasons for product failure (e.g., bad weather, air traffic controllers' problems). Then they indicated on a rating scale the extent to which they believed the airline had control over the problem or lacked control. When the passengers perceived that the airline had control over the reason for the delay, they felt angrier than when they perceived a lack of control over the cause. Furthermore, anger arose not only from control over the problem but from the firm's perceived control over a solution to the problem (cf. Brickman et al., 1982). For example, if a passenger believed that the airline could substitute another plane to solve the problem, the passenger felt angrier than if he or she believed the airline lacked a solution. Thus, a passenger may believe a delay arises from an uncontrollable problem but also believe that the airline had control over the solution to the problem and so feel angry. Similarly, a passenger might feel angry about an airline-controllable problem even though the airline lacked control over a solution.

Anger was also intensified as outcome importance increased. The more important that the passenger arrive on time, the angrier the passenger. The hostility felt by passengers led them to want to express their complaints to the airline. A path analysis showed that anger also decreased the passengers' willingness to fly the same airline again.

Telling other consumers about product failure enables the individual to vent his or her anger, gains social support for the validity of these negative feelings and also may allow the consumer some means of retaliation by discouraging others from purchasing the product. Thus it is not surprising that controllability is related to willingness to communicate with others about product failure. One study manipulated the firm's control over product failure in scenarios presented to students. Product failure controlled by the firm increased the desire to warn others against product purchase compared with instances when product failure was not controlled by the firm (Curren & Folkes, 1987).

Although I have focused on controllability and consumers' anger, controllability also appears to be important to conflict mediators. Judges and jurors in product liability cases may not feel angry about a consumer's problem but may consider controllability when determining whether sellers are to blame for the problem and so should be punished over and above providing restitution. In the achievement literature, blame is associated with failure for reasons under one's control (Weiner, 1986). An individual receives more blame for failing a test due to lack of effort than when failure is due to lack of ability. There is at least anecdotal evidence that control appears to be important in product liability cases. Controllability seems to have been taken into account when Beechnut executives were convicted of diluting apple juice for babies and were sentenced to prison. The executives could have investigated the reason for the suspiciously low price from the juice supplier.

As is obvious from the previous analysis, disputes can occur even though buyer and seller agree about the locus of the cause. Conflict occurs when buyers believe product failure is controllable by the seller but the seller does not (see Table 8.2). For example, the passenger attributes a delay to inefficient gate personnel but the airline maintains that air traffic controllers forced the airline to delay the flight. In this case the buyer feels angry and vengeful but the seller feels that his or her actions do not deserve this sort of reaction. Nevertheless, discrepancies between locus and controllability do not necessitate conflict. When the buyer attributes the problem to buyer-controlled causes but the seller attributes the problem to seller-controlled causes, conflict is unlikely. Of course, if both buyer and seller perceive product failure as controlled by the seller both should agree that the buyer should be angry. In these situations research suggests managers are even more generous when compensating the buyer than are other consumers (Resnik & Harmon, 1983).

This generosity may be partly due to a tendency to perceive sellers as having more control over product failure than buyers. Sellers have easier access to information about the product itself and to feedback from multiple buyers, whereas consumers have less expertise and are more typically isolated from each other. More generally, there may be a tendency to perceive groups as having more control over events than individuals. Further, the larger the group, the more control the group may be perceived to have. For example, a large firm's greater financial and personnel resources may be thought to facilitate problem diagnosis and solution more than for a small firm. In fact, individuals in a large firm may feel greater diffusion of responsibility over decisions and so exercise less total control over events.

Causal Stability and Expectancies for Product Performance

Discrepancies between locus and controllability can have a considerable impact on conflict due to their influence on affect and finding solutions to the problem. The third dimension, causal stability, has less impact. Causes of product failure can also be classified according to temporal stability (stable and permanent causes versus unstable and temporary causes). For example, flight delays can be perceived as caused by stable causes, such as constant understaffing or air traffic control problems, or by unstable causes, such as a temporary shortage of staff or a hailstorm. Causal stability influences expectancies for product performances, so that stable causes for an outcome lead to more confidence that the same outcome will recur than do unstable outcomes (Weiner, 1986). Thus, when products fail for stable reasons (e.g., the dishwasher stops because the product is defective or because the consumer never scrapes food off before filling the dishwasher), the consumer is more certain the product will fail again than when due to unstable reasons, (e.g., the refrigerator stops because of a power failure or because the consumer forgot to plug it in after cleaning; Folkes, 1984).

Considering the relationship of stability to expectancies it is not surprising that stability influences the type of redress preferred when a product fails (Folkes, 1984). Compared with unstable reasons, stable attributions lead consumers to prefer more strongly refunds rather than replacement of the failed product. Consumers' more pessimistic expectancies probably make replacement unattractive. However, locus also influences type of redress preferred. Preference for refunds as opposed to replacement increases when products are perceived to fail for firm-related reasons as opposed to consumer-related reasons.

Clearly, conflict can arise when sellers make unstable attributions for product failure but the buyer makes stable attributions (see Table 8.2). For example, the seller attributes a mechanical problem to a temporary glitch, but the buyer attributes the problem to poor quality parts. Buyer and seller should then disagree about what sort of redress (e.g., exchange or refund) is appropriate. Yet conflict can also spring from more complex temporal inferences. Although classifying causes into a dichotomy has proved useful in past studies examining consequences of the stability dimension, this simple system may not fully capture consumers' temporal sensitivities. Consumers may sometimes carefully analyze causes for underlying temporal patterns, which then influence their purchases. Regularities, as opposed to erratic variation, can be as important as whether causes are permanent or temporary. For example, Soviet shoppers make it a point to check an appliance's manufacturing date. Goods manufactured toward the end of the month are shunned because of common knowledge that the rush to fill production quotas leads to low-quality goods. Goods are thought to be manufactured at a more leisurely pace in the early part of the month so are sought after. When buyer and seller perceive a different temporal pattern, they are likely to disagree about future product performance.

CONFLICT OVER CONTRIBUTIONS OF CAUSES

Considering the given consequences for product failure, it is clear that attributions can provide the basis for conflict in the marketplace. Buyers and sellers may infer reasons for product failure that differ in locus, controllability, or stability. Different attributions for product failure can lead to different beliefs about what should be done about the problem (see Table 8.2).

However, conflict can also occur when buyer and seller agree about what causes are present, but disagree over the contribution of each cause. Faced with an array of possible causes, buyer and seller may disagree over how influential each cause was and what the consequences should be. For example, if the breakdown is due to the actions of both buyer and seller, a free replacement seems overly generous. In product liability cases, the courts assign a percentage of responsibility for the problem and generally allocate restitution consistent with these percentages. However, this sort of analysis seems exceptional. Considerably less effort is required to think of causes in a linear, or chain-like relationship, with each cause sufficient to lead to the effect. Judgments of responsibility are simpler to make (Brickman, Ryan, & Wortman, 1975; Johnson & Drobry, 1985). Nevertheless, research examining marital conflict suggests that observers of a conflict are more likely to explain the dispute with multiple causes than are those who take one of the participant's perspective (Howe, 1987). These results are surprising since greater involvement in the dispute would seem to lead to more effort invested in understanding its causes and so more complex explanations.

Buyers and sellers may have a general self-serving tendency to hold the other more responsible for problems when they do accept that both buyer and seller could be held responsible. For example, some retailers maintain that if the causal chain includes a buyer-related cause then the seller has no responsibility. Consistent with this notion, consumer protection manuals and product instructions discourage consumers from attempting their own repairs when product failure may be seller-related.

On the other hand, if the buyer's actions partly account for product failure, the buyer may be less likely to confront the seller with a problem. The consumer's affective reaction to being the cause of product failure is probably embarrassment and shame. Just as lowered esteem results for internally caused failures at achievement tasks (Weiner, 1986), embarrassment and shame result from having made a poor purchase decision. These internally focused affects inhibit relating the experience to others, so complaints to the seller would be lessened, even if the seller also contributed to the problem. Thus, buyer–seller conflict is less likely. The buyer's embarrassment also means that other consumers are unlikely to be informed of and so to benefit from previous users' mistakes when those previous users feel they caused the problem. The victim's reluctance to acknowledge publicly having been gullible is probably one reason why con men are often able to continue swindling others even after their victims realize they have been duped.

REDUCING BUYER–SELLER CONFLICT

Having identified how attributions can lead to buyer–seller conflict, we now turn to ways these conflicts can be reduced. Conflicts may be resolved by one party giving in to the other or by both parties compromising. But it should be noted that discrepant causal attributions need not always lead to an overt conflict between buyer and seller. Consumers often do not call problems to the seller's attention. A common response to a product problem is conflict avoidance—the consumer does nothing (Best & Andreasen, 1977; Day, 1980). Many people fear that when they return a product, the seller will disagree about where the fault lies and so put up with shoddy goods rather than involve themselves in confrontations (Richins, 1980). Thus, beliefs about the other's attributions and about the other's willingness to engage in conflict influence the expression of differences.

This conflict avoidance might seem to be an advantage for firms, but in general it works to the firm's disadvantage. When a consumer has a problem but does not complain, the firm can lose a good customer without knowing why. Complaints often stimulate product modifications that increase a firm's competitiveness. Further, if a consumer does complain, but feels the complaint is handled well, the consumer is often even more loyal to the firm than if the problem had not occurred in the first place (Richins, 1980). Thus, an attempt by sellers to discourage conflict avoidance by consumers and facilitate conflict resolution can be justified in terms of overall profit.

Conflict resolution seems to require actions to address cognitive discrepancies between buyer and seller, opportunities to express affective reactions to product failure and behaviors that redress the inequitable exchange and damaged relationship. Yet, when consumers do report problems to sellers or seek mediators to resolve problems, the solutions offered are generally conceived in the most narrow sense, in terms of providing restitution. Financial redress addresses the inequitable economic exchange between buyer and seller when a product fails, but does not acknowledge the social aspect of the exchange relationship. To repair the broken trust between buyer and seller apologies are necessary for seller-related product failure (Folkes, 1984). Perhaps apologies are atypical because complaint handlers often do not feel personally responsible for product problems and are compelled to resolve problems following policies set by others. Higher-level executives may be more sensitive to such issues because of more perceived control over the problem and more discretion over a solution. For example, a feeling of personal responsibility is clearly conveyed by Lee Iaccoca's apology when news media revealed that Chrysler had sold used cars as new. In Japan, company executives commonly publicly apologize even for minor problems with products (Christopher, 1983). Thus, consumers may find that conflicts with a firm on a proximal level are more easily resolved at a distal level.

With this chapter's emphasis on attributions as a source of conflict, it is clear that dispute resolution is more likely to be successful if it also focuses on understanding the causes of product failure. Giving excuses for product failure that are uncontrollable should reduce a consumer's anger toward the firm (Folkes et al., 1987; Weiner, Amirkhan, Folkes, & Verette, 1987). Identifying actions to take in response to problems is another important way to minimize consumers' anger at product failure. Merely informing customers where to go to solve problem can reduce retaliation, perhaps because it places some control over solving the problem with the consumer. When Parisians waiting to use a public telephone were polled on their feelings when faced with an out-of-order phone, 55% reported feeling angry and 69% reported they shook the equipment or handled it roughly (Levy–Leboyer, 1988). Observations of out-of-order phones found that fewer customers vandalized equipment when information on the phone directed the consumer to another phone and the place to obtain a refund, even though most callers did not actually seek redress.

When the firm is unwilling to accept the blame, dispute resolutions should begin with causal analysis. The information used to make the attributions would be shared. Information is generally more effective in preventing discrepant attributions for product failure if provided before product failure then afterwards. It is easier to influence beliefs before they have been created then to change them (Anderson, Lepper, & Ross, 1980). If the consumer knows how the product can be misused then subsequent misuse by the consumer leads product failure to be more likely to be recognized as consumer-controllable. Furthermore, providing an attribution before the anger associated with product failure occurs helps dissipate the anger more quickly then if the attribution occurs after anger (Schwarz & Clore, 1983). Thus, timing can influence ease of dispute resolution.

In light of the importance of cognitive processes in resolving conflict over the causes of product failure, one should consider conditions that reduce complex cognitive processing and so increase conflict. The state of heightened arousal often accompanying disputes reduces cognitive capacity and so leads to more superficial processing of information (Kim & Baron, 1988). Further, aversive emotional states increase the natural tendency to favor short-term benefits despite long-term costs and risks (Baumeister & Scher, 1988). Thus, anger may lead to escalation of conflict because it makes understanding the other's perspective more difficult. For example, a consumer's anger over the firm's perceived control over a problem may cloud the consumer's ability to understand that the firm lacks control over the solution to the problem. Perceived control over the problem's solution would intensify anger.

SUMMARY

At the heart of many disputes between buyers and sellers may be discrepant causal inferences for product performance. This chapter has reviewed research examining the sources and consequences of disparate attributions for product performance. Buyers and sellers are motivated to search for different kinds of information and have different information about sources of problems. The resulting discrepant causal attributions influence such matters as beliefs about the appropriateness and nature of redress, affective reactions and the future transactions between buyer and seller. The attributional analysis of marketplace conflicts presented here highlights cognitive and affective factors in the resolution and avoidance of conflict.

REFERENCES

Anderson, C. A., Lepper, M., & Ross, L. (1980). Perseverance of social theories: The role of explanation in the persistence of discredited information. *Journal of Personality and Social Psychology, 39,* 1037–1049.

Andreassen, P. B. (1987). On the social psychology of the stock market: Aggregate attributions' effects and the regressiveness of prediction. *Journal of Personality and Social Psychology, 53,* 490–496.

Averill, J. R. (1983). Studies on anger and aggression: Implications for theories of emotion. *American Psychologist, 38,* 1145–1160.

Baumeister, R. F., & Scher, S. J. (1988). Self-defeating behavior patterns among normal individuals: Review and analysis of common self-destructive tendencies. *Psychological Bulletin, 104,* 3–22.

Belk, R., Painter, J., & Semenik, R. (1981). Preferred solutions to the energy crisis as a function of causal attributions. *Journal of Consumer Research, 8,* 306–312.

Berscheid, E., Graziano, W., Monson, T., & Dermer, M. (1976). Outcome dependency: Attention, attribution and attraction. *Journal of Personality and Social Psychology, 34,* 978–989.

Best, A., & Andreasen, A. (1977). Consumer response to unsatisfactory purchases: A survey of perceiving defects, voicing complaints, and obtaining redress. *Law and Society Review, 11,* 701–742.

Bettman, J. R., & Weitz, B. (1983). Attributions in the board room: Causal reasoning in corporate annual reports. *Administrative Science Quarterly, 28,* 165–183.

Brickman, P., Rabinowitz, V. C., Karuza, J., Coates, D., Cohn, E., & Kidder, L. (1982). Models of helping and coping. *American Psychologist, 37,* 368–384.

Brickman, P., Ryan, K., & Wortman, C. B. (1975). Causal chains: Attribution of responsibility as a function of immediate and prior causes. *Journal of Personality and Social Psychology, 32,* 1060–1067.

Butcher, J. N., & Hatcher, C. (1988). The neglected entity in air disaster planning: Psychological services. *American Psychologist, 43,* 724–729.

Carley, W. M. (1988). In a big plane crash cause probably isn't everybody's guess. *Wall Street Journal,* March 29, 1–21.

Christopher, R. C. (1983). *The Japanese mind.* New York: Fawcett Columbine.

Clark, M. (1984). Record keeping in two types of relationships. *Journal of Personality and Social Psychology, 47,* 549–557.

Curren, M. T., & Folkes, V. S. (1987). Attributional influences on consumers' desires to communicate about products. *Psychology and Marketing, 4,* 31–45.

Darby, B. W., & Schlenker, B. R. (1982). Children's reactions to apologies. *Journal of Personality and Social Psychology, 43,* 742–753.

Day, R. (1980). Research perspectives on consumer complaining behavior. In Lamb, C. W., & Dunne, P. M. (Eds.), *Theoretical developments in marketing.* Chicago: American Marketing Association, pp. 211–215.

Dworkin, T. M., & Sheffet, M. J. (1985). Product liability in the '80's. *Journal of Public Policy & Marketing, 4,* 1–15.

Emshwiller, J. R., & Camp, C. B. (1988). On and On Grinds Fight Over Old Fords that Slip into Reverse. *Wall Street Journal,* Thursday April 4, 1988, 1–18.

Folkes, V. S. (1984). Consumer reactions to product failure: An attributional approach. *Journal of Consumer Research, 10,* 398–409.

Folkes, V. S. (1988). The availability heuristic and perceived risk. *Journal of Consumer Research, 15,* 13–23.

Folkes, V. S., Koletsky, S., & Graham, J. L. (1987). A field study of causal inferences and consumer reaction: The view from the airport. *Journal of Consumer Research, 13,* 534–539.

Folkes, V. S., & Kotsos, B. (1986). Buyers' and sellers' explanations for product failure: Who done it? *Journal of Marketing, 50,* 74–80.

159

Hamilton, V. L. (1980). Intuitive psychologist or intuitive lawyer? Alternative models of the attribution process. *Journal of Personality and Social Psychology, 39,* 767–772.

Howe, G. W. (1987). Attributions of complex cause and the perception of marital conflict. *Journal of Personality and Social Psychology, 53,* 1119–1128.

Janis, I. L. (1972). *Victims of group think.* Boston: Houghton Mifflin.

Johnson, J. T., & Drobry, J. (1985). Proximity biases in the attribution of civil liability. *Journal of Personality and Social Psychology, 48,* 283–296.

Kahneman, D., & Tversky, A. (1982). *Judgment under Uncertainty: Heuristics and Biases.* New York: Cambridge University Press.

Kelley, H. H. (1967). Attribution theory in social psychology. *Nebraska Symposium on Motivation, 15,* 192–238.

Kim, H., & Baron, R. S. (1988). Exercise and the illusory correlation: Does arousal heighten stereotypic processing? *Journal of Experimental Social Psychology, 24,* 336–380.

Levy-Leboyer, C. (1988). Success and failure in applying psychology. *American Psychologist, 43,* 779–785.

Resnik, A., & Harmon, R. R. (1983). Consumer complaints and managerial response: A holistic approach. *Journal of Marketing, 47,* 86–97.

Rethans, A. J., & Albaum, G. (1980). Towards determinants of acceptable risk: The case of product risks. *Advances in Consumer Research, 8,* 506–510.

Richards, B. (1988). Next few IUD cases could determine whether Searle faces mass tort problem. *Wall Street Journal,* September 14, 43.

Richins, M. (1980). Consumer perceptions of costs and benefits associated with complaining. In H. K. Hunt & R. D. Day (Eds.), *Refining concepts and measures of consumer satisfaction and complaining behavior.* Bloomington: Indiana University Press.

Sahagun, L. (1987). Honda's position on ATV safety disappoints state prosecutors. *Los Angeles Times,* November 18, 25.

Schwarz, N., & Clore, G. (1983). Mood, misattribution, and judgments of well-being: Informative and directive functions of affective states. *Journal of Personality and Social Psychology, 45,* 513–523.

Tversky, A., & Kahneman, D. (1973). Availability: A heuristic for judging frequency and probability. *Cognitive Psychology, 5,* 207–232.

Weiner, B. (1985). "Spontaneous" causal thinking. *Psychological Bulletin, 97,* 74–84.

Weiner, B. (1986). *An attributional theory of motivation and emotion.* New York: Springer–Verlag.

Weiner, B., Amirkhan, J., Folkes, V., & Verette, J. (1987). An attributional analysis of excuse giving: Studies of a naive theory of emotion. *Journal of Personality and Social Psychology, 53,* 316–324.

9 Conflict in Close Relationships: The Role of Intrapersonal Phenomena

Frank D. Fincham,
Thomas N. Bradbury,
John H. Grych
University of Illinois

The potential for conflict is omnipresent in social life and is perhaps nowhere more evident or significant than in close relationships. The prevalence of conflict in such relationships is suggested by the high rates of physical aggression reported in dating couples (35%, Deal & Wampler, 1986), in couples engaged to be married (38%, O'Leary, Arias, Rosenbaum, & Barling, 1986), in marriages (16%, Straus & Gelles, 1986) and in parent–child relations (62%, Straus & Gelles, 1986).[1]

Aggression and conflict should not be equated, however, as has happened in much of the psychological literature (cf. Shantz, 1987). Rather, conflict requires that two participants in a social interaction hold incompatible goals (Lewin, 1948). The goals need not be conscious and may vary from being quite specific (e.g., to cook a meal) to being very general (e.g., to be respected by others). Conflict arises when one person pursues his or her goals and in doing so interferes with the other person's goals. The interference may be quite direct (e.g., physical obstruction) or indirect (e.g., innuendos that affect the partner's emotional state). Each person may respond to the other's interference with their goals in a variety of ways. Even when partners engage the other in overt conflict, physical aggression does not occur in the vast majority of cases and hence we can assume that conflict among intimates is much more widespread than the figures cited might indicate.

The consequences of conflict in close relationships can be dramatic. In terms

---

[1]These figures are averages (across respondent sex and victim vs. aggressor roles) and reflect response rates for all items on the Conflict Tactics Scale. These items range from "threw something" to "used a gun or knife" (see original reports for further details).

of personal suffering, "an unequivocal association between marital disruption and physical and emotional disorder has been demonstrated" (Bloom, Asher, & White, 1978, p. 886). The costs to society are also high because the majority of problems for which people seek professional help are "related to some type of interpersonal difficulty—predominantly problems in a current or prior marriage" (Veroff, Kulka, & Douvan, 1981, p. 130).

For theoretical and applied reasons, therefore, it is important to understand conflict in close relationships. In the present chapter we analyze the intrapersonal or covert factors that are likely to influence conflict in close relationships, a topic that has been neglected in the psychological literature. Our goal is to facilitate research on conflict in close relationships by presenting an integrative framework that outlines the role of cognitive and affective factors in conflict. The chapter focuses on conflict in marital and parent–child relationships because these are the relationships in which conflict is most likely to arise and which are often cited as prototypes of close relationships. Our presentation is not specific to the family, however, and is intended to be applicable to close relationships in general.

The first section of the chapter provides a brief summary of what is known about conflict in close relationships and points to the need for an understanding of cognitive and affective processes in a complete psychological account of conflict. In the next section, we identify the major constructs needed for such an account of conflict. The third section describes a model of conflict in close relationships that focuses on the role of intrapersonal processes and illustrates its application. A discussion of the limitations of the model is offered in the fourth section, and the chapter concludes with a summary of the main arguments.

RESEARCH ON CONFLICT IN CLOSE RELATIONSHIPS

Although Gordon Allport (1948, p. xi) characterized it as "a particularly brilliant analysis," Lewin's (1948) ground-breaking paper on conflict in marriage has not resulted in much social psychological literature on conflict between intimates (for exceptions, see Braiker & Kelley, 1979; Kelley, 1979; Orvis, Kelley, & Butler, 1976; Sillars, 1981). Instead social psychological research on interpersonal conflict draws heavily on game theory and focuses mainly on "brief interactions among strangers or casual acquaintances . . . in contrived settings" (Peterson, 1983, p. 363). The generalization of findings from such studies to the close relationships that dominate our social lives is thus open to question.

In contrast, clinical psychologists have provided extensive data relevant to conflict in parent–child and marital relationships. Patterson's research program, for example, is particularly useful in documenting the behaviors displayed during parent–child conflict (see Patterson, 1982). His research shows that families with an aggressive child are characterized by higher rates of negative behavior than control families, and that during conflict these behaviors are reciprocated and result in bursts of negative exchanges. Such negative exchanges often escalate very rapidly as parent and child increase the intensity of their behavior. This "coercive spiral" ends when the behavior of the parent or of the child becomes sufficiently intense to force compliance on the part of the other. Because the end of the exchange involves the termination of an aversive stimulus for each person, each is negatively reinforced for their behavior. Although persuasive, this behavioral account of conflict is necessarily incomplete. Specifically, the thoughts and feelings that arise in conflict need to be investigated if it is to be fully understood.

In regard to marital conflict, clinical researchers have compared the behaviors of dissatisfied spouses and happily married spouses during conflict resolution discussions. Although a number of differences have been identified, the most consistent findings parallel those obtained in parent–child interaction. That is, dissatisfied spouses display higher rates of negative behavior and greater reciprocity of negative behavior than do happy spouses (for reviews, see Baucom & Adams, 1987; Fitzpatrick, 1988; Weiss & Heyman, in press). Despite the considerable effort expended to document the overt behaviors exhibited by dissatisfied and happy spouses in conflict discussions, little is known about the processes that give rise to such behavior. Moreover, it is important to note that the primary goal of marital researchers has been to account for variance in marital satisfaction rather than to understand conflict per se. Although satisfaction and conflict tend to co-occur, they are not equivalent. Finally, laboratory studies necessarily limit the spontaneity, duration, intensity, diversity, and ecological validity of conflicts studied. Not surprisingly, Peterson (1983, p. 396) concludes that "systematic knowledge about conflict in close relationships is severely limited."

A recent shift in focus appears to be laying the foundation for a more complete account of conflict in close relationships. More specifically, the emergence of studies on covert or intrapersonal factors in parent–child (e.g., Sigel, 1985) and marital relationships (e.g., Fincham & Bradbury, in press) points to the importance of thoughts and feelings for understanding conflict behavior. For example, mothers with a history of child abuse or neglect view the causes of their child's negative behavior as more internal to the child and more stable than mothers with no such history (Larrance & Twentyman, 1983). Similarly, dissatisfied spouses tend to make more destructive causal attributions for their partner's conflict-related behavior than do happy spouses (Fincham, 1985), and spouses' attributions for negative partner behavior affect their own behavior toward the partner (Fincham & Bradbury, 1988). Furthermore, the behaviors exhibited by distressed spouses in conflict discussions are accompanied by high physiological arousal and greater physiological linkage between spouses than corresponding measures for happy spouses (Levenson & Gottman, 1983). Attributions (Fincham & Bradbury, 1987a) and physiological arousal (Levenson & Gottman, 1985) also predict changes in marital satisfaction over time.

This new genre of research is important because it identifies factors that might increase our understanding of the behaviors that are known to occur during conflict discussions. That is, covert factors are likely to mediate the impact of conflict behavior and determine subsequent responses to it. For example, a husband may respond behaviorally to his wife's unsolicited advice (e.g., "You need to rinse the dishes before putting them in the dishwasher") differently, depending on his interpretation of the wife's action (e.g., he might see it as an attempt to be helpful or he might see it as unwarranted interference) and his affective response to it (e.g., gratitude versus anger).

Although the importance of attributions for understanding conflict is widely recognized (e.g., Gelles & Straus, 1979; Hotaling, 1980; Patterson, 1982; Peterson, 1983) detailed descriptions of the role that attributions might play in conflict are rare. Patterson (1982, p. 73), for example, notes that "the two concepts of attribution and intention potentially have much to offer a coercion theory" yet he does not specify how they might contribute to coercion theory (for application to coercion theory see the later section, *Strengths and contribution of model*). Similarly, little attention has been given to specifying the role of affect in conflict between intimates (cf. Bradbury & Fincham, 1987a). We therefore attempt to fill such gaps by offering a model of conflict in close relationships that focuses on cognitive and affective factors that are likely to influence conflict behavior. Before describing the model we will first outline its major components.

PREREQUISITES FOR A MODEL OF CONFLICT

Two important issues that arise in constructing a model of conflict in close relationships are the extent to which new concepts are introduced and the model's breadth of focus. In regard to the former, we have attempted to use existing concepts wherever feasible. The model therefore draws from research and theory on causal attribution (e.g., Weiner, 1985, 1986), responsibility attribution (e.g., Fincham & Jaspars, 1980; Shaver, 1985), attributions in marriage (e.g., Bradbury & Fincham, in press-a), and conflict in close relationships (e.g., Doherty, 1978, 1981a, 1981b; Fincham & Bradbury, 1987b). Thus, we use several concepts that have proven useful in prior research and some of the relations among them have received empirical support. Regarding breadth of focus, we have been mindful of the need for a balance between parsimony and inclusiveness. Our model is not intended to provide an exhaustive treatment of conflict. Rather, we argue that six central concepts can be used to understand the intrapersonal processes relevant to conflict, namely, an instigating event, primary processing, secondary processing, efficacy expectations, affect, and conflict behavior. The model relating these constructs is shown in Fig. 9.1.

According to the model, the occurrence of conflict requires an instigating event, which is usually a behavior by one of the partners in the relationship. This event is then processed by the perceiver. Initial or primary processing of the event establishes whether the partner behavior is self-relevant and violates expected standards of behavior. These standards are important because they reflect

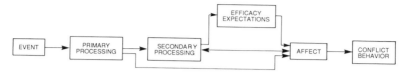

FIG. 9.1.   A model of conflict in close relationships.

assumptions about partner behavior that are integral to the perceiver's goals. To the extent that partner behavior violates such standards, a state of conflict exists. However, the perceiver's response to the conflict also depends on secondary processing, which establishes the cause of the instigating event. Primary and secondary processing of the instigating event influence the perceiver's affective state and efficacy expectations regarding their ability to resolve the problem. These two variables are the proximal determinants of the response to the instigating event. Before elaborating upon the relations in the model, we describe each of its components in greater detail.

Instigating Event

As noted, conflict begins with an instigating event. The paradigmatic case of an instigating event is a commission (e.g., statement or action) or omission (e.g., failure to do a chore, to be supportive) by one member of the relationship. However, it might also comprise an event (e.g., the birth of a child, graduation) or the action of a third person (e.g., a visit by an in-law, the action of a friend). Although they can instigate conflict, events and third-person actions do so by implicating the partner. That is, the event or the third person's behavior is translated by the spouse into a commission or omission on the part of the partner which then forms the basis of the conflict. Thus an event might give rise to conflict because it is seen to entail an omission (e.g., "the car seats wouldn't be damaged if you had closed the windows!") or because it marked an expected change in behavior that does not occur (e.g., "you were supposed to pay your own way once you graduated from high school"). Similarly, a visit by an in-law may produce conflict when, for example, the partner is "not assertive enough about telling your father that he can't just drop in anytime," a viewpoint that is not shared by the partner. In sum, instigating events involve the partner's behavior either explicitly or by implication. Without such involvement of the partner, there can be no basis for conflict in the relationship.[2]

---

[2]This brief analysis is consistent with the shift in content that is often observed in conflict. That is, the conflict may appear to be about other people or an event but is really about the partners' attitudes or behavior, a fact that may only become apparent to the participants as the conflict develops. Similarly, the conflict may fluctuate between the manifest behavior that comprises the instigating event (e.g., buying tickets for the movies) and the perceived disposition that gives rise to the behavior (e.g., "you're just inconsiderate and don't ever ask me what I want to do"). When each partner focuses on a different level of the conflict (e.g., third person vs. partner behavior, behavior vs. disposition), the conflict is likely to be particularly intractable.

Ideally, it would be useful to specify the types of events that result in conflict. This is likely to be inordinately difficult, if not impossible, because it is not clear that a unique set of events leads to conflict. Virtually any event, from the most innocuous to the most significant, can produce conflict. Even prosocial behaviors such as smiles and offers of help can lead to conflict. Thus, it is not the overt characteristics of an event that determine whether it serves as the basis for conflict. Rather, the manner in which the event is processed by the perceiver determines whether it instigates conflict, as issue to which we now turn.

Primary Processing of Instigating Event

We can infer that a person must first attend to and extract information from the instigating event before he or she responds to it. This initial processing determines the extent to which the partner is seen to have violated a standard for appropriate behavior that is considered to be self-relevant by the perceiver ("you should have. . ."). Most importantly, the partner will be seen to have acted inappropriately when his or her behavior interferes with the perceiver's goals. This reflects the fact that the standards for appropriate partner behavior are often implicit in the perceiver's goals. For example, a wife may formulate a specific career goal based on the assumption that her husband shares equal responsibility for child care. The husband will then be seen to violate a standard for behavior when he devotes insufficient time to child rearing due to the pursuit of his own career goals. In short, the standards for partner behavior often reflect assumptions that underlie the perceiver's goals.

The standards for appropriate behavior may derive from several sources, including cultural norms for interpersonal behavior and for behavior toward intimate others, experiences in past close relationships, and the history of the current relationship. Some of the standards will constitute "relationship rules" (e.g., negotiated agreements between the partners, assumptions made on the basis of past experience) and thus will be central to facilitating the goals of each person in the relationship. Knowledge of these standards for behavior may be verbalizable but is often tacit. In either case, these standards constitute part of the framework within which goals are formulated, and thus partner behavior that violates such standards and is perceived to be self-relevant, results in a state of conflict. The occurrence of such behavior thereby increases the potential for overt conflict behavior between partners.

One mechanism by which violation of standards may increase the potential for conflict behavior is the affect or emotion that it generates in the perceiver (see the later section, *Affect*). That is, it is hypothesized that primary processing can result in an affective response. Both the number and the importance of the perceiver's goals that are threatened by the violation will determine the intensity of his or her immediate affective response. Because the violation of a relationship rule is likely to interfere with numerous, important goals it will produce the most intense negative affect.

Two important observations follow from the foregoing analysis. First, the threshold for what constitutes inappropriate partner behavior may vary as a function of individual differences and relationship history. Thus, a behavior that appears to violate a standard (e.g., a failure to be polite) and appears to be quite negative to an outside observer may not be perceived as such by the participants in the relationship. Not surprisingly, spouses and outside observers show little agreement in coding partner behavior (Floyd & Markman, 1983). Second, judgments of partner behavior may be influenced by the perceiver's consideration of what she or he would do in a situation similar to that in which the partner behavior is exhibited. For example, a spouse may not see a partner behavior as a violation of a standard when his or her own response in the situation would have been similar to that of the partner.

In sum, the incongruity between partner behavior and the perceiver's standards, rather than the behavior itself, is hypothesized to determine whether an event is likely to result in conflict behavior. Provided that the event does not pose a threat to the immediate safety of the perceiver, the response to the event depends also on the outcome of a second stage of processing.

Secondary Processing of Instigating Event

During secondary processing the perceiver attempts to understand the meaning of the instigating event. This task is critical and will therefore be discussed in some detail. Fig. 9.2 depicts the processes that occur during secondary processing. The three different types of attribution incorporated in the model will be described in turn.

Causal Attribution.   Initially, the perceiver attempts to understand the meaning of the event by determining why it occurred. The causal attribution that results can be characterized in terms of the widely accepted dimensions of causal locus and causal stability. In the present context, these causal dimensions are hypothesized to carry implications for conflict behavior. The perceived locus of

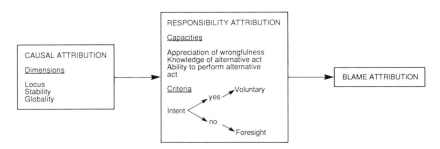

FIG. 9.2.   Secondary processing.

the cause (partner, self, relationship, outside circumstances) will determine the target of any efforts made to resolve the conflict and to avoid future conflicts. However, whether such efforts occur is likely to vary as a function of the perceiver's efficacy expectations or the extent to which he or she expects them to be successful (see the later section, *Efficacy expectations*). The perceived stability of the cause is an important factor that influences such judgments. Fincham and Bradbury (1987b) found support for these hypotheses in that judgments of causal locus and stability were correlated with target of change efforts and efficacy expectations, respectively.

The evolution of basic attribution research has revealed that the locus and stability dimensions are insufficient to capture all the psychologically significant properties of causes. A number of additional causal dimensions have been suggested in the attribution literature, including control, intent, and globality. Studies on the structure of perceived causality tend to yield results that favor control and, less consistently, intent as dimensions of perceived causality. Unfortunately, this research represents the work of "just a few investigators, often working together" (Weiner, 1986, p. 64) and tends to focus heavily on causal explanations in a single context, particularly the achievement context. In the absence of stimuli drawn from diverse contexts it is perhaps not surprising that little evidence has emerged for the global causal dimension. Moreover, as Weiner (1986) notes, different dimensions of causality may be differentially relevant across contexts.

These observations, combined with the meaningful pattern of findings obtained for the global dimension in research on learned helplessness (Peterson & Seligman, 1984) and marriage (Bradbury & Fincham, in press-a), suggest that it is premature to reject the global dimension as an important property of causes. With regard to conflict, it has been found that there is an association between the global causal dimension and the extent to which conflict initiated by a particular event affects numerous areas of the marriage (Fincham & Bradbury, 1987b). Consequently, the perceived globality of the cause constitutes a third causal dimension in our model that is hypothesized to influence the generalization of conflict behavior. In sum, causes can be characterized along the locus, stability, and globality dimensions, each of which carries specific implications for understanding conflict. For reasons outlined later, we do not include intent and control as dimensions of causal attribution.

An account of conflict that focuses solely on causal attributions is likely to be incomplete because one of the most salient features of a conflict is that it is "arousing and motivating" (Braiker & Kelley, 1979, p. 161). What contributes most to such arousal is an inference of intent. Behavior that is enacted purposefully to thwart the perceiver's goals, compared with unintended interference, will lead to greater arousal and is likely to alter substantially any behavioral response to the partner. Yet, as Weiner (1985) astutely notes, intent is not a property of causes but of a person's behavior. Weiner (1986) acknowledges that he is unable to resolve the inconsistency created by the inclusion of perceived intent as a dimension of causality and accords intent a minor role in his theory. The issue of perceived intent cannot be avoided as easily in the present context because it plays such an important role in conflict (e.g., Gelles & Straus, 1979; Hotaling, 1980; Patterson, 1982).

The solution to the problem noted by Weiner lies in recognizing that intent is central to the attribution of responsibility and blame rather than causal attribution. It is the attribution of blame, a highly evaluative judgment, that accounts for the arousal observed in conflict; a causal attribution simply constitutes a necessary condition for holding the person responsible or accountable for his or her action (except in cases of role responsibility and in some legal contexts involving strict liability).[3] The distinction between responsibility and causation tends to be overlooked in attribution theory and research. Consequently, we turn to consider responsibility attribution in greater detail.

Responsibility Attribution. The quintessence of responsibility is accountability. One is usually accountable to someone and hence perceived responsibility is especially important in interpersonal relations. Accountability arises when a person abrogates a duty or violates a standard of behavior, and its central role in conflict is therefore not surprising. As in the case of causal attribution, a number of dimensions are important for understanding responsibility attribution, and these can be grouped into two categories. The first concerns the capacities a person must possess for the question of accountability to arise and the second deals with the criteria used to determine responsibility. Each is described in turn.

We usually do not hold people accountable for their behavior if they do not possess certain capacities. Thus the question of responsibility may not arise when a 3-year-old insults a visitor to the home (e.g., "Wow, you are fat!") if the child does not appreciate that such behavior is inappropriate or wrong (Dix & Grusec, 1985). Similarly, when a husband fails to discuss his feelings with his wife he may not be held responsible if he is seen by the wife to lack the skills necessary to communicate about feelings. Based on legal analyses of responsibility (e.g., Hart, 1968), we propose that three capacities must be assumed present before partner behavior is evaluated in terms of responsibility criteria. The partner must have (a) an appreciation of the inappropriateness or wrongfulness of the behavior, (b) knowledge of an alternative conflict-avoidant behavior, and (c) the ability

---

[3]Causal attributions can account for such arousal only to the extent that they reflect such an evaluative judgment. In some circumstances, causal attributions are likely to serve as a proxy for an evaluative judgment. This is particularly true when the causal attribution pertains to the violation of a behavioral standard or a duty. For example, to infer that the partner fails to keep an appointment because she forgot about it is not a "cold" cognition. Yet a causal judgment is not sufficient for a complete evaluation of the behavior because it does not speak to the issue of whether the behavior was justified.

to carry out this alternative action. Such capacities have been found to influence adults' judgments about child behavior and their affective reactions to the behavior (e.g., Dix & Grusec, 1985; Fincham & Roberts, 1985) and may therefore be particularly important in the parent–child relationship.

Unless there is some factor (e.g., age, mental impairment) that makes capacities salient, it is hypothesized that their presence will be assumed automatically in close relationships and that perceived intent will be the focal issue in conflict. However, it is unlikely that intent alone accounts entirely for the variance in responsibility attributions. As shown in Fig. 9.2, two other criteria are evaluated once a judgment regarding intent has been made; one applies to intentional violations and the other applies to unintentional violations of behavioral standards.

In the case where intent is inferred, responsibility will be influenced by a judgment regarding the voluntariness of the behavior. A freely chosen, intentional action is the prototypical act for which one can be held responsible. The partner will not be held fully responsible for actions that are in any way involuntary. Such actions will be seen as partly, or wholly, justified, depending on the circumstances in which they occur (e.g., "I didn't really mind you ignoring me. . . . I know that you had to deal with your parents' demands"). In the case where the violation is unintentional, an inference occurs regarding the extent to which the partner should have foreseen that his or her behavior might interfere with the perceiver's goals. The partner will be seen as more responsible to the extent that such interference is considered foreseeable (e.g., "Throwing away those scraps of paper has really messed up my work. You should have realized that I left them on the desk because I needed to use them this evening.").

Although the terminology differs slightly from that used by Heider (1958), the responsibility criteria outlined earlier are the same as those he used to distinguish his "levels of responsibility." There is considerable evidence to demonstrate the influence of Heider's levels on both adults' and children's judgments (e.g., Harris, 1977; Fincham & Jaspars, 1979) and it seems reasonable to expect that they will be relevant to conflict between intimates. The connection we have drawn between Heider's levels of responsibility attribution and the responsibility criteria we propose is important because it helps us to evaluate the status accorded control judgments as a causal attribution dimension.

Fincham and Emery (1988) have shown that judgments of control are influenced by the same factors that affect responsibility and that control judgments can be used to model the impact of Heider's levels on attributions. That is, perceived control served as a summary index of responsibility criteria and predicted responsibility-related attributions. Moreover, the correlation between control and causal attributions was significantly lower than that between control and responsibility judgments. We therefore argue that perceived control is considered more appropriately as a rough, summary index for the numerous inferences related to responsibility rather than a dimension of causes. Thus, when a partner can potentially control behavior that violates a standard, he or she will be held accountable for that behavior.

Attribution of Blame.   Although the partner may be held accountable for his or her action, this does not necessarily mean that the perceiver considers him or her worthy of blame. Often, however, responsibility and blame are not distinguished in psychological research. This is understandable because the same dimensions underlie responsibility attribution and blame attribution. The difference between these two attributions is that an inference of responsibility determines whether a person should be called to account for his or her action, whereas blame is an evaluative judgment that determines the person's liability for sanctions. In addition, Shaver (1985) argues that attribution of blame ensues only after a person gives an account for his or her behavior, whereas an attribution of responsibility occurs before an account is given.

The distinction between responsibility and blame is based partly on the premise that accounts provide unique information (e.g., regarding intent) that is not available when the earlier responsibility attribution is made. Whether accounts provide such unique information is a philosophical question that we shall not attempt to resolve. It suffices to note that while some social institutions (e.g., the legal system) may reflect the logical distinction that can be made between responsibility and blame, we are not convinced that this distinction is critical to normal psychological functioning. Some intimates, especially people in very happy relationships, may not make a blame judgment until they hear the partners' account. In our experience, however, persons in close relationships readily assign blame in the absence of an account from the partner and hold such judgments with considerable certainty. Nonetheless, we maintain the distinction between responsibility and blame in our model rather than prejudge what is essentially an empirical question.

To summarize, we have drawn distinctions among causal, responsibility, and blame attributions and described the dimensions that are important in understanding each of these judgments. In doing so we have reconceptualized intent as a fundamental dimension of responsibility and blame attributions and argued that perceived control may serve as a summary index for the inferences that underlie these two attributions. We have also outlined the relations among causal, responsibility, and blame attributions.[4]

Efficacy Expectations

Following primary and secondary processing of the instigating event the perceiver attempts to determine whether the conflict can be resolved. The efficacy

---

[4]The linear relation posited among causal, responsibility, and blame attributions is a modification of the entailment model proposed by Fincham and Jaspars (1980) that has received considerable support in basic attribution research (e.g., Fincham & Roberts, 1985).

expectation represents his or her belief that constructive problem-solving behavior can be executed (see Bandura, 1977). In many cases this will involve the behavior of the couple (e.g., joint problem solving to find a means whereby both persons' goals can be achieved) but it can also involve the behavior of only one person (e.g., a partner changing his or her goal). Regardless of the behavior involved, efficacy expectations will be affected by the perceiver's attributions.[5] However, even when there are high efficacy expectations, they may not result in problem-solving behavior if they are not accompanied by the belief that the behavior will result in the desired outcome, usually a resolution of the conflict (e.g., the conflict may be seen as intractable).

Although we have expressed some concern about the applicability of efficacy theory to close relationships, especially the previously described distinction between efficacy and outcome expectations (Fincham & Bradbury, 1987b), there is an important advantage to incorporating efficacy expectations in our model at this time. Self-efficacy theory specifies three dimensions that underlie efficacy expectations—magnitude, generality, and strength—that, together with expectations about the outcome of the behavior, might allow more accurate prediction of behavior than a single expectancy judgment. Moreover, should efficacy expectations prove to be a viable construct in this context, research on close relationships can then be related to a vast literature on self-efficacy theory.

Although the ultimate status of efficacy expectations remains to be determined, an expectancy judgment of some sort is needed regarding the probability of successful conflict resolution. As in several attributional models (e.g., Abramson, Seligman, & Teasdale, 1978; Weiner, 1986), this judgment is hypothesized to mediate the relation between attributions and overt behavior. It is also likely to influence the affect experienced by the perceiver, the component of our model that is considered next.

Affect

One of the salient features of conflict is the arousal it generates. As noted earlier, primary processing can produce arousal when partner behavior is seen to violate a behavioral standard or a relationship rule. However, the perceiver's attributions for the violation will also influence his or her affective response. Following Weiner (1986), we posit that attributions determine specific emotions either directly or indirectly via efficacy expectations (see Fig. 9.3). Thus, high efficacy expectations will result in a feeling of hopefulness whereas low efficacy expectations will result in feelings of hopelessness or helplessness.

---

[5]Because causal dimensions and responsibility or "control" dimensions will be related empirically, it is not clear whether the impact of the stability causal dimension on efficacy expectations is direct or mediated by the attribution of blame. For the present, we adopt a conservative stance and assume a direct relation between causal stability and efficacy expectations so as to be consistent with existing research and theory (cf. Weiner, 1986).

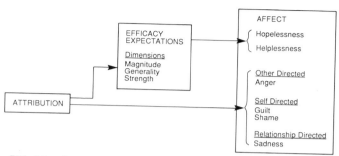

FIG. 9.3. Psychological consequences of secondary processing.

Regarding the direct impact of attributions on affect, we differ from Weiner (1986) in hypothesizing that attributions of blame, rather than causal attributions, give rise to specific emotions. The emotion most commonly associated with conflict is anger, "a highly interpersonal emotion [that] typically involves a close affectional relationship" (Averill, 1983, p. 1149). Our suggestion that an attribution of blame is the proximal cause of this emotion is consistent with the most important fact about anger, namely, that anger "is a response to some perceived misdeed" typically instigated by a "value judgment" (Averill, 1983, p. 1150).

As shown in Fig. 9.3, the emotion experienced in a conflict may be directed not only toward the partner but also toward oneself. We hypothesize that the two dominant self-directed emotions in conflict are guilt and shame, both of which ultimately affect self-esteem. Again blame attributions give rise to these emotions because they require *both* the contravention of a standard in addition to an internal causal attribution (e.g., "I should have been sensitive and not hurt her feelings"). Our position is consistent with Brewin's (1986) argument that low self-esteem in depression results from self-evaluation or self-blame rather than simply causal attributions (see also Affleck, Tennen, Pfeiffer, & Fifield, 1987). It is also consistent with the fact that the numerous studies used to demonstrate that affect mediates the association between attributions and behavior examine controllability and intent, which are dimensions of responsibility and blame attributions (cf. Weiner, 1986).

Finally, when the instigating event is attributed to the relationship the perceiver is expected to experience sadness. The frequency of such dyadic attributions is extremely low, an observation that appears inconsistent with the extent to which sadness is associated with conflict. It is therefore important to note that attributions are not the only instigators of emotion. For example, a person who, in a reflective moment during conflict, observes that he or she is arguing with a loved one may experience sadness. We shall comment further on emotion in conflict when elaborating upon our complete model.

For the present, it suffices to note that, like Weiner (1986), we hypothesize two psychological consequences of attribution. However, our cognitive consequence is an efficacy expectation that reflects several underlying dimensions rather than a single expectancy judgment. Similarly, affective consequences that are attribution-specific arise from an attribution of blame rather than a causal attribution.

Conflict Behavior

Both efficacy expectations and affect are hypothesized to influence conflict behavior directly (Fincham & Bradbury, 1987b; Weiner, 1986). Like the events that instigate conflict, however, the behaviors exhibited in conflict are numerous. Nonetheless, we propose that most responses entail either engaging in overt conflict behavior with the partner or avoiding such behavior. In the remainder of this section, we discuss briefly these two classes of response in conflict situations.

Engagement in Overt Conflict Behavior. Engagement in overt conflict with the partner may entail positive or negative behavior. Partners who believe that they can resolve the conflict are likely to engage in constructive problem solving. However, high perceived efficacy is not associated invariably with constructive responses to conflict. For example, the perceiver may not be motivated to engage in constructive problem solving and will withdraw despite high efficacy expectations (e.g., the perceiver may consider that the conflict does not warrant the energy needed to resolve it, or may have lost interest in the relationship). Similarly, the perceiver may retaliate regardless of the level of his or her efficacy expectations, a response that could lead to the escalation of conflict and ultimately to interpersonal violence. Retaliation is most likely when the partner is seen to have violated deliberately a central relationship rule for which no extenuating circumstances can be found; the partner is most likely to be seen as behaving with malevolent intent or selfish motivation. Such a situation will generate the most intense anger and may lead the perceiver to view retaliation as the partner's "just desserts."

Avoidance of Overt Conflict Behavior. Avoidance of overt conflict with the partner may similarly take positive or negative forms. Indeed, there is some evidence that happily married couples use avoidance as a primary means of coping with conflict (Raush, Barry, Hertel, & Swain, 1974). We have noted already that conflict can be avoided by partners' revising their goals without engaging in problem solving with each other. In such cases, the perceiver accepts the violation as appropriate behavior and thereby begins to redefine the standards by which subsequent behavior will be judged. However, conflict avoidance can occur also simply because the perceiver holds low efficacy expectations and sees no alternative to withdrawal (e.g., it is judged that engagement in overt conflict behavior is likely to lead to conflict escalation). When the strength, magnitude, and generality of such efficacy expectations are high, it is anticipated that the person will exhibit the behaviors associated with learned helplessness.

Summary

In sum, we have identified several concepts that constitute prerequisites for a model of conflict that highlights intrapersonal processes. The concepts involve the nature of events that can instigate conflict, the processing of these events, the psychological consequences of such processing, and the overt behavior to which they give rise. The next section outlines the relations among these concepts.

A MODEL OF CONFLICT IN CLOSE RELATIONSHIPS

At the outset of the previous section we presented briefly our model of conflict. It can be seen from Fig. 9.1 that numerous relations between components of the model were described in the last section. Some of these relations will be elaborated in the course of presenting a more detailed overview of the model.

All close relationships involve some underlying conflict of interest insofar as partners do not share all the same goals and even goals that are shared are not likely to be identical in every respect. The manifestation of conflict, however, requires the occurrence of an event that makes the conflict of interest overt *and* primary processing of that event in which the partner's action or omission is seen as inappropriate. That is, the partner is perceived to have violated a standard and thereby interfered with the perceiver's goal(s). Primary processing by the perceiver results in an affective response, with the degree of arousal varying as a function of the number and importance of the perceiver's goals that are affected by the event and as a function of individual differences in affective responsivity. At high levels of intensity, the arousal may be experienced as anxiety that could interfere with the perceiver's functioning. This possibility makes it apparent that the primary affective response is likely to affect secondary processing, an outcome that is consistent with the recent demonstration that affect influences attributions (Baumgardner & Arkin, 1988). Consequently, the arrow between attribution and affect is bidirectional.

Primary processing is followed by secondary processing, during which attributions are made. We have already described in some detail the types of attributions that occur, their underlying dimensions, and the relations among them. To provide a more complete understanding of primary and secondary processing we note three factors that might influence processing of the instigating event. Following Lewin (1948, p. 89), the first important factor is "the general level of tension" or the atmosphere in the relationship. Tension is likely to increase arousal and thereby affect information processing. In fact, Bradbury and Fincham (1987b, p. 69) hypothesized that arousal "decreases the probability of responding to negative partner behavior in terms of contextual cues and increases the likelihood of responses guided by current negative arousal."

A second factor that will affect processing is the knowledge possessed by the perceiver. Such knowledge, for example, defines the range of possible attributions that he or she might make for a particular partner behavior. Whether the perceiver will have access to the full range of possible attributions is, however, dependent on the accessibility of their knowledge when processing the instigating event. Thus, a third factor that will affect processing is accessibility of information stored in memory. The factors that affect recall of past experiences (e.g., vividness, emotion, priming, recency, and frequency of retrieval) are particularly relevant in understanding attributions. For example, when a spouse is asked to rate the extent to which a cause of a negative partner behavior affects other areas of the marriage (its perceived globality), his or her judgment is likely to be influenced by the ease with which negative partner behaviors can be recalled. The ease with which such behaviors can be recalled is, in turn, influenced by the spouse's recent exposure to negative material (i.e., "priming"), current mood state and so on (for further discussion of factors that influence processing see Bradbury & Fincham, in press-b; Fincham, Bradbury, & Scott, in press).

The attributions made during secondary processing influence the specific affect experienced by the perceiver and his or her efficacy expectations. These two variables, in turn, determine overt behavior. However, it is important to note that such behavior is constrained by several factors, including cultural and subcultural rules concerning the display of emotion, the appropriateness of the behavior, and the opportunity to engage in it. The perceiver's overt response to the instigating event becomes the stimulus for the partner, who will in turn proceed through the stages we have outlined; the course of the interaction will be sequenced accordingly.

Once the perceiver engages in overt conflict with the partner, the course of conflictual interactions will be influenced by several factors, four of which are mentioned briefly. Most obviously, any partner behavior that is perceived to be benign or conciliatory will increase the probability of a positive response and, ultimately, an end to the conflict. Second, the communication and problem-solving skills of the couple are important because appropriate skills can facilitate resolution of the conflict once this becomes a goal. On the other hand, inadequate skills can exacerbate conflict even when the goal is to bring about its resolution. Third, when a person's level of arousal or behavior toward the partner passes an acceptable threshold, or when the interactants realize they are not making progress, the conflict may be brought to an end. Fourth, the extent to which negative behaviors are seen as dominating and coercive is likely to have a particularly important influence on the course of the conflict. Such behaviors can escalate the conflict, especially when seen as purposeful attempts to control the perceiver, or can bring it to an end through violence, withdrawal or the voluntary submission of one partner. In sum, conflictual interactions can end via a number of mechanisms that range from positive (e.g., compromise) to negative (e.g., domination).

Illustration

To make the model more concrete, we provide a brief illustration of its application. Adopting the perspective of the husband, consider the following scenario: He arrives home from work knowing that his new boss is coming over for dinner that evening. His goal is to create a good impression with his boss and he is thinking about all the chores that have to be done before the guests arrive. Because he experienced a couple of serious problems at work during the day, he is in a bad mood and thinks that it is particularly important that the evening goes smoothly. A few minutes later his wife pulls into the driveway. She has work that needs to be completed for a deadline the next day and her goal is get it finished before the guests arrive. After a brief greeting, the wife sits down at the desk in the study adjoining the living room and begins her work.

Later, when tidying the living room, the husband notices his wife sitting at the desk. Primary processing of his wife's behavior leads him to experience fairly strong negative affect because her behavior interferes with an important goal and violates an implicit relationship rule based on past behavior, namely, that they both help prepare for visitors. His affective response, combined with his bad mood and the fact that the relationship has been tense lately because of disagreements about the amount of time each person devotes to work, affects the husband's secondary processing. He recalls similar occasions when he had felt let down by his wife because of her work habits and makes an internal, stable, and global attribution for her current behavior ("she is a workaholic"). He sees her behavior as intentional and voluntary and holds her responsible ("she knows that working now is inappropriate and she could be helping out"). Trying to exercise restraint, he calls her to account for her behavior: "So what's going on here? You are sitting working while I bust my gut trying to get ready for our guests." She explains that she has a work deadline but he discounts this explanation ("You let things pile up even though you knew tonight was important to me"). He sees her behavior as selfish and blameworthy. His negative affect is experienced as anger toward his wife.

The stable causal attribution made for this specific behavior confirms the husband's low efficacy expectations regarding the couple's ability to engage in effective problem solving. Although these low efficacy expectations have led him to avoid overt conflict behavior in the past, his intense anger (due to violation of a relationship rule, interference with an important goal, and perceived selfishness of partner behavior) results in his engaging the conflict with his wife: "You don't care about me, do you? I'm sick of your work messing things up. Get up and help me with the chores!" His unskilled, coercive behavior could result in an escalation of the conflict (e.g., "Watch it. I'm leaving here for the evening if you carry on like that") but his wife who has remained calm tries to de-escalate the conflict by being conciliatory ("Take it easy. . . . I didn't mean to upset you"). The husband's response to her statement is guided by his arousal rather than his wife's behavior and he again accuses her of being self-centered. Realizing that the situation might get out of hand, the wife succumbs to his demands and begins doing chores.

Having described the components of the model, the relations among them, and its application to a specific interaction, it remains to highlight the strengths of the model and its contribution to the literature on conflict in close relationships.

Strengths and Contribution of Model

Perhaps the most important feature of the model is its potential to integrate research on conflict and emotion in close relationships. Berscheid's (1983) theory of emotion in close relationships specifies that emotional experience occurs when a higher-order plan or goal is interrupted. This perspective is strikingly similar to our view of conflict. Other features of our model, in addition to this overlap in approach, are likely to facilitate integrative research. Unlike Berscheid's (1983) theory, for example, our model provides a detailed analysis of the cognitive processes relevant to emotion. Similarly, the most sophisticated cognitive model of conflict in close relationships fails to mention affect (Doherty, 1981a, 1981b; see Fincham & Bradbury, 1987b) whereas we accord emotion a central role in conflict. In sum, our model is among the first to provide an account of cognitive *and* affective processes in conflict.

A second significant feature of the model is that it represents an attempt to build on prior work relating to conflict and to basic psychological constructs (e.g., attribution, efficacy). This has two important consequences. First, it provides some empirical foundation for the model in that several of the relations specified have been supported in basic research. Further study is needed to verify that these relations also apply when studied in the context of close relationships. Second, consideration of psychological constructs and research on their interrelation in this important interpersonal context has led to the reconceptualization of basic attribution research and theory (cf. Weiner, 1985, 1986). This is particularly evident in regard to types of attributions where the distinctions drawn among causal, responsibility, and blame attributions resolve problems regarding the dimensions of perceived causation and suggest new avenues for basic research.

A third factor relevant to evaluating the model is that it appears to fill important gaps in the literature. For example, research on marital violence tends to focus on the frequency of violent acts despite numerous calls for systematic attention to intent (e.g., Margolin, 1987) and the fact that violence is often defined in terms of actual or perceived intent (e.g., "*Violence* is defined as an act carried out with the intention, or perceived intention, of causing physical pain or injury," Straus & Gelles, 1986, p. 467). Similarly, Patterson (1982) points to the potential contribution of cognitive factors, especially intent, to coercion theory. Yet, as noted, there has been no effort to fulfill this potential. In our model, intent plays a central role and it thus represents an attempt to fill such gaps in the literature. In view of the importance of this contribution, it is illustrated in relation to coercion theory.

The model contributes to an understanding of conflict escalation and thereby allows covert factors to be incorporated in coercion theory. Anger plays an important role in conflict escalation because it involves "a commitment to action if the instigating conditions do not change" (Averill, 1983, p. 1153). The two factors in the model that influence emotion are the number and importance of the goals affected by the instigating event (primary processing) and the attributions made for it (secondary processing). Thus, for example, conflict can escalate as partner behaviors are seen to threaten more and/or important goals of the perceiver. Similarly, conflict escalation may reflect changes in attribution whereby the initial attribution for the instigating event is revised or successive partner behaviors in the conflict are seen to reflect greater negative intent. These two processes are related, insofar as the affective impact of primary processing will influence attributions and their impact on emotion will, in turn, affect primary processing of the next partner behavior in the interchange. In sum, the model is among the first to address the cognitive and affective processes that can result in a "coercive spiral" (see also Gottman & Levenson, 1986).

Recognition of the role of affect in motivating conflict behavior points to a potential criticism of the model. That is, it can be argued that conflict behavior is relatively automatic and reflects stereotyped, almost reflexive patterns of responding. Indeed, it seems likely that the processing of most partner behavior in established relationships is often implicit. We agree with this observation and do not suggest that conflict always or even usually entails conscious or mindful processing. But the fact that such processing may be mindless does not thereby render it less important for understanding behavior. In addition, one needs to consider how couples establish such "automatic" patterns of conflict behavior. We argue that such behaviors result initially from the processes specified in our model. Moreover, a consistent manner of processing conflict behavior may arise in the course of the couple's conflict history. These generalized patterns or styles can then become automatic and allow the highly scripted, stereotyped exchanges seen in conflict.

In sum, the model presented builds on prior work relating to conflict and to basic psychological constructs, has the potential to integrate research on cognitive and affective factors in close relationships, and provides a more complete account of conflict between intimates that can be used to enrich existing theoretical statements.

CAVEATS

Lest it appear otherwise, we hasten to add that the model is not intended to account for all aspects of conflict in close relationships. Several limitations of the model need to be recognized and we describe some of these in this section.

An important limitation of the model is that it applies primarily to conflict that occurs over a relatively brief period of time. It would be useful to include a developmental component in future versions of the model. An understanding of how conflict develops over the course of a relationship is important for several reasons. First, it would provide information on how styles of processing get established. Second, it might clarify the relation between situation-specific judgments and judgments that simply reflect generalized beliefs. Third, it would allow us to determine the conditions under which mindful versus mindless processing occurs. These are important issues that need to be addressed in any comprehensive model of conflict.

A further limitation of the model is that it focuses primarily on the *instigation* of conflict. In principle, the processes described in the model are relevant to behaviors that occur at any point during a conflict, yet it is possible that there may be features of behavior that occur after the perceiver's initial response to the instigating event that require modifications to the model. For example, does the communication of an attribution for the instigating event during conflict (e.g., "You smiled at her because you wanted to make me feel jealous") display unique properties as a stimulus event that cannot easily be accommodated by the present model? Similarly, do the meta-attributions to which such communications can give rise (e.g., "You think I smiled at her just to make you feel jealous? You are so insecure it's unbelievable") require alteration of the processing component of the model? If these turn out to be important factors in understanding conflict, our model would be further limited by a failure to specify the conditions under which attributions are communicated to the partner versus remain private.

Finally, although it is not intended to be specific to a particular type of close relationship, application of the model to relationships involving children needs to be outlined in greater detail. For example, application to the parent–child relationship requires consideration of at least two important factors, the perceived and actual cognitive abilities of the child and the parent's role as a socializing agent. The parents' perceptions of their child's cognitive abilities influences their causal and responsibility attributions for the child's behavior (Dix & Grusec, 1985) and their role as socializing agents militates against their accepting that they cannot influence their child's behavior (Fincham & Bradbury, 1987b). Similarly, children's attributions are affected by their level of cognitive development (Shantz, 1987) and their understanding of the parental role is likely to influence their behavior in conflict situations. In sum, application of the model to relationships involving children poses significant challenges, including the task of specifying (a) How the age of the child whose behavior is at issue influences the perceiver's processing, (b) How processing is affected by the cognitive developmental level of the perceiver, and (c) How the cognitive development of the perceiver and of the target person interact (e.g., do people at different levels of cognitive development process behavior differently depending on the age of the target person?).

The foregoing discussion does not provide an exhaustive evaluation of the model. Several further questions can be raised. For example, does the model apply equally well to the perceiver's processing of his or her own behavior? Furthermore, what are the implications of making judgments about one's own behavior for processing partner behavior? Space limitations preclude the consideration of such questions and further expansion of the model to address the issues outlined earlier. Nonetheless, in its present form the model offers several advantages over existing analyses of conflict and provides a potentially fruitful framework for future research.

CONCLUSION

Starting with Lewin's (1948, p. 91) observation that "conflicts depend on the degree to which the goals of the members contradict each other" we have attempted to develop a model that describes the cognitive and affective processes that mediate behavior exchanges during conflict in close relationships. The model is prompted by the evident need for such an analysis as revealed in our brief survey of research on conflict in close relationships. This survey also outlined the emergence of a new genre of research that emphasizes the importance of covert processes for understanding behavior in marital and parent–child relationships. The influence of this research on the model is apparent as it focuses on the major variables studied in this research, namely, attributions and affect. However, the subsequent presentation of the model reveals that the relations between the components are influenced more heavily by basic research on attribution, particularly that of Weiner (1985, 1986). The attempt to draw on such diverse areas of inquiry is likely to promote integrative research and gives rise to fundamental reconceptualizations of existing theory and data. Other strengths of the model were noted as were several of its limitations.

Although we have emphasized the covert processes that occur during conflict, it is important to acknowledge that they are not equally important in all situations. For example, Bugental (1987) has found that attributions have a greater influence on the interactions of stranger adult–child pairs in unstructured, compared with structured situations. It is therefore important to acknowledge the role of explicit interactional rules on moderating the impact of the covert processes on conflict behavior. However, the role of covert processes in conflict is not negated by this observation because most "rules between intimates are undefined, implicit, and ambiguous" (Hotaling, 1980, p. 140). Research on cognitive and affective processes is therefore required to gain a complete understanding of conflict in close relationships and the model presented in this chapter represents an attempt to facilitate such research.

ACKNOWLEDGMENT

Frank Fincham was supported in the preparation of this chapter by a Faculty Scholar Award from the W. T. Grant Foundation and by grant R01 MH44078–01 from the National Institute of Mental Health. Thomas Bradbury was supported by a grant from the National Science Foundation and a National Research Service Award from the National Institute of Mental Health. The authors wish to thank Fred Kanfer for his critical comments on an earlier draft of the manuscript.

REFERENCES

Abramson, L. Y., Seligman, M. E. P., & Teasdale, J. (1978). Learned helplessness in humans: Critique and reformulation. *Journal of Abnormal Psychology, 87,* 49–74.

Affleck, G., Tennen, H., Pfeiffer, C., & Fifield, J. (1987). Appraisals of control and predictability in adapting to a chronic disease. *Journal of Personality and Social Psychology, 53,* 273–279.

Allport, G. W. (1948). Foreword. In K. Lewin, *Resolving social conflicts: Selected papers on group dynamics.* New York: Harper & Row.

Averill, J. R. (1983). Studies on anger and aggression: Implications for theories of emotion. *American Psychologist, 38,* 1145–1160.

Bandura, A. (1977). *Social learning theory.* Englewood Cliffs, NJ: Prentice–Hall.

Baucom, D. H., & Adams, A. N. (1987). Assessing communication in marital interaction. In K. D. O'Leary (Ed.), *Assessment of marital discord* (pp. 139–181). Hillsdale, NJ: Lawrence Erlbaum Associates.

Baumgardner, A. H., & Arkin, R. M. (1988). Affective state mediates attributions for success and failure. *Motivation and Emotion, 12,* 99–106.

Berscheid, E. (1983). Emotion. In H. H. Kelley, E. Berscheid, A. Christensen, J. H. Harvey, T. L. Huston, G. Levinger, E. McClintock, L. A. Peplau, & D. R. Peterson (Eds.), *Close relationships* (pp. 110–168). San Francisco: Freeman.

Bloom, B. L., Asher, S. J., & White, S. W. (1978). Marital disruption as a stressor: A review and analysis. *Psychological Bulletin, 85,* 867–894.

Bradbury, T. N., & Fincham, F. D. (1987a). The assessment of affect in marriage. In K. D. O'Leary (Ed.), *Assessment of marital discord.* Hillsdale, NJ: Lawrence Erlbaum Associates.

Bradbury, T. N., & Fincham, F. D. (1987b). Affect and cognition in close relationships: Towards an integrative model. *Cognition and Emotion, 1,* 59–87.

Bradbury, T. N., & Fincham, F. D. (in press-a). Attributions in marriage: Review and critique. *Psychological Bulletin.*

Bradbury, T. N., & Fincham, F. D. (in press-b). Behavior and satisfaction in marriage: Prospective mediating processes. *Review of Personality and Social Psychology.*

Braiker, H. B., & Kelley, H. H. (1979). Conflict in the development of close relationships. In R. L. Burgess & T. L. Huston (Eds.), *Social exchange in developing relationships* (pp. 135–168). New York: Academic.

Brewin, C. R. (1986). Internal attribution and self-esteem in depression: A theoretical note. *Cognitive Therapy and Research, 10,* 469–475.

Bugenthal, D. B. (1987). Attributions as moderator variables within social interactional systems. *Journal of Social and Clinical Psychology, 5,* 469–484.

Deal, J. E., & Wampler, K. S. (1986). Dating violence: The primacy of previous experience. *Journal of Social and Personal Relationships, 3,* 457–471.

Dix, T., & Grusec, J. E. (1985). Parent attribution processes in child socialization. In I. E. Sigel (Ed.), *Parental belief systems* (pp. 201–233). Hillsdale, NJ: Lawrence Erlbaum Associates.

Doherty, W. J. (1978, August). *Cognitive processes in intimate conflict.* Paper presented at the National Council on Family Relations Annual Meeting, Boston.

Doherty, W. J. (1981a). Cognitive processes in intimate conflict: I. Extending attribution theory. *American Journal of Family Therapy, 9,* 3–13.

Doherty, W. J. (1981b). Cognitive processes in intimate conflict: II. Efficacy and learned helplessness. *American Journal of Family Therapy, 9,* 35–44.

Fincham, F. D. (1985). Attribution processes in distressed and nondistressed couples: 2. Responsibility for marital problems. *Journal of Abnormal Psychology, 94,* 183–190.

Fincham, F. D., & Bradbury, T. N. (1987a). The impact of attributions in marriage: A longitudinal analysis. *Journal of Personality and Social Psychology, 53,* 481–489.

Fincham, F. D., & Bradbury, T. N. (1987b). Cognitive processes and conflict in close relationships: An attribution-efficacy model. *Journal of Personality and Social Psychology, 53,* 1106–1118.

Fincham, F. D., & Bradbury, T. N. (1988). The impact of attributions in marriage: An experimental analysis. *Journal of Social and Clinical Psychology, 7,* 147–162.

Fincham, F. D., & Bradbury, T. N. (in press). Cognition in marriage: A program of research on attributions. In D. Perlman & W. Jones (Eds.), *Advances in personal relationships* (Vol. 2). Greenwich, CT: JAI Press.

Fincham, F. D., Bradbury, T. N., & Scott, C. (in press). Cognition in marriage. In F. D. Fincham & T. N. Bradbury (Eds.), *The psychology of marriage: Basic issues and applications.* New York: Guilford.

Fincham, F. D., & Emery, R. E. (1988). Limited mental capacities and perceived control in attribution of responsibility. *British Journal of Social Psychology, 27,* 193–207.

Fincham, F. D., & Jaspars, J. M. (1979). Attribution of responsibility to self and other in children and adults. *Journal of Personality and Social Psychology, 37,* 1589–1602.

Fincham, F. D., & Jaspars, J. M. (1980). Attribution of responsibility: From man the scientist to man as lawyer. In L. Berkowitz (Ed.), *Advances in experimental social psychology,* (Vol. 13, pp. 81–138). New York: Academic.

Fincham, F., & Roberts, C. (1985). Intervening causation and the mitigation of responsibility for harm-doing: 2. The role of limited mental capacities. *Journal of Experimental Social Psychology, 21,* 178–194.

Fitzpatrick, M. A. (1988). *Between husbands and wives: Communication in marriage.* Newbury Park, CA: Sage.

Floyd, F. J., & Markman, H. J. (1983). Observational biases in spouse observation: Toward a cognitive/behavioral model of marriage. *Journal of Consulting and Clinical Psychology, 51,* 450–457.

Gelles, R. J., & Straus, M. A. (1979). Determinants of violence in the family: Towards a theoretical integration. In W. R. Burr, R. Hill, F. Nye, & I. Reiss (Eds.), *Contemporary theories about the family* (Vol. 1, pp. 121–146). New York: Free Press.

Gottman, J. M., & Levenson, R. W. (1986). Assessing the role of emotion in marriage. *Behavioral Assessment, 8,* 31–48.

Harris, B. (1977). Developmental differences in the attribution of responsibility. *Developmental Psychology, 13,* 257–265.

Hart, H. L. A. (1968). *Punishment and responsibility.* New York: Oxford University Press.

Heider, F. (1958). *The psychology of interpersonal relations.* New York: Wiley.

Hotaling, G. T. (1980). Attribution processes in husband–wife violence. In M. A. Straus & G. T.

Hotaling (Eds.), *The social causes of husband–wife violence* (pp. 136–154). St. Paul: University of Minnesota Press.

Kelley, H. H. (1979). *Personal relationships: Their structures and processes.* Hillsdale, NJ: Lawrence Erlbaum Associates.

Larrance, D. T., & Twentyman, C. T. (1983). Maternal attributions and child abuse. *Journal of Abnormal Psychology, 92,* 449–457.

Levenson, R. W., & Gottman, J. M. (1983). Marital interaction: Physiological linkage and affective exchange. *Journal of Personality and Social Psychology, 45,* 587–597.

Levenson, R. W., & Gottman, J. M. (1985). Physiological and affective predictors of change in relationship satisfaction. *Journal of Personality and Social Psychology, 49,* 85–94.

Lewin, K. (1948). The background of conflict in marriage. *Resolving social conflicts: Selected papers on group dynamics.* New York: Harper & Row.

Margolin, G. (1987). The multiple forms of aggressiveness between marital partners: How do we identify them? *Journal of Marriage and the Family, 13,* 77–84.

O'Leary, K. D., Arias, I., Rosenbaum, A., & Barling, J. (1986). *Premarital physical aggression.* Unpublished manuscript. State University of New York at Stony Brook.

Orvis, B. R., Kelley, H. H., & Butler, D. (1976). Attributional conflict in young couples. In J. H. Harvey, W. Ickes, & R. F. Kidd (Eds.), *New directions in attribution research* (Vol. 1, pp. 353–388). Hillsdale, NJ: Lawrence Erlbaum Associates.

Patterson, G. R. (1982). *Coercive family process.* Eugene, OR: Castalia.

Peterson, C., & Seligman, M. E. P. (1984). Causal explanations as a risk factor for depression: Theory and evidence. *Psychological Review, 91,* 347–374.

Peterson, D. R. (1983). Conflict. In H. H. Kelley, E. Berscheid, A. Christensen, J. H. Harvey, T. L. Huston, G. Levinger, E. McClintock, L. A. Peplau, & D. R. Peterson, *Close relationships* (pp. 360–396). San Francisco: Freeman.

Raush, H. L., Barry, W. A., Hertel, R. K., & Swain, M. A. (1974). *Communication, conflict, and marriage.* San Francisco: Jossey–Bass.

Shantz, C. U. (1987). Conflicts between children. *Child Development, 58,* 283–305.

Shaver, K. G. (1985). *The attributions of blame: Causality, responsibility, and blameworthiness.* New York: Springer–Verlag.

Sigel, I. E. (1985). (Ed.).*Parental belief systems.* Hillsdale, NJ: Lawrence Erlbaum Associates.

Sillars, A. L. (1981). Attributions and interpersonal conflict resolution. In J. H. Harvey, W. Ickes, & R. F. Kidd (Eds.), *New directions in attribution research* (Vol. 3, pp. 279–305). Hillsdale, NJ: Lawrence Erlbaum Associates.

Straus, M. A., & Gelles, R. J. (1986). Societal change and change in family violence from 1975 to 1985 as revealed by two national surveys. *Journal of Marriage and the Family, 48,* 465–479.

Veroff, J., Kulka, R. A., & Douvan, E. (1981). *Mental health in America: Patterns of help-seeking from 1957–1976.* New York: Basic Books.

Weiner, B. (1985). An attributional theory of achievement motivation and emotion. *Psychological Review, 95,* 548–573.

Weiner, B. (1986). *An attributional theory of motivation and emotion.* New York: Springer–Verlag.

Weiss, R. L., & Heyman, R. E. (in press). Observation of marital interaction. In F. D. Fincham & T. N. Bradbury (Eds.), *The psychology of marriage: Basic issues and applications.* New York: Guilford Press.

10 Attributions and Organizational Conflict

Robert A. Baron
Rensselaer Polytechnic Institute

Conflict is a serious matter for many organizations. Practicing managers report that they spend approximately 20% of their time dealing with conflict and its impact (Baron, in press; Thomas & Schmidt, 1976). Further, organizational conflict, once it develops, tends to exert negative effects on several important aspects of organizational functioning. It interferes with coordination and communication (Robbins, 1974), increases tendencies to stereotype various groups within the organization (Linville & Jones, 1980), and induces shifts toward authoritarian rather than participative styles of leadership (Fodor, 1976). Finally, the ill will and animosity left behind by intense organizational conflicts may persist and interfere with productivity and efficiency for months or even years following their resolution (Thomas, in press).

Given these potential costs, it is far from surprising that considerable attention has been directed, by researchers in several different fields, to the nature and causes of organizational conflict (e.g., Pruitt & Rubin, 1986; Thomas, in press). In the past, much of this work focused primarily on *structural* or *organization-based* causes of conflict (e.g., competition over scarce resources, reward systems that pit individuals or groups against one another, ambiguity over responsibility or jurisdiction; Blake & Mouton, 1984; Robbins, 1974). More recently, however, the scope of such research has been expanded to include a wide range of *interpersonal* factors—potential causes of conflict relating to the manner in which organization members interact with and think about one another (e. g., Baron, 1984). It is within this general context that knowledge about attribution is relevant to the tasks of understanding and managing costly organizational conflicts. In short, attributions can be viewed as one of several interpersonal factors that play a role in the initiation, persistence, and ultimate resolution of such conflicts.

The remainder of this chapter will focus on four major tasks. First, the theoretical and empirical basis for assuming that attributions are relevant to organizational conflict will be described. Next, the findings of research dealing with the impact of attributions on such conflict will be reviewed. Third, links will be suggested between these investigations and research dealing with closely related topics (e.g., excuses, causal accounts; Bies, Shapiro, & Cummings, 1988). Finally, some practical implications of this research for preventing or managing organizational conflict will be proposed.

THE RELEVANCE OF ATTRIBUTIONS TO
ORGANIZATIONAL CONFLICT: EMPIRICAL AND
THEORETICAL FOUNDATIONS

If several decades of research on attribution as a social process have taught us anything, it is this: Faced with the behavior of other persons, human beings often attempt to determine the causes behind these actions. In short, they wish to know *why* other persons have behaved in specific ways, not merely that they have done so (Ross & Fletcher, 1985). Is this process relevant to organizational conflict? Several considerations suggest that it is.

First, conflict situations involve actions and outcomes of considerable importance to participants. Organizational conflict has often been defined as a process in which one or more individuals perceive that one or more others has thwarted or will soon thwart their major goals (Thomas, in press). Previous research on attributions suggests that under such circumstances—where important motives or goals are at stake—human beings show strong tendencies to engage in causal analysis of others' behavior (Fiske & Taylor, 1984). Given this fact, it seems reasonable to expect that attributions will indeed play an important role in organizational conflict.

Second, conflict situations, by their very nature, often involve unexpected or unpredicted behaviors by others. Indeed, conflicts frequently begin when one individual fails to behave in an anticipated fashion, or violates the social expectations of another (e.g., by refusing a request or rejecting a specific offer; Cody & McLaughlin, 1985). Major theoretical frameworks for understanding attribution (e.g., Kelley & Michela, 1980), as well as empirical research, indicate that it is precisely in such cases that human beings are most likely to exert the cognitive effort required by causal analysis of others' behavior (e.g., Hansen, 1980). Thus, once again, there are grounds for suggesting that attributions may play an important role in organizational conflict.

Turning to empirical evidence, an extensive body of research findings point to the conclusion that attributional processes often affect the occurrence or intensity of overt aggression (Ferguson & Rule, 1983; Johnson & Rule, 1986). It has been repeatedly observed that individuals are more likely to react with anger and overt retaliation to provocative actions by others when they perceive such actions as intentional rather than accidental or unintended in nature (i.e., when they perceive provocation as stemming from internal-controllable rather than external-uncontrollable causes; Rule & Nesdale, 1976; Zillmann, 1988). For example, in one revealing study on this relationship, Johnson and Rule (1986) exposed male subjects to strong provocation from another person (actually an accomplice), and then provided them with an opportunity to retaliate against this individual through the delivery of loud, unpleasant noise. Subjects then received information offering an explanation for the accomplice's provocative behavior (mitigating circumstances). Half received this information prior to being angered; the remainder received it only after being provoked. Additionally, within each of these conditions, half of the participants received a weak explanation for the accomplice's anger-inducing actions (he was upset over a low grade on a chemistry exam but felt that it wouldn't adversely affect his grade). The remainder received a much stronger explanation (the accomplice reported that the low grade might prevent him from gaining entry to medical school). It was hypothesized that the strong-mitigation information would be more effective in reducing subsequent aggression than weak-mitigation information, and that information about mitigating circumstances would be more effective if received prior to provocation than after its occurrence. Results offered support for both predictions. In addition, subjects who received the strong-mitigation information prior to being provoked actually showed lower physiological arousal (lower heart rates) than those who received such information after being provoked, or who received only weak-mitigation information.

These findings, and those of related studies (e.g., Ferguson & Rule, 1983; Kremer & Stephens, 1983), suggest that provocative actions that are perceived as stemming from external-uncontrollable factors (e.g., another's unavoidable emotional upset) produce lower levels of anger and aggression than identical actions that are perceived as stemming from internal-controllable causes (e.g., another's intentions or motives). Since organizational conflict often develops in situations where one individual or group adopts a confrontational stance toward one or more others, it seems possible that similar attributional mechanisms play a role in the occurrence or intensity of such conflict, too. In short, confrontational actions which are attributed to external causes (e.g., orders from one's superiors, organizational rules or policies) may be less likely to result in actual conflict than identical actions which are attributed to internal causes (e.g., personal intentions or motives). It is to assess the accuracy of such reasoning, and to determine whether findings uncovered with respect to aggression do, indeed, generalize to conflict, that several recent studies have been conducted. This research will now be described.

ATTRIBUTIONS AND ORGANIZATIONAL CONFLICT: INITIAL EVIDENCE

In an initial and seemingly straightforward test of the reasoning that has been outlined, Baron (1985) asked male and female subjects to play the role of an executive in a large company, and to negotiate with another person representing a different department over division of $1,000,000 in surplus funds. Subjects' opponent in these negotiations was actually a same-sex accomplice, specially trained to adopt a consistently confrontational stance throughout the session. Thus, the accomplice began by demanding fully $800,000 for his or her department, and made only two small concessions (of $50,000 each) over the course of eight exchanges of offers and counteroffers. The accomplice's comments during the negotiations followed a prepared script, and were used to vary the apparent causes behind this person's intransigence. In one condition (the *internal-competitive* attribution group), the accomplice offered repeated comments suggesting that his or her "tough" stance stemmed primarily from personal characteristics— the accomplice's own competitive nature (e.g., "I like to come out on top so I'm not changing my last offer"). In a second condition (the *internal-sincere belief* group), the accomplice's comments suggested that his or her position stemmed from sincere beliefs concerning the importance of his or her own department ("I really believe that my department is more important and deserves most of the money"). In a third condition (the *external-uncontrollable* group), the accomplice's remarks indicated that his or her position stemmed from felt role requirements ("I represent my whole department, and they expect me to get as much as possible for them"). Finally, in a fourth, control condition, the accomplice's comments revealed no clear cause behind his or her behavior (e.g., "I don't have any special reason for making this offer; it just seems O.K. to me").

After conclusion of the negotiations, subjects rated the accomplice on several personal dimensions (e.g., not reasonable–reasonable; not willing to compromise–willing to compromise; not competitive–competitive). Then, they indicated the likelihood that they would handle future conflicts with the accomplice in each of five ways: avoidance, accommodation, competition, compromise, collaboration. These five patterns have been identified in past research as representing basic modes of behavior in many conflict situations (e.g., Rahim, 1983; Thomas, in press).

Results

Consistent with the findings of previous research on aggression, it was predicted that subjects would react more favorably to the accomplice when his or her confrontational stance during the negotiations appeared to stem from external-uncontrollable rather than internal-controllable causes. However, results offered little support for this hypothesis. Turning first to ratings of the accomplice, a

TABLE 10.1
Mean Rating of Opponent's Competitiveness as a Function of
Attribution Condition and Sex of Subjects

Sex of Subject	Attribution Condition			
	No Information	External	Internal–Competitive	Internal–Belief
Female	$4.89_{a,c}$	6.11_b	$5.78_{b,c}$	4.00_a
Male	$5.47_{a,c}$	$6.06_{b,c}$	6.33_b	$5.39_{a,c}$

Note. For each sex, means that do not share a common subscript differ significantly ($p < .05$) by Duncan multiple-range test. From Baron (1985a). Copyright (1985) by the American Psychological Association. Reprinted by permission of the publisher.

multivariate analysis performed on the data for males failed to yield significant results. In contrast, a corresponding multivariate analysis performed on the data for females yielded a significant main effect for attribution condition. (All results described as significant refer to $p < .05$ unless otherwise specified.) Follow-up univariate analyses indicated that this effect stemmed mainly from ratings of the accomplice in terms of competitiveness. As predicted, females rated the accomplice as significantly more competitive in the internal-competitive attribution condition than in the internal-belief condition. However, contrary to expectations, they rated the accomplice as more competitive in the external-uncontrollable attribution condition than in either the internal-belief or no-information conditions (refer to Table 10.1).

With respect to reported strategies for dealing with future conflicts, multivariate analyses again yielded a significant main effect for attribution condition for females. Follow-up univariate analyses then indicated that this effect stemmed primarily from the item relating to collaboration. Females reported being significantly less likely to collaborate with the accomplice in the internal-competitive conditions than in any of the others ($p < .05$).

The corresponding multivariate analysis performed on the data for males yielded a main effect for attribution condition that approached but did not attain significance. However, given the exploratory nature of this initial investigation, follow-up univariate analyses were performed despite this finding. These analyses yielded significant effects for the item dealing with compromise. Contrary to expectations, male subjects reported being significantly less likely to compromise with the accomplice in the external-uncontrollable condition than in the no-information condition ($p < .05$. In addition, they were almost significantly less likely to compromise with the accomplice in the internal-competitive or sincere belief groups ($p < .10$ in both cases). Thus, contrary to predictions, male subjects did *not* express a greater preference for handling future conflicts through compromise when the accomplice's confrontational behavior seemed to stem from external causes. On the contrary, they reported being least likely to compromise with this person under these conditions.

Finally, turning to behavior during the negotiations, results indicated that contrary to predictions, males actually made smaller concessions to the accomplice in the external-uncontrollable attribution condition ($72,220) than in the internal-belief ($140,000) or no information ($182,500) conditions. Thus, information suggesting that the accomplice adopted a "tough" stance because of external causes actually reduced rather than enhanced male subjects' tendencies to offer concessions to this person.

Discussion

The results of this initial study were somewhat surprising. On the one hand, they offered support for the view that attributions do indeed play a role in the occurrence and resolution of organizational conflict. Comments by the accomplice concerning the reasons for his or her confrontational stance did indeed affect subjects' perceptions of this person, their reported strategies for handling future conflicts with the accomplice, and their willingness to make concessions to this individual (although these findings differed for the two sexes in several cases). However, contrary to initial expectations, results were not similar to those reported in several studies concerned with the impact of attributions on overt aggression. Female subjects rated the accomplice as more competitive in the external-uncontrollable condition than in internal-belief and no information conditions. Male participants reported being *less* likely to handle future conflicts with this person through compromise when the accomplice's "tough" bargaining stance seemed to stem from external rather than internal causes. And males also made smaller concessions to the accomplice in the external-uncontrollable attribution condition than in the internal-belief and no-information conditions. Clearly, then, information suggesting that the accomplice's confrontational behavior stemmed from external causes did not lessen the likelihood or intensity of future (or present) conflict. What accounts for this disparity between the impact of attributions in the present research and in past investigations of aggression? One possibility is as follows:

In past research on aggression, information about the causes behind a provoker's behavior was provided either by a third party (typically, the experimenter), or was presented at a point in time distinct from the provocation itself. Under these conditions, there was little reason for subjects to doubt the accuracy of this information, or to assume that it was employed to manipulate or mislead them. In the present research, in contrast, attributional information was presented by the accomplice at the same time that this individual engaged in confrontational actions. Further, the accomplice had clear reasons for seeking to mislead subjects with respect to the true motives behind these actions (e.g., this person would certainly profit if subjects accepted assertions to the effect that the accomplice had no choice but to be tough during the negotiations, and then made concessions to this person because of this fact).

Together, these considerations suggest that the apparent sincerity or accuracy of information concerning the causes behind others' confrontational behavior may play a key role in determining the impact of such information on subsequent conflict. When statements of external causality are perceived as sincere, they may indeed serve to reduce negative reactions (e.g., anger, resentment) to confrontational actions. Then, the likelihood or intensity of subsequent conflict may also be reduced. In contrast, when such statements are perceived as false or misleading, opposite reactions may follow. Provocative actions may generate strong negative feelings, and conflict may be intensified rather than reduced (Rubin, Ekenrode, Enright, & Johnson–George, 1980). In order to examine this possibility, two additional studies were conducted.

ATTRIBUTIONS AND ORGANIZATIONAL CONFLICT: APPARENT SINCERITY AND THE 'MY HANDS ARE TIED' STRATEGY

The first of these investigations (Baron, 1988a) was, like the study described earlier (Baron, 1985), a laboratory simulation. Male and female subjects again negotiated with an accomplice over the division of a hypothetical budgetary surplus. As in the earlier study, the accomplice adopted a confrontational stance in these discussions, demanding $800,000 out of the $1,000,000 available, and making only two small concessions during the exchange of offers and counteroffers. Statements by this individual during the negotiations were again used to vary the apparent causes behind these actions. In two conditions (external attribution-sincere; external attribution-insincere) the accomplice stated repeatedly that he or she had been instructed to behave in this confrontational fashion by his or her department (e.g., "I've got firm instructions from my department to get as much as possible. I really have no choice—I have to do the best I can") In a third condition (the internal-competitive group), the accomplice made statements suggesting that his or her behavior stemmed primarily from the fact that he or she was simply a highly competitive person (e.g., "I'd rather stick to my guns and not get an agreement than be weak and give into my opponent. That's just the way I am").

In order to vary the apparent accuracy or sincerity of these attributional statements, subjects were informed that one purpose of the study was to determine how information about an opponent's instructions affected the course of negotiations. They were then further informed that to investigate this topic, they would receive information about the instructions their opponent had received from his or her department. In the external attribution-sincere condition, these instructions did in fact indicate that the accomplice should be tough in dealing with the subject, and try to get as much money as possible. In the external attribution-insincere condition, in contrast, they actually urged the accomplice to adopt a conciliatory stance and to make many concessions if this was necessary to reach an agreement. Thus, in the first condition, subjects received information suggesting that the accomplice's attributional statements were sincere, while in the second, they received information suggesting that these statements were insincere (i.e., this person was lying about the causes of his or her behavior). Finally, in the internal-competitive condition the instructions to the accomplice were ambiguous; they indicated that the accomplice should act in whatever ways he or she felt was best.

A third variable in the study was the apparent (time) pressure to reach agreement. This factor was introduced to examine the possibility that subjects would pay closer attention to attributional statements by the accomplice, and so be more influenced by them, when this person's behavior was unexpected or unusual than when it was more ordinary in nature (cf. Hansen, 1980). In order to test this suggestion, half of the subjects in each of the conditions described were told to assume that if they did not reach an agreement today, they could meet in the future for further negotiations (low pressure). The remaining half were told to assume that if they did not reach agreement today, the funds would be given to two other departments instead (high pressure). It was hypothesized that the accomplice's unyielding, intransigent behavior would seem more unusual or unexpected under conditions of high pressure to reach agreement. Thus, the accomplice's attributional statements (statements about the causes behind his or her behavior) would exert stronger effects upon subjects' behavior under high pressure than low pressure to reach agreement.

Following conclusion of the negotiations, subjects completed checks on the various experimental manipulations, and several items designed to assess their perceptions of the causes behind the accomplice's behavior. They also indicated their likelihood of resolving future conflicts with this person in five different ways: avoidance, competition, accommodation, compromise, collaboration (Thomas, in press).

Results

A check on the attempted manipulation of the accomplice's sincerity indicated that this was successful. Subjects rated the accomplice as being more honest in the external-sincere condition than in the external-insincere condition ($p < .05$).

Three additional items completed by subjects assessed their perceptions of the causes behind the accomplice's behavior. A multivariate analysis of variance on these data yielded a significant main effect for attribution condition. Follow-up univariate analyses indicated that as expected, subjects perceived the accomplice's behavior as stemming from instructions from his or her department to a greater degree in the external-sincere ($M = 6.11$) than external-insincere (M = 4.79) or internal-competitive conditions ($M = 4.85; p < .05$). Similarly, they perceived the accomplice's behavior as stemming from his or her personality to a

TABLE 10.2
Mean Reported Likelihood of Avoiding the Accomplice in Future Conflict Situations as a Function of Attribution Condition, Sex of Subject, and Pressure to Reach Agreement

Pressure for Agreement	Attribution Condition					
	Males			Females		
	External–Sincere	External–Insincere	Internal–Competitive	External–Sincere	External–Insincere	Internal–Competitive
Low	$2.72_{a,c}$	1.86_a	$2.86_{a,c}$	$2.86_{a,c}$	$2.81_{a,c}$	1.67_a
High	1.71_a	$3.71_{b,c}$	2.14_a	2.29_a	$3.85_{b,c}$	$2.86_{a,c}$

Note. For each sex, means that do not share a subscript differ significantly ($p < .05$) by Duncan multiple-range test. From Baron (1988a). Reprinted by permission of Academic Press.

TABLE 10.3

Mean Reported Likelihood of Competing With the Accomplice in Future Conflict Situations as a Function of Attribution Condition, Sex of Subject, and Pressure to Reach Agreement

Pressure for Agreement	Males			Females		
	External–Sincere	External–Insincere	Internal–Competitive	Internal–Sincere	External–Insincere	Internal–Competitive
Low	$4.00_{a,c}$	$4.14_{a,c}$	5.24_b	$5.14_{a,c}$	3.71_a	$4.83_{a,c}$
High	2.57_a	$4.43_{b,c}$	5.29_c	4.00_a	$6.00_{b,c}$	$4.57_{a,c}$

Note. For each sex, means that do not share a subscript differ significantly ($p < .05$) by Duncan multiple-range test. From Baron (1988a). Reprinted by permission of Academic Press.

greater degree in the internal-competitive condition ($M = 5.33$) than in the external-insincere ($M = 4.50$) or external-sincere conditions ($M = 4.82$; $p < .07$).

With respect to strategies for handling future conflicts, a multivariate analysis of variance on the data for these items yielded a three-way interaction between attribution condition, sex of subject, and pressure to reach agreement. Follow-up univariate analyses indicated that this effect was significant for avoidance, and approached significance for competition. The means for these items are presented in Table 10.2 and 10.3. Examination of these tables reveals that under conditions of high pressure to reach agreement, both males and females reported stronger tendencies to handle future conflicts with the accomplice through less constructive means (i.e., avoidance and competition) in the external-insincere condition than in the external-sincere condition. Thus, they reported negative reactions to attributional insincerity on the part of the accomplice. Consistent with initial predictions, attributional statements by the accomplice had little if any effect on subjects' behavior under conditions of low time pressure.

Turning to behavior during the negotiations, it was found that subjects asked for less of the available funds in the high-pressure than low-pressure condition. In addition, they made more concessions in the high-pressure condition ($M = 3.34$) than in the low-pressure condition ($M = 2.51$). In addition, and contrary to expectations, subjects actually made more concessions to the accomplice in the external-insincere condition ($M = 3.29$) than in the external-sincere ($M = 2.71$) or internal-competitive conditions ($M = 2.93$). A similar pattern of results was also obtained with respect to the total concessions made by subjects. Here, subjects made larger concessions to the accomplice in the external-insincere condition ($M = 219,000$) than in the external-sincere condition ($M = \$170,000$; $p < .05$).

Discussion

The results of this study offer support for the hypothesis that the impact of the "my hands are tied" strategy (attributing one's provocative actions to external causes) is indeed strongly determined by the apparent sincerity of such statements. When subjects received information suggesting that such claims by the accomplice were inaccurate, their reported preferences for resolving future conflicts through avoidance and competition were stronger than when they received information suggesting that such claims by the accomplice were accurate. Thus, subjects in this laboratory simulation reported negative reactions to attributional insincerity on the part of an opponent. Indeed, they reacted more negatively to such insincerity than to identical confrontational behavior stemming from internal causes (their opponent's highly competitive nature). In addition, the present results were consistent with the prediction that attributional statements by the accomplice would have a stronger effect on subjects' behavior in the context of high than low pressure to reach agreement. Previous studies (e.g., Hansen, 1980) suggest that human beings are more likely to engage in causal analyses of others' behavior when it is unexpected or unusual than when it is expected or ordinary. Assuming that intransigence by an opponent is more unusual under conditions of high than low pressure to reach agreement, the present findings are consistent with these earlier results.

While attributional insincerity generally induced negative effects, it did increase subjects' tendencies to make concessions to the opponent. Subjects in the external-insincere condition made more and larger concessions to the accomplice than those in the external-sincere condition. A similar pattern of current concessions coupled with stated intentions to resist an opponent in the future has also been obtained in another recent study (Baron, 1988b). In that investigation, subjects offered larger concessions to an opponent who had previously delivered harsh, offensive criticism than to one who had previously criticized them in a more constructive manner. What accounts for the tendency to offer concessions to a highly abrasive or insincere opponent? One possibility may lie in the constraints imposed by the simulated negotiations, plus subjects' perceptions that they were dealing with an extremely difficult, perhaps irrational, person. Within the present context, subjects had no choice but to seek an agreement with the accomplice; no other potential partners were available. Further, the stated goal of the negotiations was reaching such an agreement. Under these conditions, some subjects, at least, may have concluded that the only way of reaching *any* agreement, and thus fulfilling their assigned role, was that of yielding to their opponent. They might well have behaved quite differently if other potential partners were provided, or if they believed that other goals (e.g., reaching a totally fair division of the funds; protecting their own self-interests) were central. Future studies can readily examine this possibility by varying the presence or absence of other negotiating partners, and the negotiation goals assigned to subjects. Since many negotiations within a given organization do occur under constraints similar to the ones prevailing in this study, however, it seems possible that the results observed here (current concessions coupled with longer-term resistance) occur in real organizational contexts as well. Clearly, this is an empirical question deserving of further attention.

Study 2: An Extension to an Employed Sample

Taken as a whole, the results of the study just described (Baron, 1988a), plus those of the earlier investigation (Baron, 1985) suggest that information about the causes behind another's provocative behavior can indeed play a role in organizational conflict. However, both of these studies were laboratory simulations conducted under relatively artificial conditions. In order to determine whether attributions also affect conflict in actual organizations, a follow-up study was performed. In this investigation, officers of a large urban fire department

TABLE 10.4
Mean Reported Likelihood of Dealing with Conflict Through Avoidance,
Compromise, Competition, Accommodation, or Collaboration as a Function of
Attribution Condition

Mode of Dealing With Conflict	Attribution Condition			
	Internal–Competitive	Sincere Belief	External–Sincere	External–Insincere
Avoidance	3.47a	3.40a	3.13a	3.93a
Competition	3.60a,b	3.60a,b	3.47a	4.40b
Compromise	5.40a	5.00a	5.07a	4.07b
Accommodation	2.60a,b	2.87a	2.20a,b	1.67b
Collaboration	5.13a	5.60a	5.53a	3.37b

Note. Within each mode of dealing with conflict, means that do not share a sub-script differ significantly ($p < .05$) by Duncan multiple-range test. From Baron (1988a). Reprinted by permission of Academic Press.

were asked to imagine that they were experiencing conflict with another member of their department. This conflict was described as stemming from four possible causes: their opponent's personality (he was a highly competitive individual); this person's sincere belief that his position in the dispute was correct; external pressures that forced their opponent to disagree with them (e.g., orders from a superior or a group he represented); or false claims by the opponent concerning external pressures (he claimed that such pressures forced him to disagree, but in fact he was dishonest in this respect).

After reading these descriptions of the causes behind the current conflict, subjects rated their likelihood of dealing with the situation through avoidance, competition, compromise, accommodation, or collaboration. On the basis of the previous results, it was predicted that they would react negatively to attributional insincerity. That is, subjects would report stronger preferences for avoidance and competition, but weaker preferences for compromise or collaboration when the opponent's behavior stemmed from this cause than when it actually did derive from external causes. Results offered partial support for this prediction. The interaction between attribution condition and type of reaction to conflict was significant. As shown by Table 10.4, subjects reported being significantly less likely to compromise or collaborate with this person under these attributional conditions than under any of the others ($p < .05$). In addition, they reported being more likely to compete with their opponent in the external-insincere condition ($p < .05$).

Discussion

The findings of this study, like those of the laboratory simulation, offer support for the view that attributions about the causes behind provocative, confrontational behavior can play a role in subsequent conflict. Further, the results of both studies suggest that the success of the "my hands are tied" strategy—attributing such actions to uncontrollable, external causes—depends strongly on the apparent sincerity of such statements. When they are accepted as accurate or valid, this strategy may indeed be effective and reduce subsequent conflict. When they are rejected as false, however, opposite effects may result. The practical implication of these findings for persons wishing to use this strategy seem clear: Adopt it only when additional, supporting evidence for the role of external causes is available. In the absence of such evidence, statements attributing provocative actions to external factors may backfire, and exacerbate rather than reduce, subsequent conflict.

RELATED RESEARCH: EXCUSES AND CAUSAL ACCOUNTS

The research described thus far has focused directly on the role of attributions in organizational conflict. Further, it was based, in part, on earlier findings concerning the role of attributions in anger and aggression (Johnson & Rule, 1986). However, other recent research, deriving from somewhat different sources and rationales, is also relevant to this relationship. These studies have focused, respectively, on *excuses* and *causal accounts*.

Excuses: An Attributional Analysis

When individuals fail to meet social obligations, they often offer excuses for their behavior. In other words, they offer explanations for why they failed to keep an appointment, appear at a social event, and so on. Recent research by Weiner and his colleagues (Weiner, Amirkhan, Folkes, & Verette, 1987) has focused on the nature of such excuses, and provides revealing evidence about the attributional mechanisms determining their effects upon recipients. In general, the results of this excellent research suggest that excuses citing external, uncontrollable reasons are more likely to be viewed as acceptable, and less likely to induce anger and resentment, than excuses citing internal, controllable reasons. For example, in one ingenious study on this topic, an accomplice arrived 15 minutes late for an appointment, thus keeping subjects waiting. When this person arrived, he or she offered one of two excuses: a good excuse based on external, uncontrollable factors ("The professor in my class gave an exam that ran way over time. . . ."), or a poor excuse based in internal, controllable factors ("I was talking to some friends I ran into in the hall. . . ."). A few moments later, subjects completed a questionnaire on which they rated the accomplice's personality and the desirability of future social interaction with this person. As predicted, these ratings were more positive in the good excuse than poor excuse condition. Specifically, subjects rated the accomplice higher on several traits (e.g., dependability, responsibility, considerateness), reported greater willingness to interact with this person in the future, and reported lower anger, resentment, and irritation when the accomplice offered a good excuse than a poor one.

In a follow-up study, subjects were told to keep another person waiting, and then to offer either a bad excuse, a good one, or no excuse for their tardiness. Subjects wrote their excuses down before actually meeting with the person they delayed. Careful analysis of these records indicated that those told to prepare a good excuse wrote ones citing external, uncontrollable factors (e.g., "I had to take my mother to the hospital," "My midterm took longer than expected."). In contrast, those who were told to prepare a poor excuse wrote ones citing internal, controllable factors ("I forgot," "I ran into some friends and talked.")

Together, these and other studies conducted by Weiner et al. (1987) indicate that when people violate social obligations or expectations, they tend to offer excuses designed to "defuse" anger and resentment on the part of others. Further, this research suggests that the excuses most effective in this regard—the ones viewed as most compelling or convincing—cite external, uncontrollable causes. Excuses that mention internal, controllable causes, in contrast, are far less successful. Since individuals who engage in provocative, conflict-inducing actions often offer excuses for their actions, these findings appear relevant to the role of attributions in organizational conflict. Specifically, they suggest that some statements concerning conflict-inducing actions will be much more effective in reducing anger and irritation among recipients than others. For example, negotiators who propose offers extremely favorable to their company may induce less anger (and reactance) among opponents if they attribute such actions to external factors beyond their control (e.g., rising manufacturing costs, import duties, government regulations) than if they attribute them to internal ones they might, potentially, control (e.g., minimum profit margins they have established). Similarly, a manager who rejects a request from a subordinate may induce less anger in this person, and so improve future relations, if he or she attributes this action to budget constraints or formal company policy rather than to his or her own preferences or standards. This latter type of situation has recently been the subject of a considerable amount of research (Bies, 1988). Because the findings of these studies are directly relevant to the role of attributions in organizational conflict, they will now be briefly considered.

Causal Accounts and Organizational Conflict

Supervisors in functioning organizations often find it necessary (or at least expedient) to reject requests from subordinates. For example, they may refuse requests for resources (money, equipment), changes in policy or procedures, or alterations in task or job assignments. When they do, they often offer *causal accounts*—explanations as to the reasons behind their refusal. Such accounts are designed to both explain and justify the supervisor's actions. To the extent they are successful in this task, negative reactions among subordinates (e.g., anger, resentment, perceptions of unfairness) may be lessened and their future relations improved. What type of causal accounts are best in this respect? Research by Bies and his colleagues (Bies et al., 1988) provides some clear-cut answers.

In one of several studies on this topic, Bies, Shapiro, and Cummings asked employed persons currently enrolled in an evening MBA program to describe a recent situation in which they made a request or proposal to their boss which was then rejected. After doing so, they rated the extent to which a causal account was offered (the extent to which the boss indicated he or she had no choice in this decision), the adequacy of the reasoning offered in support of this claim, and the boss's apparent sincerity. In addition, subjects rated the extent to which they became angry after the refusal, the extent to which they felt they were treated unfairly, their disapproval of their boss, and the extent to which they complained about the decisions to "higher-ups."

Bies and his colleagues reasoned that merely providing a causal account (attributing the negative decision to external, uncontrollable causes) would not, by itself lessen negative reactions among subordinates. However, the more adequate the reasoning provided in support of this claim, and the greater its apparent sincerity, the more favorably would subjects react. Results indicated that this was indeed the case. Both perceived adequacy of reasoning and perceived sincerity were significant predictors of subjects' reactions. Specifically, the more adequate the reasoning in the boss's refusal and the greater his or her sincerity, the lower subjects' reported feelings of anger, unfairness, disapproval of the boss, and tendency to complain to higher-ups.

Other findings indicated that in offering explanations for their refusals, supervisors most frequently cited subordinates' own behavior (e.g., insufficient preparation, incompetence), budget constraints, upper management, the political environment within the organization, formal company policy, and company norms (traditions within the organization). These were not viewed as being equal in adequacy, however. Participants rated accounts based on company norms, budget constraints, and formal company policy as more adequate than ones focused on subordinates' own behavior, upper management, or the political environment.

These findings, as well as those of others conducted by Bies (e.g., Bies, 1988), suggest that causal explanations for refusals may play an important role in organizational conflict. When such accounts are convincing (i.e., clearly reasoned), and appear to be sincere, negative reactions to refusals and subsequent conflict may both be reduced. When they are unconvincing and seem insincere, however, they may be ineffective in reducing anger, feelings of injustice, or later conflict. In sum, research on causal accounts agrees closely with the findings of research concerned with attributional sincerity and the impact of the "my hands are tied" strategy. Together, the two lines of research indicate that attributing provocative actions to external, uncontrollable causes is not, by itself, sufficient to reduce subsequent conflict. Rather, such benefits occur only when these explanations are accepted as accurate in nature.

ATTRIBUTIONS AND ORGANIZATIONAL CONFLICT: PRACTICAL IMPLICATIONS

The research reviewed in this chapter suggests that attributions do indeed play an important role in organizational conflict. When faced with confrontational, conflict-inducing actions by others, people seem to pause and consider the causes behind these actions. If these seem reasonable or unavoidable, they may respond to provocation with relative equanimity. Then, subsequent conflict can be avoided or at least reduced. If the causes behind provocative actions seem unreasonable or avoidable, however, they may react more negatively, and conflict may become more likely or intense. Do these findings have any practical implications for managing or preventing conflict in organizational settings? In several respects, they do.

First, individuals who find it necessary to take potentially conflict-inducing actions (ones that negatively affect the interests or goals of others) should carefully consider the interpretations that others will place on such actions. Often, it seems, it is these interpretations—not the actions themselves—that more strongly shape the course of subsequent events.

Second, explanations for such actions should emphasize the role of external, uncontrollable causes. To the extent these are noted, negative reactions to even highly provocative behaviors may be quite muted.

Third, the precise external, uncontrollable causes cited should be chosen with care. Those selected should be ones consistent with current organizational conditions. For example, an explanation that cites the impact of persons at higher levels within the organization will probably fail if it is well known that they do not normally interfere with decisions at lower levels. Similarly, an explanation in terms of organizational culture or norms will be unsuccessful when it is obvious to recipients that such traditions or norms are regularly violated and exert only weak effects upon decisions.

Fourth, to be effective, causal explanations for provocative actions must be clearly reasoned and possess at least the appearance of sincerity. Explanations that are weak (hard to follow, unconvincing), or that seem insincere will prove relatively ineffective. Indeed, they may well backfire and exacerbate rather than reduce subsequent conflict.

Fifth, the timing of such information, too, is important. Information about mitigating circumstances presented prior to a provocative event will often be more effective in reducing subsequent anger and conflict than information presented only after provocation has occurred (cf. Johnson & Rule, 1986; Zillmann, 1988). Thus, such information should be offered early in negotiations or prior to making a refusal rather than at later times.

Finally, the role of attributions must be considered against a backdrop of other potential causes of organizational conflict. Even highly convincing causal accounts for provocative actions will fail to lessen conflict in situations involving long-standing grudges between opponents. Similarly, individuals possessing certain characteristics (e.g., those who are Type A or highly competitive themselves) may tend to perceive all provocative actions as internally caused, and will remain largely unaffected by an opponent's causal accounts (Baron, 1989).

Within broad limits, however, the explanations people offer for potentially conflict-inducing actions, or the explanations constructed by the persons exposed to such actions, appear to play a powerful role in organizational conflict. Left to their own devices, most people will develop causal explanations for events that impinge on their interests or goals. One important task for those wishing to manage or avoid such conflict, therefore, is that of shaping such explanations so that they are as convincing and favorable as possible within the context of a particular situation.

SUMMARY

Research on anger and aggression suggests that provocative actions stemming from external, uncontrollable causes induce lower levels of anger and retaliation among recipients than identical actions stemming from internal, controllable causes. Since organizational conflict often results when one or more individuals engage in confrontational actions, it was reasoned that attributions play a key role in this process as well.

An initial study designed to assess this possibility (Baron, 1985) yielded largely negative results. Attributions did in fact affect conflict, but not in a manner consistent with previous research on aggression. Specifically, subjects reported weaker tendencies to resolve future conflicts through compromise when an opponent attributed his or her "tough" stance during negotiations to uncontrollable external factors than when this person attributed such behavior to sincere beliefs in one's position or one's own competitive nature.

A follow-up investigation indicated that these findings stemmed primarily from subjects' skepticism regarding their opponent's causal statements. In this study, subjects who received information supporting the accuracy of statements attributing confrontational behavior to uncontrollable external causes reported weaker tendencies to resolve future conflicts through avoidance or competition than subjects who received information refuting the accuracy of such statements. As predicted, these findings occurred only under conditions of high pressure to reach an agreement with the opponent.

Related research on *excuses* indicates that when individuals violate social expectations (e.g., fail to keep an appointment), excuses that cite external, uncontrollable causes are more effective in reducing anger and resentment than excuses that cite internal, controllable causes. Additional research concerned with *causal accounts* suggests that when supervisors reject requests from their subordinates, the subordinates are less likely to become angry or complain about the boss when his or her explanations for such refusals are well reasoned and sincere than whey they are poorly reasoned or insincere.

Taken together, the research reviewed in this chapter suggests that individuals who engage in actions which negatively affect others' interests or goals should pay careful attention to the explanations they offer for such actions. Under appropriate conditions (e.g., when they are well reasoned, sincere, and introduced prior to the conflict-inducing behavior) such causal explanations can help reduce negative reactions and subsequent conflict.

REFERENCES

Baron, R. A. (1984). Reducing organizational conflict: An incompatible response approach. *Journal of Applied Psychology, 69,* 272–279.

Baron, R. A. (1985). Reducing organizational conflict: The role of attributions. *Journal of Applied Psychology, 70,* 434–441.

Baron, R. A. (1988a). Attributions and organizational conflict: The mediating role of apparent sincerity. *Organizational Behavior and Human Decision Processes, 41,* 111–127.

Baron, R. A. (1988b). Negative effects of destructive criticism: Impact on conflict, self-efficacy, and task performance. *Journal of Applied Psychology, 73,* 199–207.

Baron, R. A. (1989). Personality and organizational conflict: Effects of the Type A behavior pattern and self-monitoring. *Organizational Behavior and Human Decision Processes, 44,* 281–296.

Bies, R. J (1988). Beyond "voice": The influence of decision-maker justification and sincerity on procedural fairness judgments. Manuscript submitted for publication.

Bies, R. J., Shapiro, D. L., & Cummings, L. L. (1988). Causal accounts and managing organizational conflict: Is it enough to say it's not my fault? *Communication Research, 15,* 381–399.

Blake, R. R., & Mouton, J. S. (1984). *Solving costly organizational conflict.* San Francisco: Jossey-Bass.

Cody, M. J., & McLaughlin, M. L. (1985). Models for the sequential construction of accounting episodes: Situational and interactional constraints on message selection and evaluation. In R. Street & J. Capella (Eds.), *Sequence and pattern in communicative behavior* (pp. 50–69). London: Arnold.

Ferguson, T. J., & Rule, B. G. (1983). An attributional perspective on anger and aggression. In R. G. Geen & E. I. Donnsertsin (Eds.). *Aggression: Theoretical and empirical reviews.* (Vol. 1, pp. 41–74). New York: Academic.

Fiske, S. T., & Taylor, S. E. (1984). *Social cognition.* Reading, MA: Addison-Wesley.

Fodor, E. M. (1976). Group stress, authoritarian style of control, and use of power. *Journal of Applied Psychology, 61,* 313–318.

Hansen, R. D. (1980). Commonsense attribution. *Journal of Personality and Social Psychology, 39,* 996–1009.

Johnson, T. E., & Rule, B. G. (1986). Mitigating circumstance information, censure, and aggression. *Journal of Personality and Social Psychology, 50,* 537–542.

Kelley, H. H., & Michaela, J. L. (1980). Attribution theory and research. *Annual Review of Psychology, 31*, 457–501.

Kremer, J. F., & Stephens, L. (1983). Attributions and arousal as mediators of mitigation's effects on retaliation. *Journal of Personality and Social Psychology, 45*, 335–343.

Linville, P. W., & Jones, E. E. (1980). Polarized appraisals of out-group members. *Journal of Personality and Social Psychology, 38*, 689–703.

Pruitt, D. G., & Rubin, J. Z. (1986). *Social conflict.* New York: Random House.

Rahim, M. A. (1983). A measure of styles of handling interpersonal conflict. *Academy of Management Journal, 26*, 368–376.

Robbins, S. P. (1974). *Managing organizational conflict.* Englewood Cliff, NJ: Prentice–Hall.

Ross, M., & Fletcher, G. J. O. (1985) *Attribution and social perception.* In G. Lindzey & E. Aronson (Eds.), *Handbook of social psychology.* New York: Random House.

Rubin, J. Z., Brockner, J., Eckenrode, J., Enright, M.A., & Johnson–George, C. (1980). Weakness as strength: Test of "My hands are tied" ploy in bargaining. *Personality and Social Psychology Bulletin, 6*, 216–221.

Rule, B. G., & Nesdale, A. R. (1976). Emotional arousal and aggressive behavior. *Psychological Bulletin, 83*, 851–863.

Thomas, K. W. (in press). Conflict and negotiation processes in organizations. In M. D. Dunnette (Ed.), *Handbook of industrial and organizational psychology* (2nd ed.). Chicago: Rand McNally.

Thomas, K. W., & Schmidt, W. H. (1976). A survey of managerial interests with respect to conflict. *Academy of Management Journal, 19*, 315–318.

Weiner, B., Amirkhan, J., Folkes, V. S., & Verette, J. A. (1987). An attributional analysis of excuse giving: Studies of a naive theory of emotion. *Journal of Personality and Social Psychology, 53*, 316–324.

Zillmann, D. (1988). Cognition-excitation interdependencies in aggressive behavior. *Aggressive Behavior, 14*, 51–64.

11 An Attributional Approach to Intergroup and International Conflict

Hector Betancourt
Loma Linda University

The objective of this chapter is to present a general view of the attributional theory of motivation and emotion (for reviews see Weiner, 1985, 1986) applied to intergroup and international conflict. First, the generalizability from individual and interpersonal attribution processes to intergroup phenomena is addressed. Second, relevant aspects of intergroup conflict are analyzed from the perspective of the attributional approach to interpersonal feelings and action. Finally, practical work in international conflict is analyzed, using attribution principles to illustrate the role of causal attributions and the potential for applications.

Intergroup and international conflicts have interested social psychologists for a long time. This interest, particularly at the international level, has increased significantly in recent years (e.g., Austin & Worchel, 1979; Blight, 1987; Chilstrom, 1984; Deutsch, 1983; Fiske, 1987; Mack, 1985; Plous, 1985; Pruitt & Rubin, 1986; Stroebe, Kruglanski, Bar–Tal, & Hewstone, 1988; White, 1986a). Although attribution theory and research has focused on individual and interpersonal behavior, some authors have identified potential applications to the study and solution of intergroup and international conflicts (e.g., Betancourt, 1986; Hewstone, 1988; Horai, 1977; Kelman, 1983; Taylor & Jaggi, 1974; Tetlock & McGuire, 1986). The importance given to causal attributions in this area varies from the theoretical analysis of attribution processes in intergroup conflict (Hewstone, 1988) and the use of attributional concepts in international conflict resolution (Kelman, 1983) to a mere acknowledgment of the potential for applications.

Despite the common reference to the potential that attribution processes represent in intergroup and international conflicts, only limited aspects of causal attributions have been considered. In most cases, only factors assumed to influence locus of causality have been studied or discussed. For example, attention has been given to the fact that in a conflict situation one may be biased to attribute negative behaviors to the other party (internal to that party) rather than to the situation (external). However, locus is only one of the three general properties of attributions identified as psychologically relevant in predicting action (see Weiner, 1986). Each of the general properties or dimensions of attributions—locus, stability, and controllability—has specific psychological consequences, such as esteem-related affects, expectancy change, and interpersonal emotions, respectively. These dimension–consequence linkages, which represent the core of the theory, constitute the focus of analysis here.

FROM INDIVIDUAL TO INTERGROUP AND INTERNATIONAL PHENOMENA

Most of the research in social psychology takes place at the individual level of analysis. Hence, a legitimate question is raised as to whether or not it is appropriate to use social psychological knowledge in the analysis of conflicts that involve groups and nations. In the early work of Sherif (1958, 1966), we find a warning against the excessive reliance on knowledge based on research at the individual level to analyze intergroup behavior. However, at the same time Sheriff defined important areas of concern where individual-level research and theory could contribute to the understanding and resolution of intergroup conflicts. For example, Sheriff considered social behaviors such as competition, cooperation, and aggression as particularly important in the study of conflict and conflict resolution. If these behaviors are important in conflicts at all levels, social psychological knowledge in these areas should certainly contribute to a better understanding of interpersonal as well as intergroup conflicts. In reference to specifically cognitive phenomena, Sheriff suggested that when groups are in conflict, members of the groups engage in mutual blame, recrimination, and judgment, which leads to a vicious cycle and persistence of conflict.

A more recent development in this area has been the work of Kelman and colleagues concerning the interactional approach to international conflict resolution (Kelman, 1986, 1987). According to this approach, social psychological processes that take place in interactions between conflicting parties can produce changes at the individual level which facilitate change at the social or international policy level. Even when the political process is responsible for the settlement of an international conflict, the "psychological barriers" can make a solution impossible. Contemporary developments in attribution theory and social cognition represent important potential contributions to understanding such psychological factors.

In one of the early attempts to apply attribution principles to intergroup processes, Pettigrew (1979) identified what he called the ultimate attribution error. He suggested that phenomena similar to those observed at the interpersonal level, such as the fundamental attribution error (Ross, 1977) and the actor–observer discrepancies (e.g., Jones & Nisbett, 1972), also occur at the intergroup level. At the interpersonal level, the actor–observer discrepancies refer to an individual's tendency to attribute his or her own behavior to external causes while observers tend to attribute the same behavior to the internal dispositions of the actor. The fundamental attribution error refers to a tendency to attribute other people's behavior to more dispositional causes, underestimating the importance of situational factors. Similarly, at the intergroup level, the ultimate attribution error would take place when members of a group make attributions about the behavior of their own people (ingroup) versus the behavior of members of another group (out-group). For example, in the case of negative behavior of the ingroup, external causes are emphasized, while internal causes are emphasized for the negative behavior of out-group members. This pattern reverses for positive behavior, so that ingroup behavior is attributed to more internal factors while the out-group behavior tends to be attributed to more external factors.

Similar work by Cooper and Fazio (1979) elaborated on Jones and Davis's (1965) theory of correspondent inference in relation to intergroup attributions. For example, they define "vicarious personalism" as a group's perception of the behavior of another group as intended for them. This phenomenon is supposed to be equivalent to personalism at the interpersonal level. For example, Japanese business people may perceive a U. S. policy to impose a tax on imports as a measure against their economy, intended to harm them, even when the actual motivation may be to increase revenues or something else.

The issue of attributions in intergroup conflict has been discussed recently by Hewstone (1988). Hewstone reviewed the evidence from studies such as those conducted in India by Taylor and Jaggi (1974) using Hindu and Muslim subjects, and Hewstone and Ward (1985) in Southeast Asia, using Chinese and Malay subjects. For example, Taylor and Jaggi observed that Hindu subjects made internal attributions for other Hindus' (ingroup members) socially desirable behavior and external attributions for their undesirable behavior. On the other hand, external attributions were made by Hindus for socially desirable behaviors and internal attributions for socially undesirable behaviors of Muslims (members of the out-group). Results similar to those observed between ethnic ingroups and out-groups have been reported for causal attributions between males and females (e.g., Bond, Hewstone, Wan, & Chiu, 1985).

Hewstone (1988) extended his analysis to areas such as attributions for success and failure between ethnic and gender groups and the conception of stereotypes as schemata for attributions (Hamilton, 1979). Based on his analysis, he proposes a model to represent the role of attributions of causality in intergroup conflicts. According to the model, internal attributions for out-group behaviors that confirm negative expectancies increase the likelihood of a continued conflict, while internal attributions for behaviors of the out-group that disconfirm negative expectancies reduce the likelihood of a continued conflict.

From an attributional perspective, this model has two important limitations. First, only internal versus external attributions are considered. Both internal and external causes may also be controllable or uncontrollable as well as stable or unstable (see Weiner, 1986). Ignoring general properties of attributions that might be relevant may show a limited picture of the role of attributions in the conflict domain. Theoretically, it is controllability of attributions and not locus which influences interpersonal behavior the most. Therefore, it is the comparative study of controllable versus uncontrollable causes in relation to interpersonal feelings and reactions that represents the major potential contribution to the study of intergroup conflict and conflict resolution. In addition, stability has been the dimension most linked to expectancy.

Second, the model only focuses on the antecedents of attributions. Once an internal or external cause is made for a particular ingroup or out-group behavior it is assumed that it contributes to reducing or continuing the conflict. The analysis of the psychological consequences of attributions which mediate the effects on action should significantly contribute to a better understanding of the dynamics of intergroup conflict.

AN ATTRIBUTIONAL VIEW OF INTERGROUP BEHAVIOR AND CONFLICT

The attributional study of intergroup and international conflicts is approached here in two ways. First, developments in the attributional study of behavioral domains that are important in international conflicts are considered. For example, social behaviors such as cooperation, competition, and aggression, are assumed to be important in the study of international conflicts. If this is so, attribution theory developments in these areas represent potential contributions. Second, specific attribution principles, such as those in the area of interpersonal emotions and reactions, are applied to the analysis of conflict situations. Aspects of attribution processes that are likely to play a role in the dynamics of conflict are analyzed. In most cases, the study of causal attributions may involve either antecedents or effects of attributions. However, consistent with the focus of Weiner's theory (1986), only the consequences and not the antecedents are emphasized here.

Attributional Analysis of Relevant Behaviors

Cooperation and aggression are among the behavioral domains traditionally important in the social psychological study of conflict (Deutsch, 1973, 1986; Sherif, 1966). Although the experimental evidence concerning the role of causal attributions in cooperation is limited, there have been significant research and theoretical developments in the area of prosocial behavior.

There are obvious differences between cooperation and some forms of prosocial behavior. For example, while altruism implies an unselfish motive to help others, cooperation involves positive consequences for both parties. Nevertheless, since prosocial behavior is defined in a broad way as behavior that results in benefits for others, independent of the motives, cooperation is generally considered a kind of prosocial behavior (for a discussion, see Eisenberg & Miller, 1987).

Prosocial Behavior. Although early attributional views of helping behavior focused on locus of control as the key attributional variable (e.g., Berkowitz, 1972), research has demonstrated that controllability is the variable that is most responsible for the influence of attributions on helping (e.g., Barnes, Ickes, & Kidd, 1979; Betancourt, in press; Meyer & Mulherin, 1980; Weiner, 1980). It is evident today that locus of causality has been confounded with controllability. For example, if locus only is considered, one could erroneously assume that lower levels of help observed when a person's need is attributed to causes such as lack of effort, which is controllable, are due to the internal locus of the attribution. However, when internal causes which are also uncontrollable are considered, such as lack of ability, more positive emotions and higher levels of help are observed for internal and uncontrollable than for internal and controllable attributions. Research (for a review, see Weiner, 1986) has demonstrated that it is the perceived controllability and not the locus of causal attributions for the need or problem that most influences helping.

This confusion between the locus and controllability properties of causal attributions may also occur in contemporary analyses of intergroup attributions and behavior. When attributions are classified in terms of locus of control in order to predict the effect on conflict and conflict resolution (e.g., Hewstone, 1988; Tetlock & McGuire, 1986), the resulting differences may actually be due to controllability and not to the locus of the attribution.

According to the attributional approach, perceived controllability of causal attributions for a person's need influences the probability that one would help that individual. Although perceived controllability of causes seems to affect helping directly, it has been proposed that the most important effect is emotion-mediated. This implies that uncontrollable causes elicit positive interpersonal feelings, such as pity, which in turn increase the likelihood of helping. On the other hand, more controllable causes elicit lower levels of these emotions and higher levels of negative ones, such as anger, resulting in a higher probability of neglect (for a review, see Weiner, 1986).

Interpersonal emotions have also been important in the study of helping in relation to empathy. Empathy has been found to influence prosocial behavior (for a review, see Eisenberg & Miller, 1987). According to one of the approaches to helping behavior in this area (e.g., Batson, Duncan, Ackerman, Buckley, & Birch, 1981), empathic emotions mediate the effect of induced empathy on prosocial behavior. The key elements of this approach have been incorporated into a more comprehensive attribution-empathy model of prosocial behavior (Betancourt, in press). According to this model, controllability of the attributions one makes for a person's need influences the likelihood of helping that person. This takes place both directly and through the influence of perceived control-lability of the attribution on interpersonal emotions such as pity and anger. In addition, as observed in the empathy approach, adopting an empathic perspective induces the same interpersonal emotions as does making uncontrollable attribu-tions. In turn, these emotions increase the likelihood of helping. Moreover, induced empathic perspective influences the perceived controllability of the at-tribution for the need, so that adopting an empathic perspective toward the victim results in perception of the cause as less controllable. In sum, it is apparent that part of the effect of empathy on prosocial behavior is attribution–mediated and part of the effect of attributions is mediated by empathic emotions.

Cooperation.   In general, the cognition (attribution)–emotion–action se-quence proposed by Weiner's theory seems to also apply to cooperation, as one instance of prosocial behavior. The study of cooperation has received significant attention in the area of intergroup and international conflict. Some authors have tested different strategies to induce cooperation as a way of reducing conflict. In a series of experiments designed to test strategies to induce cooperation, Deutsch (1973, 1986) concluded that a nonpunitive (defensive deterrence) strategy was more effective than both punitive (aggressive deterrence) and altruistic (turn the other cheek) strategies in inducing cooperation and reducing conflict. When applied to international relations, this implies that threats or the development of offensive weapon systems on the part of a country, intended to force another country to cooperate, may actually discourage cooperation and intensify conflict by provoking aggressive reactions. From an attributional perspective, the differ-ential levels of cooperation induced by the strategies studied by Deutsch could be attribution-mediated. For example, an aggressive action on the part of the Soviet Union, even if it is intended to force the United States to cooperate, would be perceived in the United States as negative. As discussed previously, there is evidence that in an intergroup conflict, negative behaviors of the out-group tend to be attributed more to internal causes (e.g., evil intentions) while similar behaviors on the part of the ingroup tend to be attributed more to external causes (e.g., the situation). Therefore, it is possible that while the Soviets could per-ceive their own action as motivated by the conflict situation and the need to force the United States to cooperate, people in the United States may perceive it as intended to dominate, provoke, or humiliate, reducing the probability of cooper-ation.

The causes used to illustrate the attributional thinking of the United States and the Soviet Union in the previous example are obviously different in terms of locus of causality. However, according to the attributional theory of motivation, what really matters in inducing cooperation (prosocial behavior) is the perceived controllability of causes. In the previous example, the need to force the other country to cooperate, which can be classified as situational, is also likely to be perceived as uncontrollable. For example, during the missile crisis, the blockade of Cuba by the United States was largely attributed to the need to force the Soviets to cooperate and stop the deployment of missiles in Cuba. Such an attribution is likely to be perceived as situational or external to the United States as well as uncontrollable. On the other hand, the blockade could be attributed to an attempt to provoke or humiliate, which can be perceived as internal to the USA as well as controllable.

The attribution approach to prosocial behavior would predict that attributing a country's negative action to uncontrollable causes would result in more positive and less negative feelings and a higher likelihood of cooperation with that country in a conflict situation than attributing the same action to more controllable causes. In a similar manner, attributing a positive action to controllable causes would result in more positive feelings and higher likelihood of cooperation than attributing it to less controllable causes.

In general terms, since defensive actions are less likely than offensive ones to be perceived as negative by the other party, offensive actions might be attributed to more controllable causes. If this is the case, more negative emotions, such as anger, and less positive ones, such as sympathy, would be experienced by the other party as a result of offensive actions than as a result of defensive ones. This would in turn influence the likelihood of cooperation. In addition, such attributions on the part of people from third-party countries may influence their feelings and willingness to cooperate or help.

Concerning the role of empathy (White , 1986b) has suggested that the resolution of a conflict begins with an attempt to understand how the conflict looks from the other party's perspective. With respect to the relationship between the United States and the Soviet Union, he believes that to induce cooperation and reduce conflict there should be an attempt to empathize with the other country. In his view, although the Soviet arms build-up is normally perceived as "cold-blooded aggression," there is significant evidence indicating that insecurity and fear are the motivation as much as these are for the United States. Although White recognizes how difficult it is for U. S. citizens to empathize with the Soviet government, he believes that an attempt to see the situation from their perspective would significantly increase cooperation. Of course, the same applies for the Soviets toward the government of the United States.

This view is supported by attributional principles and evidence concerning prosocial motivation. According to the attribution-empathy model of prosocial behavior discussed previously, empathic perspective increases prosocial behavior in two ways. First, it elicits empathic emotions, which in turn influence prosocial motivation. Second, it influences perceived controllability of attributions, which influences prosocial behavior both directly and through increased levels of empathic emotions (see Betancourt, in press). In addition, there is evidence in the actor–observer literature suggesting that observers instructed to empathize with an actor make more situational attributions for negative outcomes than observers who did not empathize (Gould & Sigall, 1977; Regan & Totten, 1975). Such evidence supports the suggestion that empathy is a powerful factor in inducing cooperation and reducing conflict.

Aggression in Conflict Situations.   Although research and theory developments concerning the role of causal attributions in aggression and violence are not as advanced as in the area of prosocial motivation, there are some encouraging results. It has been demonstrated that controllability, the key property of causes in the interpersonal behavior domain, is associated with neglect in helping scenarios and with punishment in achievement scenarios (for a review see Weiner, 1986). For example it has been observed that in helping scenarios people are less likely to help (or more likely to neglect) a needy person when the need or problem is attributed to controllable causes than when attributed to less-controllable ones. In a similar manner, when a student's failure is attributed to controllable causes, punishment from the teacher is more likely than when the same outcome is attributed to uncontrollable causes.

Controllability of causal attributions has also been proposed to influence aggression and violence. Early research on aggression and retaliation suggested a role for causal explanations in the instigation of violence. For example, perception of frustration or pain as intentionally caused by other people seems to increase the likelihood and intensity of an aggressive response (e.g., Bandura, 1973; Greenwell & Dengerink, 1973).

More recently it has been proposed (Betancourt, 1986) that the attribution of frustrating or negative actions to causes perceived as controllable increases the likelihood of a violent action or retaliation in a conflict situation. For example, in one recent study college students were presented with a number of situations representing interpersonal, intergroup, and international conflicts. Results showed that subjects who attributed aggression to causes perceived as more controllable by the victim and as less-controllable by the aggressor tended to prefer violent as opposed to nonviolent solutions to conflicts. In contrast, those who attributed the same actions to causes perceived as less controllable by the victim and more controllable by the aggressor tended to prefer nonviolent (negotiated) solutions to conflicts (Betancourt, Ergas, & Ripoll, 1986).

Although a conclusion is still premature in this area, it is apparent that controllability of attributions for out-group negative behavior in addition to influencing cooperation may also affect the choice of aggression versus negotiation in conflict situations. Lower levels of perceived controllability appear to be associated with increased cooperation and negotiation as well as with a lower probability of aggression or retaliation.

AN ATTRIBUTIONAL VIEW OF INTERNATIONAL CONFLICT

The interactional approach to conflict resolution as applied to the Middle East conflict by Kelman and colleagues (Kelman, 1986; Kelman & Cohen, 1976) provides good material to illustrate the applications of an attributional analysis to international conflicts. The interactional approach focuses on the interactions between the parties in a conflict. In fact, one of the objectives of the conflict-resolution workshops conducted by Kelman and his colleagues has been to promote and provide the conditions for interactions that contribute to de-escalation and conflict resolution.

From an attributional perspective, the interactional approach is appropriate in that it recognizes the importance of social psychological phenomena such as attribution processes and provides a setting for analysis and change. The study of attribution processes and the pertinent psychological consequences within the context of an interactional approach may contribute to overcoming psychological barriers and create social psychological conditions that facilitate the political process involved in conflict resolution.

One of the assumptions of the interactional approach is that in social interactions individuals take into account each other's intentions as well as the conditions under which the interaction takes place. Under normal circumstances we make important errors in interpersonal perception and causal attributions. Some of these errors have also been observed to take place at the intergroup level, when members of a group make attributions for the behavior of out-group members (see Hewstone, 1988). These phenomena are more likely to occur or persist in international conflicts when the parties have no opportunities to interact and learn about each other. Moreover, discrepancies in perception and judgment may be increased by cultural differences (for a review, see Fletcher & Ward, in press). Cross-cultural variations have been observed not only in the attributions people make for the same behavioral events in different cultures (e.g., Triandis, 1972) but also for the perceived properties of the same attribution (e.g., Betancourt & Weiner, 1982).

The study of attribution processes in international conflicts within the context of the interactional approach is important in at least two ways. First, properties of the attributions each party makes for others' actions or positions are important to understand their feelings, motivations, and reactions. These psychological elements contribute to creating the conditions for either negotiation, cooperation, and the settlement of a conflict, or for retaliation, aggression, and escalation of the conflict. Second, it is important to understand the conditions that facilitate errors and discrepancies in attributions for each party's behavior, both at the interpersonal and the intergroup level. Such errors and discrepancies may apply to the causes to which events are attributed as well as to the perceived properties of those causes.

In previous works on the conflict between Israelis and Palestinians, Kelman considered causal attributions, but only in terms of locus of causality (Kelman, 1983, 1986). Further analysis of causal attributions in terms of their perceived controllability and stability, which influence interpersonal behavior (e.g., cooperation) and expectancy of success, respectively, should shed additional light.

One of the characteristics of the Israeli–Palestinian conflict has been the lack of direct communication and interaction between the parties, which leads to enormous possibilities for distortions in attribution processes. These distortions are likely to affect the Palestinians and the Israelis as well as other parties involved, such as the United States and the Arab world. In addition, due to the persistence of the conflict, important changes in attitudes or objectives may have taken place over the years. Failure to perceive or acknowledge these changes may be associated with persistent causal explanations that could have been correct in the past but may now be wrong. These false attributions may be contributing to the persistence of psychological barriers impeding objective communication between the parties, therefore blocking the political process that could lead to a solution.

In his social psychological assessment of the prospects for a resolution of the Israeli–Palestinian conflict, Kelman (1983) provided an analysis of a series of conversations with Yasser Arafat, head of the Palestine Liberation Organization (PLO). In his analysis, Kelman refers specifically to the tendency in opponents of the PLO to dismiss Arafat's changes toward a more compromising position, attributing these changes to situational (external) causes, such as a deceptive tactic due to external pressures or the need to maintain a good public image. At the same time, they continue to attribute any hostile statements and actions to internal causes such as a commitment to eliminate Israel or Zionism in Palestine. According to Kelman, these kinds of attributions lead Israel and the United States to disregard any positive change on the part of Arafat, contributing to the persistence of psychological barriers that make direct negotiations impossible.

The attributional pattern described previously is consistent with predictions based on Hewstone's (1988) analysis of intergroup attributions, particularly in the case of an extremely hostile view of the out-group. For example, the Israelis are likely to have negative expectancies about Arafat. If this is the case, a positive behavior such as Arafat's signaling interest in negotiations with Israel would disconfirm expectancies. Therefore, the Israelis are likely to attribute such behavior to situational (external) causes, which would contribute to the continuation of the conflict. At the same time, a hostile statement from Arafat, which confirms expectancies, is attributed to dispositional (internal) causes, also contributing to the continuation of the conflict. Although this view of intergroup attributions is interesting, a more sophisticated analysis of attributions, including properties and consequences, is necessary in order to understand whether or not a given pattern of attributions would lead to the continuation or reduction of conflict.

If Israel or the United States attributes Arafat's positive behavior to a deceptive strategy caused by external pressures, in addition to being situational, this attribution represents low levels of controllability and stability. Theoretically, the attribution of positive outcomes to causes that are low in controllability elicits less positive and more negative interpersonal feelings. These feelings in turn relate to negative interpersonal evaluation and low levels of motivation to help or cooperate. At the same time, low stability of causal attributions leads to low expectancy that such behaviors will persist or occur again. The consequence is a low probability of positive reactions on the part of Israel or the United States.

The attribution of hostile statements to Arafat's plans or intentions to destroy Israel, in addition to being internal can also be perceived as controllable and relatively stable. Theoretically, high controllability of negative actions relates to negative emotions, such as anger, which have been found to mediate aggression and high levels of punishment. Since the intention to eliminate Israel is consistent with the Palestinian National Covenant, attributing negative statements or attitudes to causes associated with it implies relative stability. If this is so, a high expectancy of such negative behaviors and a very low expectancy of change are predicted. Hence, prospects for negotiation and peace are lowered as the prospects for hostility and aggression increase.

In the previous example, the causal attributions for Arafat's positive behavior were external, as the attributions for his negative behavior were internal. However, the attributional analysis suggests that not the locus but the controllability and stability of the attributions are responsible for the effects. Although in this case internal causes for negative behavior were also controllable and stable, in other instances an internal attribution could be uncontrollable and unstable. In a similar manner, external causes for positive behavior could be controllable. This represents the possibility of different effects on feelings, motivation, and reactions, leading to predictions that would be different from those based on the locus only analysis. The situation is analogous to what Weiner and his colleagues demonstrated in the achievement and helping-behavior domains (see Weiner, 1986).

The implications of this attributional approach can be further illustrated by analyzing some of Arafat's attributions for Israeli actions as reported by Kelman (1983). Of particular interest is the analysis of Arafat's acknowledgment of change in Israel and of differences in attitudes and purpose among Israeli officials. He also recognized that these changes could be attributed at least in part to the peace process between Egypt and Israel. In one of his conversations with Kelman, Arafat also stated that the Israelis were "stupid" because they linked their fate to the interests of the United States in the Middle East instead of trying to negotiate peace with the Palestinians.

From an attributional perspective, it is interesting that Arafat attributes the fact that Israel does not seek direct negotiations with the Palestinians at least in part to situational, external causes; mainly, the interests of the United States. However, it is apparent that he sees this cause as unstable and controllable by Israel. Theoretically, the attribution of a negative action (or the lack of positive action) to controllable causes elicits negative emotions, such as anger, and a negative interpersonal evaluation. The reference to Israeli officials as "stupid" or "idiots," suggests the perception of their behavior as controllable. In addition, accepting that Israel has changed and that the change is partly the consequence of Sadat's peace efforts, suggests the perception that it is possible that such changes in Israel may be partly controllable by the other party. In sum, it seems that Arafat perceives the causes of the conflict as complex, unstable, and subject to volitional control, primarily on the part of Israel but also on the part of the PLO. The implications are that despite the negative remarks on the part of Arafat toward Israel, he perceives change as possible and seems to be willing to make efforts toward the settlement of the conflict, even if it implies direct negotiations and the recognition of Israel.

The perception of Israel's failure to seek peace with the Palestinians as controllable and unstable, in addition to situational, sheds light on important psychological consequences. These consequences, such as feelings and expectations, may be important factors in understanding the conflict situation, thereby creating the social psychological conditions that may facilitate the political process for conflict resolution.

In the previous illustrations, we have considered causal attributions as reported by external observers. However, it is theoretically possible that what we perceive as internal, controllable, or stable, is not similarly perceived by members of the PLO or the Israelis. According to the theory, the perceived properties of causes and not necessarily the causes themselves are associated with the psychological consequences. Hence, it is not enough to know only the causal attributions. It is important to know how the conflicting parties perceive the properties of causal attributions in order to predict the corresponding psychological consequences of those attributions.

Differences in causal attributions as well as in their perceived properties are particularly expected in international conflicts, or in conflicts between ethnic groups. In such conflicts, culture is an additional factor that may play an important role. For example, it is possible that even when the Israeli government and the governments of Arab countries attribute Arafat's statements to the same causes, the properties of those causes are perceived to be different by Israelis and Arabs. This could be the case when a negative statement by Arafat is attributed to the PLO's commitment not to recognize Israel's right to exist. The cause of such a statement could be perceived as very stable by the Israeli government but not so stable by the government of some Arab countries such as Egypt. If there are differences in the perception of reality between Israelis and Arabs, these perceptions are very likely to cause differences in attribution processes. Similar differences may exist between the United States and third-world countries, which may make the settlement of conflicts more difficult.

Interactional workshops such as those implemented by Kelman and his colleagues in the case of the Middle East provide an excellent setting for attributional analysis and change, which can in turn increase the effectiveness of such interventions. Attribution processes can be analyzed and much can be learned about the cultural differences that may be relevant to social psychological phenomena and the political process involved in solving a conflict.

SUMMARY

The generalizability of attribution theory, developed at the individual level of analysis, to intergroup and international behavior was first discussed. Although some caution has been recommended, the conclusion is that a variety of social psychological phenomena are relevant to the study of conflict and its resolution at the intergroup and international levels of analysis.

Concerning attribution theory, several areas are considered important for the study of intergroup and international conflict. First, some authors suggest that although the solution of an international conflict requires a political process, social psychological factors which take place at the individual or interpersonal level can either facilitate or prevent such a process. This would be the case for attribution principles. Second, some attribution principles have been investigated at the intergroup level. Research in this area represents a unique potential contribution to the understanding of intergroup and international conflict. Third, there are behavioral domains that are important to understand conflict at all levels. The attributional study of phenomena such as prosocial behavior (particularly cooperation), competition, and aggression appears to have implications for the study of conflict. Finally, the application of attributional principles to the study of conflict and conflict resolution is illustrated through an analysis of part of Kelman's work on the interactional approach to conflict resolution in the Middle East. The direct analysis of international conflicts based on attributional principles represents the possibility of important contributions.

AUTHOR NOTES

Correspondence to the author should be sent to the following address: Department of Psychology, Loma Linda University, Riverside, California 92515.

REFERENCES

Austin, W., & Worchell, S. (Eds.). (1979). *The social psychology of intergroup relations*. Monterey, CA: Brooks Cole.

Bandura, A. (1973). *Aggression: A social learning analysis*. Englewood Cliffs, NJ: Prentice-Hall.

Barnes, R., Ickes, W., & Kidd, R. (1979). Effects of perceived intentionality and stability of another's dependency on helping behavior. *Personality and Social Psychology Bulletin, 5,* 367–372.

Batson, C., Duncan, B., Ackerman, P., Buckley, T., & Birch, K. (1981). Is empathic emotion a source of altruistic motivation? *Journal of Personality and Social Psychology, 40,* 290–302.

Berkowitz, L. (1972). Social norms, feelings, and other factors affecting helping and altruism. In L. Berkowitz (Ed.), *Advances in experimental social psychology* (Vol. 6). New York: Academic.

Betancourt, H. (in press). An attribution-empathy model of helping behavior. *Personality and Social Psychology Bulletin*.

Betancourt, H. (1986, June). *Attribution processes in violent and non-violent solutions to conflicts*. Paper presented at the ninth annual scientific meeting of the International Society of Political Psychology, Amsterdam.

Betancourt, H., Ergas, R., & Ripoll, R. (1986, August). *Antidemocratic attitudes, causal attributions and the use of violence*. Paper presented at the 94th annual convention of the American Psychological Association, Washington, DC.

Betancourt, H., & Weiner, B. (1982). Attributions for achievement-related events, expectancy, and sentiments: A study of success and failure in Chile and the United States. *Journal of Cross-Cultural Psychology, 13,* 362–374.

Blight, J. G. (1987). Toward a policy-relevant psychology of avoiding nuclear war: Lessons for psychologists from the Cuban missile crisis. *American Psychologist, 42,* 12–29.

Bond, M., Hewstone, M., Wan, K., & Chiu, C. (1985). Group serving attributions across intergroup contexts: Cultural differences in the explanation of sex-typed behaviors. *European Journal of Social Psychology, 15,* 435–451.

Chilstrom, G. (1984). Psychological aspects of the nuclear arms race. *Journal of Humanistic Psychology, 24,* 39–54.

Cooper, J., & Fazio, R. (1979). The formation and persistence of attitudes that support intergroup conflict. In W. G. Austin & S. Worchel (Eds.), *The social psychology of intergroup relations*. Monterey, CA: Brooks Cole.

Deutsch, M. (1973). *The resolution of conflict: Constructive and destructive processes*. New Haven, CT: Yale University Press.

Deutsch, M. (1983). The prevention of World War III: A psychological perspective. *Political Psychology, 4,* 3–31.

Deutsch, M. (1986). Strategies of inducing cooperation. In R. White (Ed.), *Psychology and the prevention of nuclear war* (pp. 162–170). New York University Press.

Eisenberg, N., & Miller, P. (1987). The relation of empathy to prosocial and related behaviors. *Psychological Bulletin, 101,* 91–119.

Fiske, S. (1987). People's reactions to nuclear war: Implications for psychologists. *American Psychologist, 42,* 207–217.

Fletcher, G., & Ward, C. (1988). In M. Bond (Ed.), *The cross-cultural challenge to social psychology*. Newbury Park, CA: Sage.

Gould, R., & Sigall, H. (1977). The effects of empathy and outcome on attribution: An examination of the divergent-perspective hypothesis. *Journal of Experimental Social Psychology, 13,* 480–491.

Greenwell, I., & Dengerink, H. (1973). The role of perceived versus actual attack in human physical aggression. *Journal of Personality and Social Psychology, 26,* 66–71.

Hamilton, D. (1979). A cognitive-attributional analysis of stereotyping. In L. Berkowitz (Ed.), *Advances in experimental social psychology* (Vol. 12). New York: Academic.

Hewstone, M. (1988). Attributional bases of intergroup conflict. In W. Stroebe, A. Kruglanski, D. Bartal, & M. Hewstone (Eds.), *The social psychology of intergroup conflict.* New York: Springer–Verlag.

Hewstone, M., & Ward, C. (1985). Ethnocentrism and causal attribution in Southeast Asia. *Journal of Personality and Social Psychology, 48,* 614–623.

Horai, J. (1977). Attributional conflict. *Journal of Social Issues, 33,* 88–100.

Jones, E., & Davis, K. (1965). From acts to dispositions: The attribution process in person perception. In L. Berkowitz (Ed.), *Advances in Experimental Social Psychology* (Vol. 2). New York: Academic.

Jones, E., & Nisbett, R. E. (1972). The actor and the observer: Divergent perceptions of the causes of behavior. In E. Jones, D. Kanouse, H. Kelley, R. Nisbett, S. Valins, & B. Weiner (Eds.), *Attribution: Perceiving the causes of behavior.* Morristown, NJ: General Learning.

Kelman, H. (1983). Conversations with Arafat: A social-psychological assessment of the prospect for Israeli–Palestinian peace. *American Psychologist, 38,* 203–216.

Kelman, H. (1986). An interactional approach to conflict resolution. In R. White (Ed.), *Psychology and the prevention of nuclear war* (pp. 171–193). New York University Press.

Kelman, H. (1987). The political psychology of the Israeli–Palestinian conflict: How can we overcome the barriers to a negotiated solution. *Political Psychology, 8,* 347–363.

Kelman, H., & Cohen, S. (1976). The problem-solving workshop: A social psychological contribution to the resolution of international conflicts. *Journal of Peace Research, 13,* 79–90.

Mack, J. (1985). Toward a collective psychopathology of the nuclear arms competition. *Political Psychology, 6,* 291–321.

Meyer, J., & Mulherin, A. (1980). From attribution to helping: An analysis of the mediating effects of affect on expectancy. *Journal of Personality and Social Psychology, 39,* 201–210.

Pettigrew, T. (1979). The ultimate attribution error: Extending Allport's cognitive analysis of prejudice. *Personality and Social Psychology Bulletin, 5,* 461–476.

Plous, S. (1985). Perceptual illusions and military realities: The nuclear arms race. *Journal of Conflict Resolution, 29,* 363–389.

Pruitt, D., & Rubin, J. (1986). *Social conflict.* New York: Random House.

Regan, D., & Totten, J. (1975). Empathy and attribution: Turning observers into actors. *Journal of Personality and Social Psychology, 50,* 1123–1133.

Ross, L. (1977). The intuitive psychologist and his shortcomings: Distortions in the attribution process. In L. Berkowitz (Ed.), *Advances in experimental social psychology* (Vol. 10). New York: Academic.

Sherif, M. (1958). Superordinate goals in the reduction of intergroup conflicts. *American Journal of Sociology, 63,* 349–356.

Sherif, M. (1966). *Group conflict and co-operation: Their social psychology.* London: Routledge & Kegan Paul.

Stroebe, W., Kruglanski, A., Bar–Tal, D., & Hewstone, M. (1988). *The social psychology of intergroup conflict.* New York: Springer–Verlag.

Taylor, D., & Jaggi, V. (1974). Ethnocentrism and causal attribution in a South Indian context. *Journal of Cross-Cultural Psychology, 5,* 161–171.

Tetlock, P., & McGuire, Jr., C. (1986). Cognitive perspectives on foreign policy. In R. White (Ed.), *Psychology and the prevention of nuclear war* (pp. 255–273). New York University Press.

Triandis, H. (1972). The analysis of subjective culture. New York: Wiley.

Weiner, B. (1980). A cognitive (attributional)–emotion–action model of motivated behavior: An analysis of judgments of help-giving. *Journal of Personality and Social Psychology, 39,* 186–200.

Weiner, B. (1985). An attributional theory of achievement motivation and emotion. *Psychological Review, 92,* 548–573.

Weiner, B. (1986). *An attributional theory of motivation and emotion.* New York: Springer–Verlag.

White, R. (Ed.). (1986a). *Psychology and the prevention of nuclear war.* New York University Press.

White, R. (1986b). Empathizing with the Soviet government. In R. White (Ed.), *Psychology and the prevention of nuclear war* (pp. 82–98). New York University Press.

Author Index

Italics denote pages with bibliographic information

A

Abelson, R. P., 105, *120*
Abrams, R. D., 93, *98*
Abramson, L. Y., 5, *12*, 53, 56, 57, 59, 61, *73, 74*, 103, 110, *118*, 124, 127, 128, *136*, 172, *182*
Ackerman, P., 210, *218*
Adams, A. N., 163, *182*
Adler, T., 34, *35*
Affleck, G., 80, 93, *98*, 118, *119*, 173, *182*
Ajzen, I., 57, *73*
Albaum, G., 152, *160*
Aldwin, C., 88, *98*
Allen, D. A., 80, 93, *98*, 118, *119*
Alloy, L. B., 61, *74*, 110, *118*, 131, 132, *137*
Allport, G., 162, *182*
Altmaier, E. M., 88, 90, 94, 96, *98*
Amirkhan, J. H., 5, 11, 77, 83, 86, 87, 88, 90, *98*, 157, *160*, 198, 199, *204*
Anderson, C. A., 128, *137*, 158, *159*
Anderson, C. M., 114, 116, *119*
Anderson, K., 53, 57, *75*
Andreasen, A., 157, *159*
Andreasen, N. C., 115, *119*
Andreassen, P. B., 148, *159*
Andrews, G. R., 126, 128, *137*

Antaki, C., *119*, 129, *137*
Arias, I., 161, *184*
Arkin, R. M., *51*, 80, 87, 88, 94, 95, *99*, 129, *137*, 175, *182*
Asher, S. J., 162, *182*
Atkins, A., 108, 109, *120*
Atkinson, J. W., 1, 2, 3, 7, 8, 12, *12*
Auerbach, S. M., *98*
Austin, W., 205, *218*
Auvergne, S., 38, *50*
Averill, J. R., 85, *98*, 152, *159*, 173, 179, *182*

B

Bachmann, M., 23, 24, *36*
Bailey, S., 53, 57, *75*
Bandura, A., 40, 45, 46, *50*, 83, 89, 90, 91, 95, *98*, 112, 172, *182*, *218*
Barker, D. G., 83, 86, 88, *102*
Barker, G., 25, 26, 27, 28, 29, 30, 31, *35*
Barling, J., 161, *184*
Barnes, R., 209, *218*
Barnett, K., 31, *35*
Baron, R. A., 185, 188, 191, 196, 202, *203*
Baron, R. S., 11, 33, *35*, 141, 158, *160*

221

Barrett, L. C., 60, 70, *74*
Barry, W. A., 174, *184*
Bar-Tal, D., 205, *219*
Bartlett, F. C., 133, *137*
Batson, C. D., 104, 105, 106, *119*, 210, *218*
Baucom, D. H., *137*, 163, *182*
Baum, A., 90, *99*
Baumgardner, A. H., 80, 87, 88, 94, 95, *99*, 175, *182*
Baumeister, R. F., 158, *159*
Beach, S. R., 129, *137*
Beaucom, D. H., 129, *137*
Bebbington, P., 115, *119*
Beck, A. T., 11, 60, *73*, 124, 130, 134, 135, *137*
Becker, J., *101*
Beckman, L., 128, *138*
Belk, R., 151, *159*
Bell, R. J., 89, 90, *100*
Benesh-Weiner, M., 48, *52*
Bentler, P. M., 45, *50*
Berkowitz, R., 116, *120*, 209, *218*
Berman, J., 105, 106, *119*
Berscheid, E., 149, *159*, 178,*182*
Berzins, J. I., 82, *99*
Best, A., 157, *159*
Betancourt, H., 11, 141, 205, 209, 210, 212, 213, *218*
Bettes, B. A., 58, *74*
Bettman, J. R., 146, *159*
Biermann, U., 23, 24, *36*
Bies, R. J., 186, 200, *203*
Billings, A. G., 85, 86, 89, 90, *101*
Birch, K., 210, *218*
Bird, A. M., 48, *50*
Birley, J. L., 112, 113, *119*
Blake, R. R., 185, *203*
Blaney, P. H., 82, 84, 88, 96, *99*
Blight, J. G., 205, *218*
Bloom, B. L., 162, *182*
Bohm, L. C., 80, 83, 87, 90, 94, 96, 97, *101*
Bond, M., 207, *218*
Bonett, D. G., 45, *50*
Boyd, J. L., 116, *119*
Bradbury, T. N., 103, 118, *119*, 141, 162, 164, 168, 172, 174, 175, 176, 178, 180, 182, *182*
Braiker, H. B., 162, 168, *182*
Brawley, L. R., 38, 43, 48, 49, *50, 52*
Brayfield, F., 81, *99*
Brehm, J., 55, *75*

Brewin, C. R., 103, 118, *119*, 123, 128, 129, 132, *137*, 173, *182*
Brickman, P., 106, 153, 156, *159*
Brockner, J., *204*
Brooks, D. R., 39, *51*
Brophy, J., 28, 32, 33, *35*
Brown, G. W., 112, 113, *119*
Brown, J., 19, *35*
Buckley, T., 210, *218*
Bukowski, W. M., 38, *51*
Bugenthal, D. B., 181, *183*
Bulman, R. J., 93, *99*
Buss, A. R., 111, *119*
Butcher, J. N., 145, *159*
Butler, D., 161, *184*
Butterfield, E., 81, *99*
Byrne, D., 85, *99*

C-D

Cain, M., 61, *73*
Calicchia, J. P., 82, *99*
Cameron, R., 89, 90, 94, 96, *99*
Camp, C. B., *159*
Campbell, D. T., 69, *73*
Carley, W. M., 145, *159*
Carr, J. E., 87, *101*
Carstairs, G. M., 113, *119*
Cash, T. F., 82, *99*
Chilstrom, G., 205, *218*
Chiu, C., 207, *218*
Chodoff, P., 93, *99*
Christopher, R. C., 157, *159*
Clark, M., 144, *159*
Clayton, S., 28, *35*
Clore, G., 158, *160*
Cluss, P. A., 48, *51*
Coates, D., 106, *119*, 153, *159*
Cody, M. J., 186, *203*
Cohen, J. B., 80, 85, *100*
Cohen, L. J., 85, *101*
Cohen, S., *99, 219*
Cohn, E., 106, *119*, 153, *159*
Collins, J., 46, *51*
Colvin, D., 62, 70, *74*
Compas, B., 88, 89, 96, *99*
Comstock, G. W., 79, *100*
Cooper, H., 33, *35*
Cooper, J., 207, *218*

Copeland, D. R., 83, 86, 88, *102*
Cottler, H. F., 81, *98*
Covington, M., 25, *36*
Coyne, J. C., 123, 128, *137*
Cromwell, R., 81, *99*
Cummings, L. L., 186, 200, *203*
Curren, M. T., 153, *159*
Curry, J., 81, *99*
Dabbs, J. M., 81, *100*
Daniels, D., 34, *36*
Darby, B. W., 151, *159*
Darcie, G., 31, *35*
Davis, E. R., 67, 70, *74*
Davis, K. E., 37, *51,* 207, *219*
Day, R., 147, 148, 157, *159*
Deal, J. E., 161, *183*
Debus, R. L., 126, 128, *137*
de la Salva, A., 113, 115, 117, *120*
DeLongis, A., 87, 88, *99*
Dengerink, H., 112, *218*
Dermer, M., 149, *159*
Detchon, C. S., 129, *137*
DeWolfe, A. S., 82, *100*
Deutsch, M., 205, 208, 210, *218*
Dishman, R. K., 48, *51*
Dix, T., 169, 170, 180, *183*
Doane, J. A., 117, *119*
Dodge, D., 79, *99*
Doherty, W. J., 164, *183*
Doubleday, C., 21, *35*
Douvan, E., 162, *184*
Drobry, J., 149, 156, *160*
Dubos, R., *99*
DuCette, J. P., 86, *100*
Duncan, B., 210, *218*
Duncan, T. E., 11, 16, 40, 41, 42, 44, 46, 49, 50, *51*
Dunkel-Schetter, C., 87, 88, *99*
Dweck, C. S., 21, *35,* 47, *51,* 59, *73,* 128, *137*
Dworkin, T. M., 149, *159*

E-F

Eberlein-Vries, R., 116, *120*
Eccles, J., 34, *35*
Eisenburg, N., *35,* 209, *218*
Eiser, J. R., 48, *51,* 128, 129, *137*
Ekenrode, J., 191, *204*
Ell, K. O., *99*

Elliott, D. J., 87, 91, *99*
Elliot, E., 21, *35*
Ellis, A., 11
Emery, G., 134, *137*
Emery, R. E., 170, *183*
Emshwiller, J. R., 143, *159*
Enright, M. A., 191, *204*
Epstein, L., 48, *51*
Ergas, R., 112, *218*
Evans, J. W., 86, *101*
Fadden, G., 115, *119*
Falloon, I. R. H., 114, 116, 117, *119*
Fazio, R., 207, *218*
Felton, B. J., 88, 90, *99*
Ferguson, T. J., 187, *203*
Festinger, L., 5
Fifield, J., 173, *182*
Fincham, F. D., 11, 61, *73,* 103, 118, 129, *137,* 141, 142, 162, 164, 168, 170, 171, 172, 174, 175, 176, 178, 180, 182, *182*
Finesinger, J., 93, *98*
Fischman-Haustad, L., 113, *119*
Fishbein, M., 57, *73*
Fiske, D. W., 69, *73*
Fiske, S. T., 186, 205, *203, 218*
Fitzpatrick, M. A., 163, *183*
Flaherty, J., 86, *101*
Fleming, R., 90, *99*
Fletcher, G. J. O., 113, 186, *204, 218*
Floyd, F. J., 167, *183*
Fodor, E. M., 185, *203*
Folkes, V. S., 11, 141, 146, 148, 152, 153, 155, 157, *159, 160,* 198, 199, *204*
Folkman, S., 63, *73,* 80, 82, 84, 85, 86, 87, 88, 89, 90, 91, 97, *99, 100*
Follette, V., 80, 95, *99*
Försterling, F., 11, 17, *35,* 47, *51,* 77, 103, 123, 126, 127, 129, 130, 136, *137*
Forsyth, D. R., 40, 41, 43, *51*
Forsythe, C. J., 88, 89, 96, *99*
French, R., 128, *137*
Friedman, S. B., 93, *99*
Frieze, I. E., 6, *13,* 126, 128, *138*
Frieze, I. H., *12*
Fusillo, A., 89, 90, *100*

G-H

Galvin, K. S., 103, *119*
Ganellen, R. J., 82, 84, 88, 96, *99*

Garrity, T. F., 81, *100*
Gauthier, J., 83, 89, *98*
Gelles, R. J., 161, 164, 179, *183, 184*
Gilderman, A. M., 116, *119*
Gill, D. L., 47, *51*
Girgus, J. S., 61, *73*
Glass, D. C., 80, *99*
Gleason, J. M., *51*
Goldburg, E. L., 79, *100*
Goldstein, M. J., 113, *120, 133, 139*
Good, T., 33, *35*
Goss, A., 82, *100*
Gossard, D., 83, 89, *98*
Gotlib, I. H., 123, 128, *137*
Gottman, J. M., 163, 169, 179, *184*
Gould, R., 112, *218*
Grace, G. D., 86, *100*
Graham, J. L., 152, 153, *159*
Graham, S., 11, 15, 16, 19, 20, 21, 22, 25,
    26, 27, 28, 29, 30, 31, *35, 36,* 148, *159*
Graziano, W., 149, *159*
Greenwell, I., 112, *218*
Gross, A. R., 88, *100*
Gross, J. B., 39, 40, 41, 42, 43, 47, *51*
Gruen, R. J., 87, 88, *99*
Grusec, J. E., 169, 170, 180, *183*
Grych, J., 118, 141
Guarino, P., 21, *35*
Haan, N., 85, *100*
Haisch, I., 129, *137*
Haisch, J., 129, *137*
Hamburg, D. A., 93, *99*
Hamilton, D., 207, *219*
Hamilton, V. L., *160*
Handley, R., 112, *120*
Hansen, R. D., 186, 192, *203*
Happ, D., 88, 90, 94, 95, *98*
Harari, O., 25, *36*
Hardy, C. S., 39, *52*
Harmon, R. R., 154, *160*
Harris, D. V., 39, *51*
Harris, B., 170, *183*
Hart, H. L. A., 169, *183*
Harvey, J. H., *51,* 103, *119, 120*
Hatcher, C., 145, *159*
Heider, F., 1, 2, 3, 5, 6, *12,* 130, *137,* 170,
    183
Heim, M., 128, *138*
Hempelman, M., 23, 24, *36*
Henher, B., *139*
Heppner, P. P., 80, 87, 88, 94, 95, *99*

Hertel, R. K., 174, *184*
Herzberger, S., 57, *75*
Hewstone, M., 205, 207, 209, 213, 214, *218,*
    219
Heyman, R. E., 163, *184*
Hinkle, L. E., 79, *100*
Hiroto, D. S., 55, *73*
Hogarty, G. E., 114, 116, *119*
Holland, C., 31, *35*
Holmes, T., 79, *100*
Holtzworth-Munroe, A., 80, *100*
Hooley, J. M., 113, 116, *120*
Horai, J., 205, *219*
Horowitz, L. M., 128, *137*
Hotaling, G. T., 164, 169, 181, *183*
Hountras, P. T., 81, *100*
Houston, B. K., 81, *100*
Howe, G. W., 156, *160*
Huang, M., 38, *51*
Huddleson, S., 47, *51*
Husaini, B. A., 86, 90, *100*

I-J-K-L

Ickes, W., 103, *120,* 209, *218*
Jacobsen, B., 81, *100*
Jacobson, N. S., 80,. 95, *99, 100*
Jaggi, V., 205, 207, *219*
James, M. K., 38, *51*
James, W., 4, *12*
Janis, I. L., 145, *160*
Jaspers, J. M., 164, 171, *183*
Jauna, C. D., 114, *119*
Jenkins, C. D., 79, *100*
Jenkins, J. H., 113, 115, *120*
Johnson, J. E., 81, *100*
Johnson, J. T., 149, 156, *160*
Johnson, S., *51*
Johnson, T. E., 187, 202, *203*
Johnson-George, C., 191, *204*
Jones, E., 37, *51,* 185, *204,* 207, *219*
Jordan, J. S., 103, *120*
Kaczala, C., 32, *36*
Kahneman, D., 148, 149, *160*
Kamen, L. P., 60, 70, *73*
Kanner, A., 80, *100*
Karno, M., 113, 115, 117, *120*
Karuza, J. Jr., 106, *119,* 153, *159*
Kaslow, N. J., 61, *74*
Keane, A., 81, *100*

Kelley, H. H., 1, 3, 5, 8, *12*, 18, *36*, 37, *51*, 80, 110, *120*, 124, 130, 132, 136, *138*, 148, *160*, 162, 168, *182, 184*, 186, *204*
Kelly, G., 11
Keller, M. L., 87, 96, *101*
Kelman, H., 205, 206, 213, 214, 215, *219*
Kendell, P. C., 81, *98*
Keyson, M., 82, *101*
Kidd, R., 209, *218*
Kidder, L., 106, *119*, 153, *159*
Kim, H., 158, *160*
Kobasigawa, A., 31, *35*
Koenigsbert, H. W., 112, *120*
Koletsky, S., 148, 152, 153, *159*
Kopta, S. M., 105, 106, *120*
Kornblith, S. J., 114, *119*
Kotsos, B., 146, 148, *159*
Keyson, M., *101*
Krantz, S. E., 87, 88, 90, *100*
Kremer, J. F., 187, *204*
Kruglanski, A., 205, *219*
Kuipers, L., 115, 116, *119, 120*
Kukla, A., *12*, 24, *36, 126, 138*
Kukla, R. A., 6, 8, *13*, 162, *184*
Kun, A., 24, 25, *36*, 48, *52*
Kuger, J. E., 63, 70, *75*
Lambley, P., 82, *100*
LaMontagne, L., 86, *100*
Landers, D. L., *51*
Langer, E. J., 105, *120*
Larrance, D. T., 118, *120*, 162, *184*
Latham, G. P., 61, *73*
Lawson, M., 20, *36*
Lazarus, R. S., 63, *73*, 80, 85, 86, 87, 88, 89, 90, *99, 100*
Leacock, E., 23, *36*
Leff, J. P., 113, 115, 116, 117, *120, 121*
Leggett, E., 21, *35*
Lepper, M., 158, *159*
Lerman, D., 40, 42, *52*, 80, *102*
Levenson, R. W., 163, 179, *184*
Leventhal, E. A., 80, 87, 96, *101*
Leventhal, H., 80, 81, 87, 96, *100, 101*
Levitt, N. R., 81, *98*
Levy-Leboyer, C., 158, *160*
Lewin, K., 1, 2, 3, 5, 12, *12*, 162, 175, 181, *184*
Lichtman, R. R., 80, 83, 84, 86, 90, *101*
Linville, P. W., 126, 127, *139*, 185, *204*
Locke, E. A., 61, *73*

López, S., 11, 77, 105, 106, 108, 109, 111, 113, *120, 121*
Lottman, T. J., 82, *100*
Lowe, C., 33, *35*
Lowery, B. J., 81, 86, *100*
Luborsky, L., 58, *74*

M-N-O-P

Mack, J., 205, *219*
Madonia, M. J., 114, *119*
Maehr, M. L., 33, *36, 43, 51*
Maier, S. F., 54, 56, *73, 74*
Maiuro, R. D., *101*
Magnusson, D., 83, 87, 89, *100*
Magnusson, J., 116, *121*
Margolin, G., 178, *184*
Mark, M. M., 39, *51*
Markman, H. J., 167, *183*
Marrow, A. J., 1, *12*
Marston, A. R., 113, *119*
Martin, D. S., 38, *51*
Martin, W., 79, *99*
Maruyama, G. M., 129, *137*
Marz, B., 104, *119*
Masuda, M., 79, *100*
McAuley, E., 11, 16, 39, 40, 41, 42, 43, 44, 46, 49, 50, *51*
McElroy, M., 40, 46, *51*
McGill, C., 116, *119*
McGovern, M. P., 105, 106, *120*
McGrade, B. J., 80, 93, *98*, 118, *119*
McGuire, C. Jr., 205, 209, *219*
McHugh, M., 128, *138*
McLaughlin, M. L., 186, *203*
McMillan, J. H., 40, 41, 43, *51*
McMurray, N. E., 89, 90, *100*
McQueeney, M., 118, *119*
Mechanic, D., 85, *101*
Meece, J., 32, *36*
Meichenbaum, D., 89, 90, 94, 96, *99*
Metalsky, G. I., 56, *74*, 110,*118*
Meyer, J., 209, *219*
Meyer, W.-U., 23, 24, *36*, 132, 133, *138*
Michela, J., 18, *36*, 129, 132, *138* 186, *204*
Midgley, C., 34, *35*
Miklowitz, D. J., 113, *120*
Miller, A. T., 21, 34, *36*
Miller, I. W., 55, *73*

Miller, P., 209, *218*
Miller, S. M., 85, *101*
Mintz, J., 113, *120*
Monck, E. M., 113, *119*
Monson, T., 149, *159*
Moore, D., 38, *51*
Moos, R. H., 85, 86, 89, 90, *101*
Morgan, W. P., 48, *51*
Morgan, M., 89, 90, *100*
Morosku, T. E., 82 , *100*
Moss, H. B., 116, *119*
Mouton, J. S., 185, *203*
Mulherin, A., 209, *219*
Mutrie, N., 39, *51*
Neale, J. M., 87, 96, *101*, 116, *120*
Nesdale, A. R., 187, *204*
Newman, F. L., 105, 106, *120*
Nierenberg, R., 133, *139*
Nicholls, J., 19, 21, 25, 34, *36*, 43, 48, *51*, 52
Nisbett, R., 19, 21, 25, 34, 43, 48, 125, *138*, 207, *219*
Nolen-Hoeksema, S., 61, 62, 68, *73*, *74*
Norman, W. H., 55, *73*
Nuechterlein, K. H., 113, *120*
Obitz, F. W., 82, *101*
Oettingen, G., 59, *75*
Olah, A., 83, 87, 89, *100*
Oldridge, N. B., 48, *52*
O'Leary, A., 83, 89, *98*
O'Leary, K. D., 161, *184*
Olson, J. M., 123, 125, *138*
Olsen, S., 115, *119*
O'Quin, K., 105, 106, *119*
Orley, J., 113,*120*
Orvis, B. R., 162, *184*
Overmier, J. B., 54, *73*
Oziel, J. R., 82, *101*
Painter, J., 151, *159*
Palmon, N., 83, 93, *101*
Parkes, K. R., 82, 87, 88, *101*
Pascuzzi, D., 38, *52*
Patterson, G. R., 162, 164, 169, 179, *184*
Peplau, L. A., 128, *138*
Perlick, D., 108, 109, *120*
Parsons, J., 32, *36*
Perry, R. P., 116, *121*
Peter, N., 25, *36*
Peterson, C., 5, 11, 16, 53, 55, 56, 57, 58, 61, 62, 63, 64, 65, 66, 67, 68, 70, 72, *74*, *75*, 128, *138*, 162, 164, *184*

Peterson, D. R., *184*
Pettigrew, T., 207, *219*
Pfeiffer, C., 173, *182*
Phillips, S., 80, *99*
Piaget, J., 133, *138*
Pintrich, P. R., 64, 70, *74*
Plant, W. T., *101*
Plöger, F., 23, 24, *36*
Plous, S., 105, 106, 107, *120*, 205, *219*
Potepan, P. A., 126, *139*
Prohaska, T. R., 80, 87, 96, *101*
Pruitt, D. G., 185, *204*, 205, *213*
Pych, V., 105, 106, *119*

R-S

Rabinowitz, V. C., 106,*119*, 153, *159*
Rabkin, J. G., 79, *101*
Rahe, R. H., 79, *101*
Rahim, M. A., 188, *204*
Ratzan, S., 80, 93, *98*
Raush, H. L., 174, *184*
Raw, M., 48, *51*, 128, 129, *137*
Razani, J., 116, *119*
Reed, L., 6, *13*, 126, *138*
Reifman, A., 68, 70, *74*
Reisenzein, R., 123, 125, *138*
Reiss, D. J., 114, 116, *119*
Rduch, G., *137*
Regan, D., 112, *219*
Rejeski, W., 38, 43, 49, *52*
Repucci, N. D., 128, *137*
Rescorla, R. A., 131, 132,*138*
Resnick, A., 154, *160*
Rest, B., 6, *13*, 126, *138*
Rethans, A. J., 152, *160*
Revenson, T. A., 88, 90, *98*, *99*
Richards, B., 143, *160*
Richins, M., 145, 157, *160*
Richman, J., 86, *101*
Richters, J. E., 116, *120*
Riordan, C. A., 38, *52*
Ripoll, R., 112, *218*
Robbins, S. P., 185, *204*
Roberts, C., 170, 171, *183*
Roberts, G. C., 38, 43, 49, 50, *52*
Robins, C. J., 57, *74*
Rodin, J., 80, 83, 87, 90, 94, 96, 97, *101*, 125, *138*
Rohrkemper, M., 28, *35*

Rosenbaum, A., 161, *184*
Rosenbaum, M., 83, 93, *101*
Rosenbaum, R. M., 6, *13*, 126, *138*
Rosenn, M., 85, *98*
Rosenshine, B., 33, *36*
Ross, L., 123, 125, *138*, 158, *159*, 207, *219*
Ross, M., *138*, 186, *204*
Ross, W., 82, *99*
Roth, S., 55, *74*, 85, *101*
Rothbaum, F., 86, *101*
Rotter, J. B., 1, 2, 3, 5, 6, 7, 8, 11, *12*, 81, 82, 85, 86, 89, *101*
Rotter, Julian, 1, 2, 3, 5, 6, 7, 8, 11
Rubin, J., 185, 191, *204*, 205, *219*
Rubovitz, P., 33, *36*
Rule, B. G., 187, 202, *203, 204*
Rush, A. J., 134, *137*
Russell, D., 39, 40, 41, 42, 43, 49, *52*, 80, *102*, 117, *120*, 128, *138*
Russell, R., 39, 40, 41, 49, *51*
Russo, J., 87, *101*
Rutter, M., 113, *119*
Ryan, K., 156, *159*
Saari, L. M., 61, *73*
Sahagun, L., 143, *160*
Santana, F., 113, 115, 117, *120*
Schachter, S., 124, *138*
Schaefer, C., 80, *100*
Scharf, M., 81, *100*
Scher, S. J., 158, *159*
Schill, T., 86, *100*
Schlenker, B. R., 151, *159*
Schmidt, A., 105, 106, *121*
Schmidt, G., 28, *36*
Schmidt, W. H., 185, *204*
Schwartz, N., 158, *160*
Scott, C., 176, *183*
Seeman, M., 86, *101*
Seligman, M. E. P., *5, 12*, 53, 54, 55, 56, 57, 58, 59, 60, 61, 66, 70, 72, *73, 74, 75*, 94, *101*, 103, *118*, 123, 124, 127, 128, 130, 135, *136, 138*, 172, *182, 184*
Semenik, R., 151, *159*
Semmel, A., 56, 57, *74*
Shantz, C. U., 161, 180, *184*
Shapiro, D. L., 186, 200, *203*
Shaver, K. G., 164, 171, *184*
Shaw, B. F., 134, *137*
Shaw, K. N., 61, *73*
Sheffet, M. J., 149, *159*
Shenkel, R. J., 105, 106, *121*

Sherif, M., 206, 208, *219*
Sigall, H., 112, *218*
Sigel, I. E., 163, *184*
Silbowitz, M., 82, *100*
Sillars, A. L., 161, *184*
Silva, J. M., 39, *52*
Simpson, G. M., 116, *119*
Singer, J. E., 90, *99*, 124, *138*
Slavin, R. E., 33, *36*
Smith, D. A. F., 64, 70, *74*
Smithyman, S. D., 82, *101*
Snyder, C. R., 105, 106, 107, 111, 113, *120*
Snyder, K. S., *120*
Southern, M. L., 81, *101*
Spiller, H., 23, 24, *36*
Spink, K. S., 43, 49, 50, *52*
Stack, J. J., 82, *99*
Stein, N., 87, 91, *99*
Stern, P., 20, *36*
Stipek, D., 18, 19, 34, *36*
Stephens, L., 187, *204*
Stone, A. A., 87, 96, *101*
Straus, M. A., 161, 164, 169, 179, *183, 184*
Stroebe, W., 205, *219*
Storms, M. D., 125, *138*
Struening, E. L., 79, *101*
Sturgeon, D., 116, *120*
Sutton, S. R., 48, *51*, 128, 129,*137*
Swain, M. A., 174, *184*
Sweeney, P. D., 53, 57, *75*

T-Z

Tabachnik, N., 131, 132, *137*
Tanenbaum, R. L., 61, *73*
Tarico, V., 49, *52*
Taylor, C. B., *98*
Taylor, D., 205, 207, *219*
Taylor, M., 33, *36*
Taylor, S. E., 80, 83, 84, 86, 89, 90, *101*, 129, *138*, 186, *203*
Teasdale, J. D., 5, *12*, 53, 59, *73*, 113, *118, 120*, 124, 127, 128, *136, 182*
Telles, C. A., 113, *120*
Tennen, H., 57, *75*, 80, 93, *98*, 173, *182*
Tetlock, P., 205, 209, *219*
Thomas, J. S., 38, *52*
Thomas, K. W., 185, 186, 188, 192, *204*
Thornton, K. M., 68, 70, *74*
Thornton, N., 68, 70, *74*

Topping, G. G., 113, *119*
Totten, J., 112, *219*
Triandis, H., 113, *219*
Trief, P. M., 87, 91, *99*
Tversky, A., 148, 149, *160*
Twentyman, C., 118, *120*, 163, *184*
U.S. Department of Health and Human Services, *52*
Vaillant, G. E., 53, 58, 72, *74*
Vallerand, R. J., 40, 41, 43, 47, 49, *52*
Van der Plight, J. L., 48, *51*, 128, 129, *137*
Vaughn, C. E., 113, 115, 117, *121*
Verette, J., 157, *160*, 198, 199, *204*
Veroff, J., 162, *184*
Villanova, P., 57, 63, 70, *74, 75*
Visintainer, M., 86, *101*
Vitaliano, P. P., 87, *101*
Von Baeyer, C., 56, 57, *74*
Von Frank, 86, 90, *100*
Wack, J. T., 80, 83, 87, 90, 94, 96, 97, *101*
Wallston, B. S., 82, 86, *101*
Wallston, K. A., 86, *101*
Wampler, K. S., 161, *183*
Wan, K., 207, *218*
Ward, C., 113, *218, 219*
Weary, G., 103, *120*
Weiner, B., 1, 6, 7, 8, 9, *12*, 15, 17, 19, 20, 21, 24, 28, *36*, 37, 38, 39, 40, 41, 42, 43, 44, 45, 46, 47, 48, 49, 50, *52*, 59, *75*, 80, 84, 85, 88, 91, 97, *101, 102*, 103, 107, 108, 109, 110, 111, 112, 115, 116, *121*, 124, 126, 128, 129, 132, 133, *138, 139*, 144, 150, 152, 153, 155, 156, 157, *160*, 168, 172, 173, 174, 178, 181, *184*, 198, 199, *204*, 205, 206, 208, 209, 212, 213, 215, *218, 219*
Weiner, G., 28, *36*
Weintraub, S., 116, *120*
Weiss, R. L., 163, *184*
Weitz, B., 146, *159*
Whalen, C., *139*
Wheaton, B., 82, 84, 88, 89, *102*
White, R., 210, *219*
White, S. W., 162, *182*
Williams, J. M., 48, *50*
Wilson, T. D., 126, 127, *139*
Wing, J. K., 112, 113, *119*
Wolfer, J., 86, *101*
Wolff, H. G., 79, *100*
Wolkenstein, B. H., 11, 77, 106, *121*
Wong, P., 41, *52*, 80, *102*
Wood, J. V., 80, 83, 84, 86, 90, *101*, 129, *138*
Worchel, F. F., 83, 86, 88, *102*
Worchell, S., 205, *218*
Wortman, C. B., 55, *75*, 93, *99*, 156, *159*
Zillman, D., 187, 202, *204*
Zimbardo, P. G., 105, 106, 107, 108, *120*, 125, *138*
Zuckerman, M., 133, *139*
Zullow, H., 59, *75*

Subject Index

A

Ability
 attributions to, 6–7, 10, 15, 17, 38, 126, 133
 development of, 34, 48
 entity vs. incremental, 21
 indirect cues to, 18, 33
 related to helping behavior, 27–30
 related to pity, 20–22
 related to praise and blame, 24–27
 self-efficacy and, 46, 95
Academic Performance, 60–62, 65
Accounts, 199
Affect
 see Emotion
Aggression, 177, 202, 212–213
Anger
 as an indirect attributional cue, 22–23, 30
 attributional determinants of, 7, 20, 129, 173, 187
 buyers' experiences of, 152–53
 clinicians' experiences of, 104, 109
 development of, 21
 family members' experiences of, 112, 115, 117
 following athletic failure, 40–41
 helping behavior and, 210
 marital partners' experiences of, 10, 177, 179

organizational conflict and, 190–191, 199, 202
 teachers' experiences of, 18–19
Apology, 151, 157
Arousal, 125–126
Athletes' Performance, 11, 32–50, 66–73
Attributional Style Questionnaire, 56–57, 61–65, 68
Attributional Therapy, 11, 17, 78, 123–136
Attributions
 antecedents of, 8, 18, 30
 actors vs. observers, 207
 buyers vs. sellers, 145–147, 152
 clinicians, 102–112
 development of, 19–21, 25–31, 34, 48
 employees, 197
 ingroup vs. outgroup, 207–208, 210
 family members, 112–118
 marital partners, 163, 177
 parents, 118, 163
 teachers, 18–19

B

Beck Depression Inventory, 60
Blame
 as an indirect attributional cue, 23–26
 attribution to, 169, 173, 178
 effort and, 24

Blame (*cont.*)
  responsibility attributions and, 171
  teacher reactions of, 18, 32
  related to product failure, 145, 151, 158

C

Causal controllability, 7, 37, 80, 168
  aggression and, 212
  athletes' attributions and, 40, 44–46
  clinical judgment and, 108–109, 115, 118
  family members' expressed emotion and, 114–115
  helping behavior and, 28
  intergroup conflict and, 208
  product failure and, 151–154
  prosocial behavior and, 209–211
  organizational conflict and, 198–200
  related to pity and anger, 20–21
  related to reward and punishment, 7
  related to stress and coping, 84, 88, 92, 95
  social emotions and, 10
Causal Dimension Scale (CDS), 39–41, 49, 117
Causal globality, 10, 55, 57–59, 67–68, 94, 128, 135, 168
Causal intentionality, 10, 169
Causal locus, 6–7, 10, 37–40, 84
  clinical judgment and, 104, 106–107
  coping and, 88, 92, 95–96
  emotion and, 44
  explanatory style and, 55–59, 67
  intergroup conflict and, 208, 214
  marital conflict and, 167
  organizational conflict and, 187–188, 190–197
  product failure and, 150–151, 156
  prosocial behavior and, 209
  self-esteem and, 55, 127, 156
Causal responsibility, 149, 169, 170, 178
Causal search, 8, 144, 149
Causal stability, 4, 6, 37–38, 84, 126, 129
  as a determinant of expectancy, 7, 10, 37, 88, 96, 133, 135
  athletes' attributions and, 41–43
  clinicians' attributions and, 107–109, 118
  cognitive therapy and, 135
  explanatory style and, 55–59, 67–68
  marital partners' attribution and, 167
  perceived illness relapse and, 117–118

  product failure and, 151–152, 154–155
  learned helplessness and, 127
  self-efficacy and, 168
  stress and, 92–96
CAVE procedure, 58, 66, 68
Classical conditioning, 124, 131–132, 136
Clinicians
  ethnicity of, 105–106
  judgments of, 103–112
Cognitive therapy, 11, 124, 130, 134–36
Compensatory schema, 24–25, 27, 30
Conflict
  buyer-seller, 143–158
  couples, 163, 177
  intergroup, 207
  international, 205–217
  Israeli-Palestinian, 214–215
  parent-child, 162–162, 180
  resolution of, 156, 201, 206, 213
Consistency information, 131–132, 136
Control beliefs, 84, 90–92
Cooperation, 210–211
Cooperative learning, 33
Coping, 64, 77, 79–98
  emotion focused, 86–87, 89, 91
  problem focused, 63, 86–87, 89, 93
  social support and, 86–87
Covariation principle, 3, 8, 124, 130–133, 136

D

Depression
  attributional therapy for, 11, 124, 134–136
  clinicians' judgments of, 110
  cognitive therapy and, 134–136
  explanatory style and, 60–62, 94
  locus of control and, 5
Direct Instruction Model, 33
Disappointment, 41
Dissonance theory, 2, 5, 12
Distinctiveness information, 131–132, 136

E

Effort
  attributions to, 6, 17–18, 38
  development of, 20–21, 25, 48
  evaluation and, 6, 24

indirect cues to, 18, 20
learned helplessness and, 128
related to anger, 20–22
related to helping behavior, 27–30
related to praise and blame, 24–27
self-efficacy and, 46, 95
Embarrassment, 156
Emotion
as an attributional consequence, 18–19,
172–175, 209
athletes' attributions and, 40–41, 43–45,
47–49
causal dimensions and, 7, 37
causal locus and, 7, 11, 96
outcome-dependent, 8, 42, 91
related to helping behavior, 209–210
self-efficacy and, 209–210
teacher, 20, 22–23, 32
Empathy, 210–211
Evaluation, 6, 24
Excuses, 157, 198, 200
Expectancy
as a motivational determinant, 7
at chance tasks, 4–5
at skill tasks, 4–5
causal stability and, 7, 10, 37, 44, 88, 96,
109, 133, 135
coping and, 94
product failure and, 154–155
self-efficacy and, 46
related to ability and effort, 17–19, 126
teachers' attributions and, 18–19
Expectancy-value-theory, 2–5, 7
Explanatory style, 53–73, 94–95
Expressed emotion, 112–114, 116–117

F

Fundamental Attribution error, 207

G

Goal setting, 61, 63
Gratitude, 40–41, 44, 48
Guilt
athletes' experience of, 41–42
blame attributions and, 173
causal controllability and, 10, 80, 88, 93, 104
development of, 48

H

Health locus of control, 4, 82–83
Hedonic bias, 2
Help seeking, 62
Helping behavior
as an indirect attributinal cue, 28–32
causal controllability and, 11, 28, 109, 209–
210, 215
clinicians' attributions and, 109
cooperative learning and, 33
empathy and, 209–210
family members' expressed emotion and,
115–117
related to pity and anger, 115, 210

I

I-E Scale, 4, 12, 81
Information processing
primary, 164, 166, 175, 177
secondary, 165, 167, 175–176

L

Learned helplessness, 53–59, 63, 67–72, 103,
127–128, 136
Locus of control, 4, 81–82, 85–86, 89–90, 95
Luck, 7, 20, 38, 133

M

Marital conflict, 156, 161–182, 129
Marital satisfaction, 116
Misattribution, 125–126
Minority children, 33

N

Necessary vs. sufficient schemata, 110
Need for achievement, 7–8

P

Pity
as an indirect attributional cue, 22–23, 30

Pity (*cont.*)
  attributional determinants of, 7, 20
  clinicians' experience of, 104, 109
  development of, 21, 34
  family members' experience of, 112, 115,
    117
  helping behavior and, 210
  teachers' experiences of, 18–19, 21, 33
Praise
  as an indirect ability cue, 23–27, 30
  effort and, 24
  teacher reactions of, 18, 32
Pride, 7–8, 10, 40–42, 44
Psychotherapy, 130–136
Punishment, 6–7

R

Reasons, 111
Reward, 6–7

S

Sadness, 173
Satisfaction, 42, 44
Schizophrenia, 103, 107, 112, 114–115
Self-efficacy

attributions and, 40, 45–46, 168
  coping and, 91, 95
  of marital partners, 171–172, 177
Self-esteem, 10, 17–18, 42, 80, 88
Shame
  athletes' experience of, 40–42
  attributional determinants of, 7, 47, 80, 88
  buyers' experience of, 156
  marital partners' experience of, 173
  stress and, 93
Stigma, 116
Stress, 5, 79–98
Surprise, 40–42
Sympathy
  See Pity
Systematic desensitization, 132

T

Task difficulty, 20, 38
Test anxiety, 129
Two-factor theory of emotion, 124

U

Ultimate attribution error, 207

DATE			

BAKER & TAYLOR